D1339737

IGNITING INNOVATION

IGNITING INNOVATION

Inspiring Organizations by Managing Creativity

KARI LAMPIKOSKI
JACK B. EMDEN

JOHN WILEY & SONS
Chichester · New York · Brisbane · Toronto · Singapore

Other Wiley Editorial Offices

John Wiley & Sons, Inc., 605 Third Avenue,
New York, NY 10158-0012, USA

Jacaranda Wiley Ltd, 33 Park Road, Milton,
Queensland 4064, Australia

John Wiley & Sons (Canada) Ltd, 22 Worcester Road,
Rexdale, Ontario M9W 1L1, Canada

John Wiley & Sons (Asia) Pte Ltd, 2 Clementi Loop #02-01,
Jin Xing Distripark, Singapore 0512

Library of Congress Cataloging-in-Publication Data

Lampikoski, Kari.
    Igniting innovation : inspiring organizations by managing
creativity / Kari Lampikoski, Jack B. Emden.
        p. cm.
    Includes bibliographical references and index.
    ISBN 0-471-96367-4 (cloth)
    1. Creative ability in business.   2. Employee motivation.
I. Emden, Jack B.   II. Title.
HD53.L36   1996
658.3′14–dc20   95–50659
                                                          CIP

British Library Cataloguing in Publication Data

A catalogue record for this book is available from the British Library

ISBN 0-471-96367-4

Typeset in 10/12pt Palatino by Dobbie Typesetting Ltd, Tavistock, Devon
Printed and bound in Great Britain by Bookcraft (Bath) Ltd
This book is printed on acid-free paper responsibly manufactured from sustainable forestation,
for which at least two trees are planted for each one used for paper publication.

Contents

Chapter 12

Chapter 13

Chapter 14

Chapter 15

Acknowledgements

The authors gratefully acknowledge the contribution of the Wihuri Foundation which funded the basic research upon which this book is based. IMA associates in a number of countries have been generous in allowing us to use the information which they have gathered in their surveys, seminars and consulting practices.

For the preparation of the drawings and self-assessment forms, Timo Lampikoski merits a special vote of thanks for a job well done. Our friend and colleague, Kari Korpelainen, has been a source of insight and helpful discussion. Among those who have read, commented, encouraged and criticized as the book progressed are Professor Keith Rawson-Jones, Moscow State University, and Lauri Leppänen, Institute of Marketing. Pat Vaughn provided an insightful and highly professional critique, while Margaret Sanders alternately provoked, criticized and encouraged, starting from the first tender sprouts. Ira Germanova and Lorenzo Emden made valuable observations while the work was in progress.

For their great help in gathering masses of information as well as sorting it out, special thanks are due to Tommi Lampikoski and to the Information Services of the Institute of Marketing. Dr Liz Burge and Professor Lynn Davie were unfailing in their support during the Toronto period, when the idea for the book first developed. We would particularly like to thank Daniel, June, William, Max, Lenty, Jari, Patricia and Robert who represent composites of the many thousands of managers who have participated in our seminars on Creativity and Innovation Management and SAI around the world. We acknowledge a special debt to the Institute of Marketing, Finland, for their cooperation.

To Senior Editor Diane Taylor at John Wiley & Sons who encouraged the project and Geoff Farrell who provided his no-nonsense marketing expertise, our heartfelt thanks, as well as to Pirjo Kavander for her work on the format.

Chapter 1

Wanted: Innovation Explosion!

In the 1960s the talented Polish actor Zybigniew Cybulski performed an impressive role in the film *Ashes and Diamonds*. That title popped into mind when we were thinking about how to describe role profiles of various innovative managers. The solution was simple, once thought of. Why not describe the role profile by finding the "diamonds" and "ashes" in their personalities.

We were aware of the problems of describing living innovative personalities, mainly as a positive characterization. Anyone who has enough experience with the realities of business life knows that the phenomena of so-called "great personalities" have their dark or shadow sides as well, though mostly forgotten or ignored by those authors who write success stories of well-known present-day innovators and managers.

Our aim is to describe the role profiles of innovative managers as possessing necessary and beneficial traits for a company's success and survival — and also to criticize and point out the weaknesses which often accompany the role being enthusiastically carried out. We also clarify the threats to the companies which are consequences of these weaknesses in the innovative manager's role behaviour. Our approach is supported by the research done at INSEAD (The European Institute of Business Administration) by Paul Evans and Fernando Bartolome[1] which shows that "The well adjusted and upbeat executives have been through an extensive process of exploitation that has taught them to recognize their own strengths and weaknesses."

The purpose of the extensive description of each role profile is to support your effort to assess your own qualities as an innovative manager. By implementing a concept of "re-creating management" we emphasize the need and challenge of continuous self-development and suggest ways of enhancing your own and your teams' innovativeness. As a CEO your main concern may be to evaluate your managers' role behaviour in order to develop the greatest assets of your company, the human managerial and leadership skills. As a student of managerial sciences or practices you benefit from exploring lively characterizations of innovative managers each one of whom has a different background, position and business situation.

The role-profile model of the innovative manager is based on the research performed by one of the authors, Kari Lampikoski, supported by intensive discussions and analysis together with Jack Emden. This research work is supported by the Wihuri Foundation[2]. It started by creating a theoretical model of innovativeness in the modern company and pointed out how greatly the managers influence the innovativeness of the whole company with their role behaviour. Peter Drucker[3] wrote an often-cited passage, "Because it is its purpose to create a customer, any business enterprise has two—and only two—basic functions, marketing and innovation". Desphandé et al.[4] make an interesting note that although marketing concept is extensively discussed and developed, "little attention has been devoted to Drucker's second 'basic' function, innovation".

Devotion to creativity and innovations is the way to go. "Creativity is both feasible and worthwhile in business; get innovative or get dead", says Tom Peters[5]. By creativity we mean the process of imaginative thinking (input) which produces new ideas; while innovations are the output, ideas implemented successfully in practice.

In recent years there have been a number of trends in managerial practice, such as Re-engineering, The Learning Organization, Total Quality Management, Teamwork and Networking. We are not proposing a new "ism", but rather underscore the idea that in each of these major trends that have caught fire, there is a common denominator—that is, managers must behave innovatively in order to stimulate their people and make these concepts work successfully. On the other hand, innovations, in order to be a source of distinctive capability to the firm, require the development of a powerful range of supporting strategies, such as quality management, teamwork and supportive networks, as John Kay[6] points out in his analytical book of business strategies. Any successful business must be associated with many different factors. Central to corporate survival and maintenance of excellence is innovative management behaviour. This is far from easy to achieve. It is not restricted to R&D and pioneering a stream of new products. It requires excellence in managing quality, downsizing costs and a number of other activities that contribute to creating the company's image. Top innovative companies excel in adding value to everything they do. Fortune's selection of the US's most admired company Rubbermaid, Inc. was chosen by a panel of CEOs, financial analysts and outside directors on the basis of the company's overall excellence in the entire gamut of corporate activities.

Recent research by the UK Department of Trade and Industry[7] has found common features in nine out of ten of the most successful companies. They are led by visionaries, emphasize developing the creative potential of their people, know and exceed customers' expectations, and constantly introduce new, differentiated products and services. John Plender, reporting the research, points out that many companies reacted to the research results by saying that "this is nothing new, we are doing it already". "Yet the inquiry's finding revealed *a big gap between what business leaders claimed they regarded as important and the priorities they set for themselves and their companies in practice*", says Plender[8].

In the US Robert Johnston recently reviewed past studies of Fortune 500 companies dating back to the 1940s[9]. His main conclusion was: "Companies lose their Fortune 500 status because they cannot maintain, over time, a successful innovative edge with their products and services." According to him, American businesses need to rethink their one-shot approach to innovation and implement instead a systems approach to supporting and managing innovation. The importance of innovativeness is recognized in Japan as well. "Creativity and innovativeness form the most important megatheme as Japanese corporations get ready for the Age of Creation", say Murakami and Nishiwaki at the Nomura Research Institute in Tokyo[10].

The EU Commission gives a high priority to programmes to develop creativity and innovation capabilities within the EU countries in order to maintain their competitive power. The research projects[11] of IRDAC (Industrial Research and Development Advisory Committee of the Commission of the European Communities) and ERT (European Round Table of Industrialists) emphasize strongly the need to learn the new roles of management of innovations and innovativeness. There is need for adaptability and flexibility combined with the imagination and anticipation of change. Organizational creativity and innovativeness also depend upon skills for leading other people to more intensive and effective cooperation and teamwork.

As progressively more people in companies engage in creative work such as R&D, information services, marketing and new business development, the managers of these creative people need to behave innovatively if they want their full contribution.

Germany has taken these recommendations seriously by appointing the nation's first cabinet level minister with the responsibility to expand creativity and innovativeness in the whole nation — "a minister for the future". The need for higher innovativeness is not restricted to profit making organizations.

Public organizations need creativity and innovativeness as much as business organizations do to be able to survive in the progressively more difficult economic conditions and under environmental and political pressures.

Our intention has been to conceptualize and clarify one important part of the phenomenon of innovativeness in organizations: innovative management behaviour. The role pattern of the innovative manager was described at an early stage of the research as consisting of a number of behavioural dimensions. The first version of the survey instrument was based on a thorough analysis of previous questionnaires and instruments, the oldest, developed by General Motors, dating back to the 1950s. Later surveys were examined, especially those done in the US, the UK and Germany. The selection of role dimensions was based on an analysis of these models according to:

• the relative frequency of dimensions (subroles) in previous models
• an estimation of the relative weight or importance of these dimensions.

Role descriptions were selected that covered satisfactorily the area of innovative managerial behaviour. A survey was then conducted among approximately seven hundred managers, using a two hundred item questionnaire, based on the original role pattern. Following analysis of the empirical material supplemented by in-depth interviews and results of group discussions, the renewed role pattern which we used was established as a Managerial Profile.

The conclusion of our inquiry was the recognition that a manager reaches his or her objectives according to each one's own personal style. Within the dynamic of the actual situation, each one acts to generate unique innovative solutions. Our goal has been to crystallize their various behavioural models and to note the special characteristic differences between them. However, we also observed that the role profiles have some degree of overlap. The role concepts are dominant ones rather than mutually exclusive. Most managers do have some characteristics of each role but one type of role emerges as the conspicuous one.

The role behaviour seems to be influenced by the manager's position in the firm and by situational factors, but we have not experienced essential differences between the national or cultural areas. James Brian Quinn CJ[12] concludes, after researching innovation management in a two and a half year worldwide study, that more striking than the cultural differences between the companies are the similarities between innovative small and large organizations and among innovative organizations in different countries. *Effective management of innovation seems to be the same, regardless of national boundaries.* Our experience leads us to the same conclusion. The innovative managers' role profiles resulting from our tests show a surprising similarity in various countries. The ethos of innovation is much stronger than national and cultural characteristics. However, the approaches to innovativeness may follow various paths.

As we perceive it, many managers may be highly creative themselves, but it is even more important that they eagerly welcome, support and stimulate creativity and innovativeness among their people at all company levels.

Innovative managers must be more than just creative dreamers. They must be able to implement creative ideas successfully in practice and maintain profitability.

Each chapter begins with a theoretical and practical overview of the question: how can we seek for innovativeness in the company by following a certain innovative role pattern? The description of a typical "real life" manager follows. We have included several case studies and observations of existing companies to legitimize our anecdotal descriptions. Though the basis of the description of managerial behaviour in this book is based on the research work mentioned above, we do not follow it strictly. Instead, we have created for each of these role concepts an imaginary manager personality. That solution has given us more flexibility. The charm of this approach is that it has required from us a certain degree of creativity and permitted us to avoid simply recording what managers told us. We were also inspired by a challenge to overcome the often perceived general lack of creativity in books about the subject.

It has been an interesting task to create a model person who acts out a role in a real life play. These manager personalities, became very real to us. We couldn't avoid thinking at the end of each chapter that they are alive: "Every story could be true to life", even though none was taken literally from any one of the subjects studied in the survey. And yet, if you should happen to find any similarity to some manager or executive you know, we say "What a coincidence!"

In describing the innovative managers, we have characterized each role according to four main aspects:

DIAMONDS
Those characteristics and strengths which make the role holder successful.

PEARLS
The opportunities for future success and career development which this role opens.

STONES
The weaknesses and deficiencies of the manager and his/her personality traits which weigh like heavy stones and become obstacles and barriers to business success.

ASHES
The real threats which the role, when inflexibly executed, may cause to the person and to the company. The early successes produced by great creativity may vanish like ashes in the wind.

Chapter 2

Coming up with Great Business Ideas: The Manager as a Creator

The Creator as a manager is himself/herself willing and able to generate a flow of original thought and is inclined to change things. He/she is an entrepreneur and inventor by nature, usually a quick thinker, fluent in expression of ideas and has the courage to take risks in order to implement promising ideas.

There is strong evidence in business history that companies need managers capable of generating bright ideas in order to be innovative. This applies especially to managers who operate in the focus of a company's everyday operations. Top executives should also be idea-generators because they have to develop strategies and envision the corporate future.

Creativity is an essential part of innovativeness, the starting point of a process which, when skilfully managed, brings an idea into innovation. Creativity is more than just dreaming up grand schemes. In business life ideas, insights and problem solutions must be original, useful and feasible. Idea-generation is only meaningful when implemented into practice, and this requires that the Creator has the courage to engage in a deliberate decision-making effort.

Innovativeness is a characteristic of an individual, team, organization or even of a nation. Innovativeness is a capacity to create ideas and develop them to be usable in practice. This involves skilful use of a company's core capabilities for supporting the implementation process. Thus, innovativeness is a managerial skill to initiate change and give impetus towards the innovation goals. While maximizing and directing innovativeness a company may, in financial terms, gain consistent earning and return for innovation investments and thereby secure its future.

Innovations may consist of incremental improvements, in which there is no need to change the underlying rules or principles. The product and the basic production method remain essentially the same. Breakthrough innovations are those in which the basic rules and principles have been broken and the demand for new procedures, systems and perhaps also management methods is more urgent. Real breakthrough inventions are rare and most innovations are improvements of existing products or processes. Actually, breakthrough products, such as the micro oven or blockbusters like Glaxo's Imigran, an antimigraine drug, are created by an accumulation of successive and simultaneous discoveries and incremental improvements. Creative copy cats may also be successful as Steven Schnaars[1] has described. Creative innovators try to counteract imitators' moves by designing or redesigning their innovations in such a way that they are difficult to copy or replicate.

In the context of public organizations we may speak about social innovations which are novel and workable solutions to problems of productivity or customer satisfaction.

In practice, innovations fulfil the expectations of inventors, marketers, management and shareholders. Innovations attract the interest of consumer-innovators in the marketplace, who themselves often show imagination in their use of products and services.

DOING THE UNEXPECTED

There are many ways and means to solve problems creatively and produce ideas and innovations. The biographies of famous creative artists and inventors tell about various personal habits, work methods and modes of thinking. They describe how these geniuses solved difficult problems creatively with their ingenuity, expertise and experience. Many super-innovative entrepreneurs have been "lone wolves" building their businesses with a strong confidence in their personal creative capability and with their ability to work without close social support.

The majority of entrepreneurs seem to consider idea-generating as a very important characteristic in an entrepreneur's own self, but as a relatively unimportant criterion when they hire employees for their company. However, they want to hire ambitious people, not yes-men, as the survey conducted by Donald Rumball[2] reveals. Creators as managers are inclined

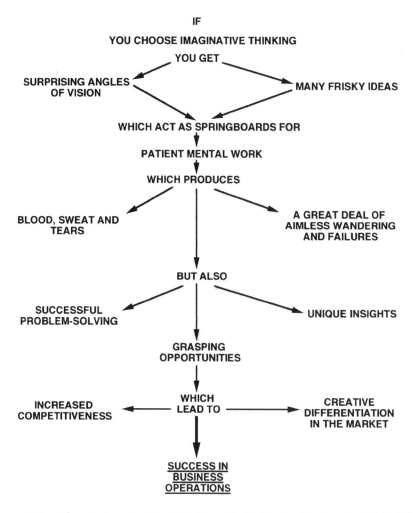

Figure 2.1 Why is Imaginative Thinking Profitable in Business? (Printed by Permission of IMA)

to rely on their own individual capacity in problem-solving situations rather than asking others to produce ideas and initiatives. There are numerous conditions and situations in business life where it is indeed quicker, more cost effective and secure to solve problems as an individual managerial task rather than as team work e.g., when you need the solution to the problem overnight, working on a matter of company secrecy or you happen to be the top creative person.

The time to develop further your creativity is at hand. Start it NOW! *Training* journal[3] argues, "The 90's emphasis on quality, innovation and cost cutting means a bull-market for good ideas."

Innovativeness is a core component in Business Development. Every manager needs creativity to:

- *cope successfully with his/her key tasks*
- *solve personal and everyday operational problems*
- *generate new product ideas*
- *devise new procedures, practices and systems*
- *promote and make innovative experiments in his/her unit*
- *be able to offer his/her input in strategic planning and management*
- *have some fun*
- *make a profit . . . in order to insure survival*

A CREATIVE MIND AT WORK

There are many ways and means available for learning the Creator's role. We have selected the ones which, in our consulting and training context over the years, we have found to be most useful.

CLEAR TIME AND SPACE FOR CREATIVITY

Life is composed mainly of routine actions, repeated day after day, an endless course from home to work, from work to home. Instinctive automatic behaviour, routine, repetition and time killing seem to dominate people's lives. It may be surprising that research conducted in many countries has revealed that even top management spends the majority of their time in routines. What does this tell us? Well, it may be that management considers that routines are important because they secure the existing base of the organization, or perhaps that management has delegated the innovative work to others in the company. It is obvious that in most organizations management values rationality over creativity in business. Stanley M. Davis[4] in his brilliant book, *Future Perfect*, argues how in large organizations rationality is found more often than creativity. "Rational types focus on facts, and facts are about the past . . . *The faster things change, the less you can use facts and the more you need imagination*", says Davis.

Routine-mindedness brings the dangers of dogmatism, control and pyramiding. Nestlé's managing director Helmut Maucher indicated that one of his main objectives in reshuffling Nestlé in the early 1980s was "to get rid of preconceived ideas—to be less dogmatic and more pragmatic . . . and to reduce pyramiding of layers of management"[5]. Red tape is a symbol for

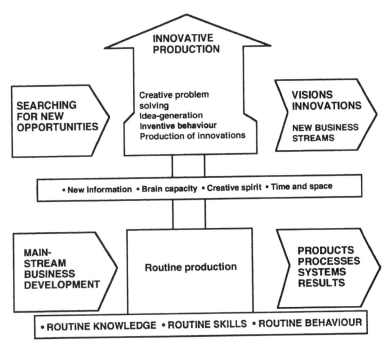

Figure 2.2   Need of Increasing Creative Productivity. (Printed by permissio of IMA)

the dominating power of time-wasting bureaucracy in organizations. Efficiency is their goal. This is attained by repetition, seldom questioning the effectiveness of the action. Dr Jerry White[6] at the University of Toronto argues that "The bureaucracy is simply the dominant organizational form followed by the overwhelming majority of businesses, as well as not-for-profit organizations and governements throughout the world." Some organizations are extremely reluctant to change their traditional organiza-tional forms. In a recent speech Professor Frank Newman referred to a study which revealed that among the organizations which have continued with the same organization chart since the sixteenth century are the Catholic and Lutheran Churches, the parliament of Ireland and sixty-two universities!

Management in business organizations as well as in public organizations works within the limits of strategies, budget expectations, deadlines, resource limitations and customer restraints. Production based on routine knowledge, skills and behaviour keeps the main stream business running steadily. Don't underestimate its value to the company. The downside is that when managers are so occupied with the daily routines, there is little energy left for creative endeavour.

If you interview managers you will find that they are not satisfied with the situation. Indeed, today's companies urgently need to make larger investments in innovative production based on "creativity factors", such as human brain capacity, information processing, creative spirit and time and space for creativity.

TIME TO SEE: RECALLING FROM THE PAST

Robert Ornstein[7] tells about Carlos Castañeda who spent several years in Mexico with an Indian shaman Don Juan. He found the way Don Juan sensed the human consciousness very fascinating. Once Carlos recounted how he enjoyed to chat in the darkness because talking was the only thing he could do besides just sitting around. But Don Juan could not understand that Carlos had not learned to use the darkness. "What can you use it for?", Carlos asked. Don Juan replied that darkness was the best time to "see", explaining that "when you close your eyes and ears, it induces a sensory deprivation in which you are able to listen to your inner self and to come in closer contact with your inner resources"[8].

Every manager's creative potential lies in the wonderfully complex structure and function mechanism of the brain. The cortex of the cerebrum contains billions of neurons or nerve cells. The memory capacity of the brain is immense. There we have a "databank" of our past experiences, perceptions, memory traces and images of things and movements. Most of these are repressed and can only be brought back to consciousness by skilful creative thinking. *The utilization of the memory reserve is absolutely the most cost-effective way to search and process information in problem-solving situations.* Creative managers have related that images and ideas often pop into their minds when they are inactive or just relaxing, sitting down or lying in the bath. That is most likely to happen if one is incubating a difficult problem. The length of time is immaterial. Insights and ideas can be traced even in a few moments. More important is that we really profit from our inner resources, the multi-sensory nature of our brains. We are able to see, hear, smell, feel and taste the events and experiences in our past. In active recalling we create rich, colourful, lively images from the past and relate them as means to problem-solving tasks.

PLACE TO THINK

Most creative individuals need, according to Arieti[9], aloneness. He argues that "A solitary individual is not constantly and directly exposed to conventional stimulation and is less in danger of being overcome by the cliches of society." Indeed, the normal working life exposes managers to routine stimulations and repetitive group activities which leave little space

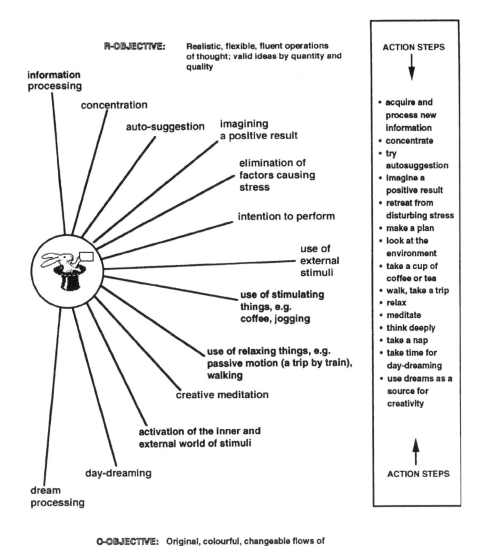

Figure 2.3 How do we Create Ideas by Raising and Lowering our Activation Level? (Printed by Permission of IMA)

for creativity. Creative managers function in diverse ways. Some need a place to be removed from distractions and noise by leaving their work environment. This may entail using the sauna, an ambient preferred by many North Europeans to stimulate original thought, or solitary walks on the beach preferred by Mediterranean types. A number of managers have developed a useful practice of blocking off communication totally during the first hour of their working day, even if it means arriving an hour early. But while some of us need solitude to get the inspiration flowing, others seem to be able to produce ideas wherever they happen to be. They seem to need distractions, noise, stimulation and especially other people. Their secret is the ability to concentrate on the problem at hand, use effectively their inner capacity and to react quickly. Why not benefit from opportunities for creative thinking in any of modern business life's inconvenient situations like waiting in airport lounges, or when stuck in rush hour traffic jams, not to speak of jams on the information superhighway or 4 am insomnia.

FLASH AND CAPTURE: FREE-THINKING

The creative capacity as a kind of reservoir of images and memory traces remains mainly at the subconscious level. The manager has to transform this capacity into creative performance by guiding and directing the thinking process in order to produce something concrete and valuable. According to Arieti[10], in free thinking the person permits his/her mind to wander in any direction without restraints or organization. This situation is similar to the state of inactivity where the continuous sequences of images and memories quite randomly flow in our mind partly stimulated by our inner perceptions (memories) and external signals (sights and sounds we happen to see or hear). Free thinking is seldom productive in business life without supportive thinking aids like creativity methods which help the idea-generation process to be directed to creative performance. There are a number of practical creativity methods to be found in the literature. Most of them follow more or less the classic pattern of creative thinking: problem finding, fact finding, idea-generation, evaluation, incubating of ideas, reworking the ideas, selecting the best ones and acting. Some may argue that creative thinking cannot be learned, one is either born with the ability or not. But it is now generally accepted that, although it may be difficult or impossible for a layman to gain top creativity in the arts or sciences, "workable" creativity in business life is accessible to all. *Creative problem solving processes can be modelled and consequently learned.*

CHOOSE AND DEFINE YOUR PROBLEM WITH CARE

We as managers usually have some burning problems to be solved. They pop into our mind even when we do not want to think about them. It is axiomatic that if a difficult problem is precisely defined it already is half solved. Try to define problems in ways that do not restrict your thinking. Look for causes rather than effects in problem definition. Trace the problem's original sources.

PRODUCE A GREAT NUMBER OF IDEAS

Alex Osborn, who originated Brainstorming, advises that the more ideas you produce, the more original and better quality ideas you will find among them. The statistical assessments of ideas show that the most original ideas in brainstorming will appear after 60–80 ideas. Take a challenge: "I will create 80 ideas for solving my problem X . . .". When generating ideas, develop effective ways to CAPTURE them. One manager described the process of finding ideas saying that "Ideas are the ghosts which appear surprisingly when you do not expect them." Use a desk notepad, Post-it notes, a diary's idea section, dictaphone, microcomputer, electronic mail or personal flip-chart. Fax your ideas. Use your mobile phone to dictate urgent notes to your secretary.

Create Idea-Chains

Some ideas act effectively as springboards for idea-chains. They often are by nature frisky, surprising, challenging our further thinking. When searching for them, incubate your problem, let your dreaming produce unique and original ideas for you, or use random objects around you (perhaps a newspaper, magazine, book) to trigger unconventional ideas. You will find out how these "springboard ideas" FLASH into your mind as insights and that you may have found something very interesting. But even old and familiar ideas get new life as they form chains and open new routes for associations. You may also use a checklist produced by Osborn or some extension of Osborn's checklist to be found in the literature of creativity.

LOOK AT IMAGINATIVE SOLUTIONS

The ability to imagine processes and outcomes beforehand is extremely important to designers of new business concepts and products. Top creative designers can sit for hours just imagining how the final product could look and play with thoughts for several imaginative alternatives. In a similar way, you may try to create several new, original alternatives in your private brainstorming session. The more odd, strange, fantastic ideas you create, the more chances you have of ending up with new original problem solutions. The advantage of imaginative thinking is that it is unconventional and you look at something that already exists from a different perspective. You may generate solutions which work as idea sprouts, from which new thoughts and more developed ideas continuously spring up. Significantly, as you search for solutions you may be more ready to accept mistakes and failures.

Hardly any absolute criteria of originality can be found. Most often orginality can be defined on the basis of spontaneous first impression: an idea seems to be novel, original and fresh. One has not felt or experienced this or done it in this way before. You may be helped by computer software like the IdeaFisher program published by Fisher Idea Systems or Idegen+++ published by CAC-Research. They include a huge amount of questions to provoke your creative thinking. The Faculty of Commerce at the University of British Columbia has developed a software called GENI for generating ideas. The inventors of GENI claim that the use of the program leads to the development of significantly more creative alternatives than traditional brainstorming.

DELAY YOUR CRITICISM

While struggling to find a solution for a difficult problem, our mind reacts by giving a number of ideas continuously. Unfortunately, the more imaginative or weird they are, the more probable it is that our rational control mechanism, 'superego' as Freud called it, knocks them out. Instant criticism will nearly always cause rejection of a far-out idea. We may even fear to give conscious expression to our wild ideas. Creativity becomes a risky business. The complete abstaining from criticism at the stage of ideation guarantees a number of imaginative, original ideas. Delay your criticism to the assessment stage.

REWORK YOUR IDEAS

Mark all ideas with numbers, evaluate and select the best ones, give them the finishing touch. Ideas produced by brainstorming usually are raw ideas which need further development. There is often a need to add to the *originality-power* of the idea by combining raw ideas, producing idea flurries, imagining far-out ideas or searching for analogies. In other cases there is a need to develop the *solution-power* of a raw idea by producing a more workable one, generating alternative ways to overcome obstacles or means to persuade others to accept the idea. This procedure is developed in an interesting way in the creativity method called IMAGINE![11]. The ideas to be reworked will be put on different sectors of an "idea space". Ideas which are considered to be original are put on the O-sector, practical ideas on the P-sector and floating ideas — the ones difficult to decide upon are placed outside of the idea space. The objective is to develop ideas so that they are both original and practical. By using Post-it notes, written ideas are easily transferable to any part of the space but the sought-after direction is always toward recommendable ideas and especially to OK! top ideas which contain remarkable solution power (see Figure 2.4).

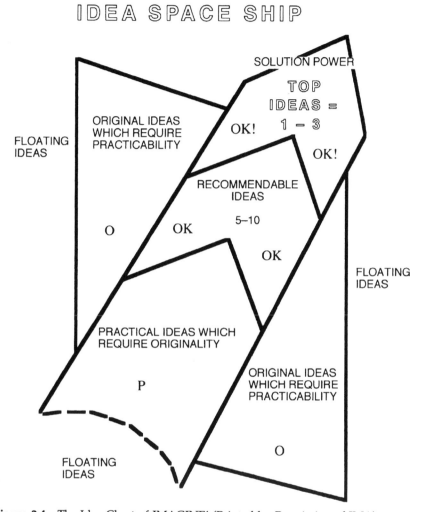

Figure 2.4   The Idea Chart of IMAGINE! (Printed by Permission of IMA)

25 Means for Coming up with Great Business Ideas

1. *Create* a new product or service for your old market
2. *Create* new market segments for your product or service
3. *Create* a renewed product for your old market
4. *Create* a renewed product for new market segments
5. *Create* a new use or habit for your old product
6. *Create* some new value of the product for your customers

7. *Renew* your service concept
8. *Renew* your marketing delivery system
9. *Renew* your marketing campaign
10. *Find* a market gap, search for latent needs
11. *Imagine* something universally applicable
12. *Combine* products or services in an unconventional way
13. *Combine* previously unconnected products or functions
14. *Change* some function or attribute of your product
15. *Replace* or add some function or attribute of your product
16. *Devise* some service or product for midnight, midday, midsummer, midcourse, midlife, and perhaps for a growing "midsection"
17. *Profit* from the new trends – don't ignore contradictory ones
18. *Profit* from the residual markets, markets left behind by big companies
19. *Fly* on the wings of growing new markets
20. *Find* the simplest, most cost-effective solution to some problem
21. *Hunt* the problem which asks for a commercial solution
22. *Scan* your environment for new ideas. Build your network. Surf in Internet.
23. *Ease* the practical life of "forgotten" people with your solution
24. *Add* to the attractiveness of your product or service
25. *Benchmark* attractive successful products or services

DEPARTURE FROM TRADITIONAL CONCEPTS

Creative thinking is often understood as an unconventional combination of items, i.e. linking images and making associations that are normally far from each other. Our mundane approach teaches us that one and one equal two. With an imaginative leap, our minds can be stretched to accept that one and one can be three when innovation is added as a multiplying factor. A friend of ours was teaching a group of six year olds their first lesson in arithmetic and had just explained to them that one and one equal two. She then asked the class: "How much is two and two?" Their answers ranged from five, to seven and ten. When the teacher told them that the correct answer was four, one little girl asked incredulously "How in heaven can it be four?" Little children and great geniuses share this capacity to question conventional wisdom.

Alan MacDonald, the head of Citibank Global Finance in North America, has generated several "laws" of wholesale banking. His first law is that, "one plus two plus three equals 75!" He outlines an important idea that the first three companies into any business get 75% of the fees or income. Within that 75%, the first will get most, followed by the second, then the third. "I want to be the preferred supplier of the stuff that I am good at", says MacDonald[12].

In the literature creativity is sometimes symbolically expressed by using the formula:

An+Bn=C!

where *A* and *B* are items (objects) and *n* means a certain condition of that item. If we combine these items together we get something (a discovery) assuming that these items with these specific conditions have not been connected together earlier. *C!* indicates an original, surprising pattern as the result.

One of the authors held the Innovation Management seminar in Perm, Russia, for local executives a couple of years ago. A few months after returning home he got a letter from one of the participants who explained how they had solved a difficult production and marketing problem in his factory. Before Perestroika they had manufactured gas masks for the Red Army. As the market suddenly ceased to exist the factory faced shutdown. But the inventive manager found a great solution. He perceived that in Russia alone there was a potential market of about 100 million people who needed hard-to-get refined carbon tablets, used for stomach ailments. Also the carbon filters from the masks filled an urgent need to purify water by using a similar device. Imaginative new uses for the same material and technology — swords into ploughshares.

In conventional thinking we do not normally link together items far away from each other, but in creative thinking this approach has a high relevance. *Analogy* means the similarity of the function mechanism between compared objects, such as products, devices, articles, creatures or natural phenomena. In analogical thinking we seek to generate ideas in problem-solving situations by examining objects (mechanisms) comparable to the object that is the focus of our attention. The strategic approach is:

What ideas do we find when we examine the functions and mechanisms of the comparable (analogical) objects? The more comparable analogical objects you find the better, especially if you are able to examine objects which are far from your focus-object and you are able to make analogy conclusions about them. Let us assume that you are interested in bright new ideas to improve the performance of your staff. If you try to create ideas right away they are likely to be quite conventional. Instead, for example, examine how the top performers in art or sport operate: the Berlin Philharmonic, the Rolling Stones (still going strong!), Orlando Magic, Dream Team or the Brazilian national soccer team. Find some performance mechanisms (training strategies or recruitment methods) which are the most interesting and try to trigger analogical conclusions as to how you could motivate your staff to follow these examples.

VERBALIZE YOUR IDEAS

Many people may have excellent ideas but are not able to communicate them. Roger Firestein says that those people are good at "In Thinking" but bad at "Out Thinking". Corporate culture is usually verbal (and of course digital in the sense that budgets and sales figures play an important role, but even the interpretation of figures is verbal). The successful creative manager has the skill to verbalize ideas and concepts and explain purposes and intentions fluently. He/she also writes fluently and effectively and uses rich powerful language. He/she is good at OUT THINKING!

Reporter Distinction

How have reporters learned their exceptional, powerful and fluent writing ability? By exercising and using their talent, writing again and again for their selected audience. What could you do in your case? The answer is simple: write and write again. Writing a lot does not mean writing lengthy treatises. General Electric's CEO John J. Welch is said to recommend that a company's strategy should be able to be summarized in a page or two.

Copywriter Distinction

Take a look at an excellent advertising brochure which has been written by some skilful copywriter. She/he naturally tries to persuade you to become a new customer of the company. Notice the striking use of language. The message is clearly targeted, the facts are concise and effectively expressed, the benefits attractively formulated, headlines provocatively written with the intention of stimulating the reader's interest. But even more important, a unique written statement, a creative concept, a "BIG IDEA" is devised and expressed by the copywriter. Here you have a model for training verbal fluency: follow the guidelines of copywriting.

Thesaurus Distinction

In many cases the manager's problem in out thinking is simply a poverty of vocabulary, especially when dealing with abstract concepts. There is no better way to create a vivid, fresh expression than to look for synonyms, antonyms and phrases which you find in any extensive thesaurus or other "word-power" book. Sometimes you have to create your own original word. As Arthur Fry says, "New ideas often don't even have words to describe them to start with."[13]

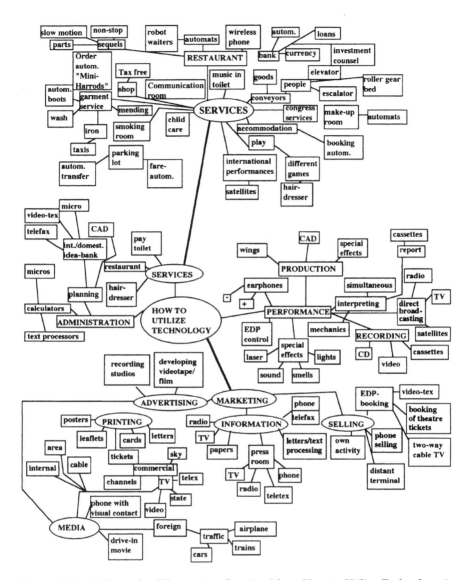

Figure 2.5 An Example of Expressing Creative Ideas: How to Utilize Technology in the Services of a New Opera House. MJD-Teamwork at the Institute of Marketing

Designer Distinction

Why not make a real improvement in your language power by using the designer's way to express ideas and thoughts in various materials, forms, colours and other means. Think first to whom, when, how and in which context you really want to express your ideas. Have courage to use original, unusual ways, means and materials in expressing your thoughts.

VISUALIZE YOUR THOUGHTS

In creative thinking, images come before words. Try, for example, to explain the concept of a spiral. Your first thought is surely visual. The ability for visual imagination results in taking full advantage of one's inner and outer visual perceptions. Why not try some of the following:

- Learn to observe, capture and scan visual images and stimuli in your environment
- Look at objects from different angles, levels, viewpoints
- Catch the original, interesting, novel, surprising figures and forms
- Visualize your ideas by drawing diagrams and figures
- Connect and combine unconnected visual objects in an original way
- Profit from visual information sources, such as scrapbooks, slides, videotapes, films, advertising campaigns, posters, models and prototypes
- Visit great museums and exhibitions
- Produce your own visuals using different media like photography and video films
- Take advantage of computer-based visual and graphic production
- Learn visualization solutions in a hypermedia or multimedia study programme
- Take a correspondence course in drawing
- Daydream with visual images
- Imagine by capturing visual images and project them on your "eyes' screen"
- Experiment with an attitude: no borders and constraints in visual design

By effectively visualizing and verbalizing your BIG IDEA you will be able to communicate its power to solve the problem with a unique and perfect fit.

EVALUATE IDEAS

The effective evaluation of ideas requires that management give real thought to ideas generated within the organization. Reworking ideas, as described earlier in this chapter, is a natural evaluation procedure. Management may organize permanent idea evaluation and screening systems to include evaluation teams or committees, feasibility studies and external consulting. Kodak's Innovation Office is an excellent example of the clear understanding that the real purpose of idea evaluation is not the elimination of ideas but supporting promising ideas to become great business successes. Customers' evaluations are always useful, especially when experimenting with a new idea. If the "guinea pigs" accept your idea, your are on your way to success.

DANIEL FABUN: A CREATOR'S MIND AT WORK

A man told his friend about his problem. He would wake up at night with lots of good ideas in his mind, but all were gone when he finally got up in the morning. "What shall I do ?", he asked. "It's simple", advised his friend. "Just place a pencil and a piece of paper on your night table and write ideas down whenever they pop into your mind." And so he did. Again he woke up one night with a bright idea and hastened to write it down. The next morning he was eager to see what the superb idea would be. He took the paper and there it was, clearly written:

"This is a hell of a good idea!"

We met Daniel the first time at a conference held in Venice in the mid 1970s. He came to talk to us after our presentation and asked us to have dinner with him that evening. He promised to pick us up in the lobby of our hotel at 7 pm. He came at eight, with a wide smile and a fanciful story about his business partner, who was an excellent chef—as we would later find out. He was accompanied by a charming Italian lady whom he presented as a "friend".

The reason for his lateness, which we could hardly understand through the continuous flow of talk, was that he'd had an exciting idea during our speech which he absolutely wanted to try out immediately. It actually had little to do with the content of our talk but he had picked up the concept of "the chain of flowers" (the symbolic meaning of the chain of visual concepts in persuasive communication).

Daniel admitted openly that he did not listen very much to our speech after that because he was concentrating on developing his idea with paper and pencil design. It was spring. Venice was covered with flowers and full of tourists, families and pairs of lovers wandering along the fabulous Venetian walks beside the canals and over the bridges. And as we all know so well, Daniel smiled, women love flowers.

"The chain of flowers" meant to him an endless chain of female customers in whose hair he personally wanted to fix a flower as they waited to be seated. "So simple an idea, my friends, you are thinking. That's what they do in Tahiti. No, what I had in mind was to divide our restaurant's space into flower sectors—*every sector distinguished clearly in a certain colour*: a pink sector, yellow sector, red (for lovers, of course) and a blue sector. And I would give every woman a flower with the colour which could easily identify the part of the large restaurant where she and her party would be seated. It would always be easy to find at first glance your table wherever you go in the restaurant. And while listening to your talk I could hardly stay in the lecture hall, envisioning my restaurant full of flowers, colours and scents and the charming ladies with flowers in their hair. That would be VENICE SPRING."

So he had rushed from the place after making the appointment with us and, he continued, "You can imagine the chaos in my restaurant when I ordered the people right away to accomplish my idea. Several people ran to the marketplace after the *flowers, others after the new flower vases. A couple of waitresses protested when I told them to throw even fresh 'old' flowers into the garbage. Okay, you take them home, if you wish, I said. So they did. The headwaiter tore his hair calling store after store to find the small gadget needed to fix the flowers in the ladies' hair. I wanted something special, not the usual stuff. Finally he found them in Venice-Mestre, skilfully fashioned in the shape of a butterfly. And the chef lost his temper when his assistant was drafted to help in organizing the flower tables to be on time when the restaurant opened in the evening."*

So, we were taken by the restaurant's gondola through the marvellous Venetian canals. (By the way one of his ideas was to have the restaurant's name and location clearly shown by paintings on both sides of the boat.) He happily described his business visions while serving us his own personally selected house wine. Entering the restaurant we could understand the reason why he absolutely wanted to have a lady friend with him. The headwaiter fixed a pink orchid into her hair and we were accompanied to the pink area. What a view!

We were reminded of this event when reading our colleague Dr Roger Firestein's fascinating book Why didn't I think about that?

TWENTY YEARS LATER

Now almost twenty years later, Daniel is the main owner, CEO and chairman of the board of directors of a conglomerate of about seventy restaurants and hotels. Actually he made a major move soon after we met in Venice. He enlarged his restaurant business to include the US, realizing the opportunities for faster growth there. His corporation has grown from that memorable Venetian canal-side restaurant to a world-scale chain which is acknowledged as one of the innovative prime movers in the hospitality business.

Daniel calls himself a "life-long student". He never had time or opportunity for any longer, formal studies, but he assures us that as a foster child, reared in a genuine Italian family where most of the members were in the restaurant business, he has the knowledge and secrets of the Italian kitchen at his fingertips. He has reached the status of guru in the hospitality business thanks to his inexhaustible energy and creativity as well as accumulated experience and perseverance. He enjoys operating abroad and speaks several languages. His multicultural experience helps him to understand ethnic diversity and to cope with customers' problems, needs and preferences around the world.

Whenever time permitted he took part in seminars and courses organized by the National Restaurant Association and the Cornel University's Center for Studies in the Hospitality Business. Today he is a recognized and sought-after speaker in the industry. He keeps audiences alert by telling humorous stories about his innovations, many of which were in the beginning total failures. He speaks in a fast and lively manner, using metaphors and anecdotes, his hands revolving like a windmill. He enjoys people asking him questions and presenting problems, usually *being able to come up with quick solutions. Someone from the audience asked why he was in this business, and his prompt answer was: "Simply because this is a fascinating business field where you can always find a new opportunity by experimenting with new things. And you can demonstrate your own ability to innovate new business — something to be proud of."*

DIAMONDS

Daniel Fabun is a fluent idea-generator himself. He is a typical "right-brain thinker", picking up ideas in situations and under conditions in which other people would most likely just let things slide by. That's because he is a sharp observer. When you visit with him in one of his restaurants, already at the doorstep he can see at a glance what is going on there. How things are — customers, table settings, activities of the personnel, problems and areas of neglect. It seems like Daniel has the highly developed capacity to execute in practice the "Four Walls Theory" of D. R. Scoggin, TGI Friday's chief executive, which proclaims that you have to be able to locate and solve problems within the four walls of your restaurant. It's simply that. And Daniel is also able to think of solutions to the problems quickly.

With CREATOR managers like Daniel, it is typical to start thinking fluently of solutions to problems immediately as they are observed. Not only in their own business, but in others as well. The CREATOR is an excellent companion when you want fresh and original ideas for your business. If you sit down and have dinner with Daniel, you'll find him to be an incredible source of new ideas. Just stimulate him and then listen.

PEARLS

Daniel Fabun manages impulsively, taking eagerly every business opportunity. He is an innovator and entrepreneur by nature who can sniff new things out and has a natural instinct for the next trend or fashion. He senses intuitively good opportunities to make money. Daniel is very energetic and runs a lot of things at the same time preferring situations and events where new business ideas are needed. A typical example of his ability to scent new business areas was when he began to discuss with his company's board of directors the challenges which the new Pacific Rim area's mass tourism would bring with it. Earlier in the 1960s and into the 1970s, tourism to the Pacific was mainly concentrated in Hong Kong and Singapore — where Daniel had already made some contacts. Having had innumerable discussions with hotel clients about places like Bali, Guam and other "island paradises", he decided that this is where future tourism would likely be directed when the time was ripe. He convinced the board to search for suitable ways to develop the hospitality business in those areas. They have now launched a cost-effective, high quality food, combined with good accommodation service which meets the needs of the less affluent Far East travellers. Daniel's activities are now directed to China, where his company has already gained a foothold by granting low-interest financing to several promising joint ventures. When we asked how profitable business is there, Daniel answered with a sly glint in his eye — "anyway, we don't lack for customers, our hotels operate the year round with over 90% occupancy. Where, folks, could you find such a record in the West?"

STONES

We must observe, though, that there are some weaknesses in Daniel's management style — even though he does things in a most creative way, or perhaps just his way. His company's operations are often amusing, interesting and fast in tempo. He often surprises his own staff with his drive and new ideas. Unfortunately Daniel sometimes is an impatient manager. He wants his GREAT IDEAS to be accomplished at once, not tomorrow.

This demands great effort from the local managers and staff. They are required to change even recently instituted operations and behaviour to which they have hardly had time to understand and accommodate themselves. If obstacles exist on the way to implement the new ideas, which are often very complex, Daniel may easily lose interest, and go on to invent something new. The members of the board of directors are often confused because he lacks the patience to go through the painstaking process of idea-screening and evaluation.

Daniel often puts more trust in his own instincts than in the staff's financial analyses and profitability projections of his new business ideas. He finds board meetings boring if they concern old business, cost control, sales reports and the like. He is an idea-egoist, seeming to feel that only his ideas are bright, important and valuable. This may frustrate colleagues and staff, and they are often reluctant to offer their suggestions. This egoistic characteristic of Daniel reminds us of a sea captain who always used to say, when sending messages to ports: "I am landing, I am arriving . . ." However, when he once navigated onto a sand bar he wired: "We ran aground."

Daniel is, according to our observations, impatient with slow thinkers on his staff and may just push on ahead if they cannot match his fast pace. As a result, the company can easily grow to rely on continuous stimulation by his impulsive ideas.

ASHES

A large corporation, if not managed strategically, may find its results turning to ashes. Daniel sometimes seems to give little thought to an overall strategy. We remember when he started to expand his hospitality business. Because his flourishing core business, hotels and Italian restaurants, was very successful, he started to diversify into areas somewhat connected, but in which he had no hands-on experience. Furthermore, as a creative dreamer he overestimated the travel flow from Russia and East European countries and timed the trend too early.

Daniel soon found it very troublesome to control a number of sites, each of which was used to operating according to its own policies and procedures. He simply tried to keep too many balls in the air. Despite much travel and work with the local managers to try to resolve the problems, Daniel had to admit that his business was on a downhill slide. He didn't give enough thought to what local managers told him because he was too confident of his own ideas and ability to solve problems. The real risk was hidden in his egocentric attitude. He might have had a "memorandum of renewal needs and means" in his head but he was reluctant to write it down, murmuring that "written papers are the first sign of red tape ahead". The local managers could perhaps have been able to formulate more systematic plans, but for that he should have given them clear direction with freedom and authority to act. As we observed his operation, it is likely that he did have some strategic guidelines in mind, but he produced ideas, plans and changes so rapidly — and often in his well-known chaotic manner that the local managers could not keep up with the flow. The turning point came when he had to get rid of most of his unrelated businesses to save the core operation. Now he took the time to think about his real mission. Daniel seems to forget the obvious fact that creativity does not insure business success. There are many cases of new ventures and top creative companies which have gone under; one of the most notable is EMI, which invented computer tomography. It often takes a very long time to attain commercial success even with great ideas. Patience and tenancity are needed of any top management.

Our message to Daniel:

- *KEEP your inspiration alive as an idea-generator. By exercising and using it, your creativity as an innovative manager will last to a very old age*
- *KEEP your attitude and habits as an entrepreneurial person. Continue to love risks and be tolerant of failures as necessary steps to business success*
- *KEEP your ability to seek out new business opportunities but learn to screen and select them*
- *KEEP your way to encourage informal development by protecting the organization from red tape*
- *LEARN to give opportunities to your colleagues and staff. Learn to listen to their opinions, viewpoints and ideas. With your exciting and creative mind you will be able to fascinate them and stimulate them to create ideas and innovations in partnership with you*
- *LEARN to understand that creativity is not the same as business performance. Give time for implementing changes and process transformation in the organization. Communicate and consult with your staff in the early stages of implementation*
- *LEARN to plan and operate the business with a well-thought-out strategy*
- *LEARN to overcome idea-narcissism, the inclination to think that only your own great idea is worthwhile and unique*

Chapter 2

Self-Assessment: Creator

HOW DO YOU RATE YOURSELF AS A "CREATOR"?

Please take a few minutes to rate yourself according to the following items.
Place one numerical rating in the left hand column and one in the right.

How do you rate yourself in the following activities? (Select numerical rating.)		How important is this to your managerial career? (Select numerical rating.)	
VERY GOOD 7.....6.....5.....4.....3.....2.....1 #		VERY IMPORTANT 7.....6.....5.....4.....3.....2.....1 #	
a	Perceiving problems	a	
b	Using my imagination	b	
c	Intuitive thinking	c	
d	Expressing ideas in brain-storming sessions	d	
e	Finding solutions by incubating problems	e	
f	Coming up with original ideas	f	
g	Patient reworking of ideas	g	
h	Visualizing my thoughts	h	
i	Creating new business ideas	i	

Plot your ratings in the matrix as follows:

- First plot those items (a to i) which you consider that you perform well *and* that are also important to you (scored with 5 to 7). Place in quadrant B
- Next, select those items (a to i) in which your estimate of performance is not so good *and* not of importance (items evaluated 1 to 4). Place in quadrant C
- Next, select those items which you consider that you perform well (5 to 7) but which are *not* of particular importance to you (1 to 4). Place in quadrant D
- Finally, select those items which you consider that you perform unsatisfactorily (1 to 4), *but* which are important to you (5 to 7). Place them in quadrant A

The functions of creative behaviour in quadrant A are the ones which we recommend that you give special consideration. How will you develop those in the future?

I am inefficient (1–4)	I am very good (5–7)
IS VERY IMPORTANT A	IS VERY IMPORTANT B
IS NOT IMPORTANT C	IS NOT IMPORTANT D

MY TOP FIVE DEVELOPMENT CHALLENGES AS A "CREATOR":

1 _____

2 _____

3 _____

4 _____

5 _____

Chapter 3

Provoking Creative Behaviour: The Manager as a Stimulator

> The Stimulator as an innovative manager "catalyses" his/ her staff into idea-generation, persuades and encourages employees to bring up ideas and suggestions and to go on developing them into innovations. The Stimulator strives to create an open, communicative, supportive culture in the company.

Let's look at both the cultural and the communicative aspects. Looking at the "creativity continuum" we find that the Stimulators are themselves not necessarily highly creative. Their major effort is to get the maximum from their staff's creativity which in itself, of course, can entail imaginative effort.

STIMULATING ORIGINAL ACTIONS

Most managers are trained to be "advocates" as Peter Senge has argued. Especially the Creators are able to solve problems easily and address the solutions to other people to be implemented in practice. However, as managers rise to senior positions they find out that their own experience, skills and time are not sufficient to satisfy the continuous demands for innovative problem solving. They need other people's input. The basis for getting real involvement and commitment to innovativeness is a stimulating corporate environment. Innovative Management Associates, IMA, has accumulated information through surveys of how managers themselves and their subordinates assess the innovativeness of their organization. Though many executives claim to be able to sense their organization's culture intuitively, by walking around and through informal discussions with their people, these surveys reveal remarkable differences between the managers' own evaluations and those of their subordinates. For example, the *managers almost always overestimate the creativity of their company or unit compared with subordinates' opinions.*

Apart from IMA, there are a number of consulting and training organizations[1] that have systems and instruments to analyse organizations' culture, climate and character: CRA (Corporate Renewal Associates in London), MIT Systems Dynamics Group (originated by Peter Senge at the Massachusetts Institute of Technology), Belbin Associates Ltd (Cambridge, England) and Meridian (Berkeley, USA) are active in the field.

Innovativeness is a core factor in Corporate Culture Development. A manager needs innovativeness to:

- *assess his/her organization's culture*
- *develop visionary corporate symbols*
- *develop inspirational rites*
- *establish a supportive environment*
- *stimulate kaleidoscopic thinking*
- *reorganize activities*
- *stimulate curiosity*
- *activate dialogue, cooperation, participation and involvement*

BLOW UP THE SPIRIT

People's behaviour in companies depends on their feelings even more than on logical, rational thinking. Most people react sensitively to the organizational and environmental pressures and when they produce creative results, expect rewards and recognition. The Stimulator knows that the spirit of the organization has a remarkable effect on the performance of individuals and teams. But is it possible to actively seek creative spirit?

First, you as a manager can develop symbols. The company's environment includes a great number of overt and latent symbols that indicate to the receivers—one's own staff, customers, suppliers—the nature of the organizational climate. These include, for example, office furnishings, paintings, flags, celebrations, products and services. But the spirit is also indicated by the inner language and behavioural norms. Why not create symbols which evidence your organization's drive for creativity?

The Stimulator understands that *creativity can only flourish in an environment where people feel free to express even their wild, far-out ideas openly*. In an atmosphere of mutual trust and respect, people will be encouraged to experiment with new ideas that will benefit the company without having to fear the consequences of failure. People often hide their self-consciousness and fear of failure by silence when asked for far-out ideas and suggestions in problem-solving situations. A humorous atmosphere created by the manager can reduce stress and critical self-judgement. Joking, smiling and laughing are very positive indicators.

Second, you as a manager can develop inspirational rites. Organizational behaviour is often expressed in the form of rites, rituals and ceremonies which focus on making employees feel that they are an important part of their company. They spread the culture among newcomers and renew everyone's understanding of what the management considers to be really important in the organization. Most company rites are routine, such as annual celebrations, sales competitions and birthday parties. Too few of them blow up creative spirit: idea competitions for the whole staff with original presentation ceremonies, patent celebrations, a really exciting open day for customers and the public. It is you as a manager who must stimulate people to devise imaginative rites.

Third, establish a supportive environment. Vincent Nolan[2] has observed that because creativity is connected with newness, it is directly associated with risk. Beside the fact that the risk can be objective, tangible (e.g. loss of money), the risk even more often is subjective by nature: emotional, risk of feeling foolish, embarrassed or hurt by criticism.

Most managers willingly listen to people's suggestions which they evaluate to have a high probability of successful implementation. However, we know by experience that these kinds of suggestions rarely result in any landmark discoveries or inventions. Risky proposals also deserve attentive and empathetic treatment by management if a real creative expansion is sought.

TWIST AND SHAKE

The Stimulator as a manager seems to understand creativity in quite different terms than the Creator. Where a Creator would define creativity as a process of inventing new ideas and things, a Stimulator would describe it as a way to profit from existing elements and combine and reorder the elements for a totally new output. Our profile manager in this chapter, June Hayward, as a director of an advertising agency, would give a good explanation for that:

> If you look carefully at the total field of advertising, you will observe that new ideas or inventions very seldom appear. Virtually everything has already been

invented, produced and used in the past history of advertising and so the probability that you will find a totally new invention is pretty small. But you can keep striving for ingenious ways to combine and link already existing elements like visuals, words, concepts, auditive elements and spatial dimensions, and plan these combinations in new ways to meet the customers' variable needs, expectations, dreams, tastes and resources.

Rosabeth Moss Kanter names this kind of creativity "kaleidoscopic thinking"[3]. As in a kaleidoscope you form entirely new patterns by shaking and twisting it; in creative thinking you will emerge with new realities by rearranging the already existing pieces. Most of the thinking in companies follows the "microscopic thinking" model: learn to do better things which you already manage well and follow the long-established practices or standard operating procedures also in your private thinking. You will be safe if your thinking proceeds in an orderly, sequential, logical fashion. The Stimulator breaks down this pattern in discussions by shaking and twisting the machinery of dominating logical, rational thought.

Shake-up can also be done by reorganizing activities. Murakami and Nishiwaki[4] put forward *a deliberate shake-up of an organization within a period of three to five years for keeping people creative and fresh.* This kind of effect could be reached, for example, by a recombination of personnel, movement of personnel among divisions and departments or enrichment of individual work. They refer to the successful Japanese company Komatsu which substantially revamps the organization every four years.

ADJUST THE MOOD

Brain researchers have found out how important it is for creativity to adjust the mood and arousal (activation level) to the optimal level. Sometimes the optimum is total relaxation, where you calm down by seeking to reach detached imagery. Sometimes the optimum is a very energetic, alert mind, for example in brainstorming, when you are expected to produce a large quantity of ideas in a short time and blurt them out without inhibition. High arousal with good mood releases energy, increases courage to tackle difficult situations and confidence in one's ability to solve complex problems or to take risks and to try the impossible.

The Stimulator knows how to alter and affect people's mood and arousal in order to achieve creative productivity (see Figure 3.1).

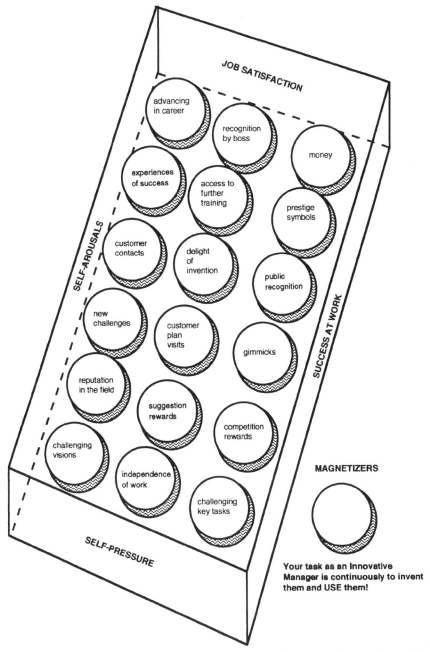

Figure 3.1 How do We Energize the Magnetic Field of Company Spirit? (Printed by Permission of IMA)

STIMULATE CURIOSITY

In a popular TV show professional comedians were simulating the bedtime moment when the anxious "father" tries to get his "baby" to sleep by starting to tell once again the popular fairy tale "Red Riding Hood". "Once upon a time there was Little Red Riding Hood", the father started. "Why was it only once?", asked the baby. "Why was the Riding Hood red?" "Why wasn't the Hood green?" Why wasn't there first the wolf?" An endless series of questions followed every sentence during the father's narration. Children's creativity is based on their inclination to look at the world with wonder and curiosity. When curiosity is discouraged and diminished by judgement and criticism, the child learns to hide this trait.

Even the adult's creativity is, however, stimulated by child-like curiosity. Top creative people are sensitive to new things around them and they have a capacity to be surprised. They are confident enough to ask "stupid and intellectually naive questions", to talk about the aspects they don't understand, to make several guesses and suggestions and let their mind follow an unpredictable path.

Managers are often annoyed by "dull", routine papers submitted to them. Quality could be improved if the manager when requesting the report would indicate the important matters to be covered and clearly state the questions to be answered. The Stimulator knows how to do this. The Stimulator understands how to wake up and encourage people's natural curiosity even when listeners are initially not much interested in the issues under discussion.

Mental excitement as a mood state is often observed to be connected with inspiration and creative insights. *Webster's New Collegiate Dictionary* defines the meaning of excite: "to arouse an emotional response by appropriate stimuli, enthusiasm for something" — exactly what you should look for as a Stimulator.

Appropriate stimuli can be *catalytic questions* which you can use during discussions, in agendas, memoranda and on notice boards (e.g. E-mail bulletin board). "Please produce some ideas or solutions regarding our problem of . . .", "Combining these factors, the end result can be interesting. Could someone elaborate some more ideas . . .", "This idea is our springboard . . . now it is your turn to develop . . .". By guided questioning you awake receivers from their routine behaviour. You bombard their brains with novel stimuli and cause a state of enrichment of neural circuits which brain researchers call "overloading". When Stimulators are drawn into intense discussions, instead of dominating the exchange with their own ideas, they skilfully use catalytic questions which arouse enthusiasm and excitement and stimulate receivers to find fresh ideas and suggestions.

ASK AND LISTEN

The Stimulator is a good listener and collects a great deal of information about problems and needs of customers, suppliers and staff as well as their plans and suggested changes. It is well known that people's ideas must be treated sympathetically if they are expected to be produced continually. Customers are an excellent source of ideas and information. When you ask and listen to them they will tell how they perceive the quality of your products and services, how you could improve them and in which aspects your offers differentiate your company from its competitors. Most customers will enjoy sharing their ideas and suggestions with you as to their present needs and interests and how they try to satisfy them.

Many companies have interesting stories about how great ideas have been found through listening to customers and probing their opinions. Sam Walton, the founder of Wal-Mart discount stores, strongly encouraged, by his own example, all managers to do a lot of travelling to visit stores all over the US. The most admired CEO in Fortune's 1993 ranking list, David D. Glass, the president of Wal-Mart, is said to spend much of his time in Wal-Mart's and competitors' stores around the US. *Fortune* magazine[5] describes how Mr Glass makes sharp observations and asks pertinent questions about sales, competition, special offers, differentiation, work conditions and pricing. Returning to the Bentonville headquarters he has his notebook full of questions, ideas and solutions. All Wal-Mart managers are required to meet employees and customers and have intensive discussions with them. They find out how the personnel in a particular store are able to respond properly and successfully to the needs of their customers. The managers in Wal-Mart act as Stimulators, starting their travelling on Monday and returning Friday with a bag full of ideas and suggestions for business improvement. These suggestions are then discussed during the board meetings every Saturday.

The manager as a Stimulator builds up a similar continuous exchange of views in close relationship with customers and suppliers. This provides a valuable source of creative improvements, such as speeding up the delivery of materials and equipment on a just-in-time basis or reducing defects. Complaints and grievances of an employee or customer are useful material for the Stimulator because they often are signs that there is a need for creative problem-solving. The Stimulator is able to treat complaints as constructive suggestions.

A Stimulator must be able to harmonize the ideas and initiatives of others, with his or her own imaginative input. The manager's most powerful source of influence is his or her credibility based on personal competence to solve key problems and make incisive suggestions for the firm's development. Excessive reliance on questions may be counterproductive. If the questions are either too vague or too complex, others may perceive the continuous questioning as irritating or time wasting. Peter Senge has observed that just asking a lot of questions can be a way of avoiding learning and hiding one's own view behind a wall of incessant questioning. The art is to find a suitable balance between stimulating others to create and using one's own creative capacity.

HONOUR YOUR PEOPLE

The Stimulator knows how to motivate achievement by keeping people's creative inspiration continuously at a high level. He or she can stimulate self-pressure by assigning challenging key tasks, stating expectations and giving clear directives. Stimulators respect people and understand that this means providing one's team with the opportunity to take risks while accepting the possibility of failure.

Stimuli may sometimes be more subtle and the person's desire to try something new may more likely be awakened by self-arousals like perception of an interesting problem or a preliminary idea. In these situations, profitable creativity seems to come about through stimuli which are characteristic of artistic endeavour; a sort of playful excitement based on curiosity. Achievements and success at work will create job satisfaction increasing the motivation for people's long-term creative activity.

JUNE HAYWARD: A STIMULATOR OF ORGANIZATIONAL CREATIVITY

KL relates . . .

June phoned me in Toronto and asked if I knew anything about the ladies' marathon in Helsinki. "Sure", I responded. "It is so well known and publicized in Finland that everyone knows it there." June is, as I was told, a very bright young manager of a big Canadian advertising agency. We met in her office, which in a word was weird, decorated mainly with question marks — some very small, one very large — the meaning of which I discovered later.

After serving decaffeinated coffee she questioned me about the interests, habits, attitudes and conditions of Finnish women. I described them generally by pointing out that they've got an equal, or even better, education than most men. Most of them work outside of the home, striving hard nowadays for equal status and pay. In many sectors this is the reality in Scandinavian work life. She went on to ask me about their hobbies and other interests. I mentioned that Finnish women generally are culturally more active than men, and that they take part actively in political and social life. They take even better care of their physical and psychological condition than the men do. June's interest was particularly aroused as I spoke about a research project concerning the growth of feminism, conducted by one of my colleagues, Elina, a professor of sociology at Helsinki University. Elina interviewed a number of persons attending the Ladies' Dances, a unique Finnish institution. At these dances the ordinary working people, professionals, housewives — women sitting together in groups or even alone — take the initiative to ask men to dance. These dances are, as Elina could tell you, symbolic of women's striving for equality. But there is also a humorous element and one can become quite breathless from the exercise, as the women who ask men to dance are so active.

June turned to questions about feminism in Finland. I replied that the feminist groups started by using aggressive tactics; blaming, attacking and accusing men and the political system of being chauvenistic. What actually happened was that these early movements aroused a defence mechanism among men and even many women who did not view these activities with sympathy. Also their orientation was essentially negative, as the protests, demonstrations and public display mainly evidenced anger and hate.

This excited her interest and she asked if other alternatives were tried. I replied that some thoughtful women were worried about the negative developments between the sexes and started to consider more positive approaches that might encourage women to participate in demonstrations. Two of these "feminist innovators" were business professionals who got the idea to organize "LADIES' TEN", a 10 kilometre run for women only, to take place in Helsinki during the month of May. They had observed that among the participants in different events, such as the Helsinki marathon and other shorter runs, more and more women were participating. "Why not organize one for just women", they thought. Their friends and acquaintances were not all that enthusiastic. "Ten kilometers is too long a run for most of the women", they were told. "Many women could be reluctant to participate in a public event." "It could be very difficult and costly to organize and publicize by private persons."

"And how did they answer?", June asked. "All right, let's organize it so that one can either run, walk or even push a pram, just as you like. We have to take some risk investing our money, but we'll get a return on our investment from registration fees and by seeking sponsors who will advertise on our printed leaflets. We should start to recruit participants mainly through large organizations and companies. Let's try to get as many company teams as possible by offering a reduction of the entrance fee according to the number of participants. Let's try to get publicity through newspapers, women's magazines, local radio and television. Yes, we absolutely have to get some teams from broadcasting companies to insure that we get coverage on the television channels." "And were they successful?", June asked. "Yes, very", I replied. "Over all, they exceeded even their most optimistic plans. The number of participants has grown year after year, increasing to several thousands so that the originators of LADIES' TEN were able to sell the idea and system to the National Athletic Association. I estimate that the selling price of the rights might have been about 10 million FMK (about 3 million Can.$)." "Not bad for an idea like that!",

June admitted. "How was the idea finally realized?", she wanted to know. "Very much as planned", I answered.

"I think all of us in Finland were surprised at how eagerly women started to take part in LADIES' TEN, more than 30,000 in recent years. Many individuals and teams trained the year round. Newspapers, magazines, radio and TV publicized the run. The run itself winds through the most beautiful part of Helsinki — the seaside parks. Boyfriends, husbands with kids, male coaches from the companies which have competing teams and thousands of other spectators from all over south Finland gather along the route to encourage and applaud the runners. Thousands of participants, smiling, laughing and joking women dressed in the most diverse, colourful and imaginative sport and other costumes, running along the route, is a powerful demonstration which gathers and binds masses of women together in an arena which traditionally has been a male perogative. I would judge it to be a positive and powerful approach to strengthening the feminine identity."

"Kari, do you think that kind of run could also be a success here in Toronto?", June continued questioning. I admitted that having been here about half a year by no means qualified me as an expert to answer that question, but I could envision that a Toronto Spring Run for women could also be a success. Living near High Park, I had observed that running, jogging and walking were popular among young women in Toronto. As many of them also seemed to participate in sports like tennis, swimming, golf, aerobics and fitness training, I would expect their condition to be good enough to make the run. Also Toronto has very beautiful lakeside avenues, and particularly for Europeans, who could be potential participants, the run through the skyscraper area and China Town could be an attraction. "Perhaps even through Eaton's Mile" (a very large shopping mall in downtown Toronto), we joked together. "Why not do it in May, when Toronto has emerged from the long winter season to blossom in the spring. People are more inclined to wander out and seek physical exercise."

"North Americans love parades. Could this be used somehow in this connection?", she asked. "It would be very difficult to compete with them, but the idea of a Toronto Spring Run could certainly use some of a parade's elements", I replied. "Maybe you could organize something at the conclusion." "Fine", she said. "Let's go ahead. Perhaps we could have a workshop to discuss further innovations." I replied that I would gladly participate whenever needed. And so it happened. Today the Toronto Spring Run, organized by June and her associates, is a great event, ending up at the Sky Dome with an exciting parade and a Ladies' Dance. A curiosity perhaps worth mentioning is a yearly charter flight full of participants from Helsinki, coached — guess by whom?

STIMULATOR OF ORGANIZATIONAL CREATIVITY

June Hayward joined her first advertising agency as a copywriter in a newly formed television department after earning her MBA at Buffalo State University. There she had been impressed by the studies in creativity which had been funded by the noted advertising executive, Alex Osborn, who was, incidentally, the originator of the brainstorming technique.

June was convinced that she could get a good start in her business career by beginning at the core point where the producer's messages to customers are designed — the level requiring the greatest creativity. As it developed, although she was not particularly successful as a copywriter, her boss discovered that she possessed considerable team management skills and offered her a job which would utilize this talent as well as require the increased customer contacts she had wished. June accepted the proposal and soon developed into a successful negotiator and team leader, able to attract important new customers to the agency. Her major responsibility was to plan and launch the main corporate image campaigns for companies like Canadian Air, Mobil Corporation, Philip Morris and Tandy. These clients, I was told, were very enthusiastic about her teams' ability to generate novel ideas and excitement in their campaigns. Despite a degree of personal success, she was not comfortable with the leadership style or the general atmosphere of the organization and left to join a newly formed advertising agency in Toronto as a creative director. The agency's mission was to create advertising strategies for clients in the service industries. The board of directors gave her a free hand to create an agency environment and working methods according to her own ideas and standards.

During the past seven years the agency has shown a yearly growth well above the average for the industry in North America. A great part of this success has been due to the innovative managerial style of June Hayward. She has combined research, creative campaign planning and the use of the most modern media. The forecast for the business remains quite positive.

DIAMONDS

In June Hayward's view it is important that managers stimulate an atmosphere that encourages everyone in a company to bring up seemingly crazy, wild ideas without fear of ridicule. She has observed many times during her career that ideas which may sound crazy when you hear them the first time, often serve as a useful basis for solutions which are original, and differentiate the company and its products from its competitors. As she expresses it: "What we are aiming for in our advertising are original, novel concepts. To beat our competition we have to be able to develop unique solutions for our customers' problems, giving them creative and cost-effective advertising — real value for every dollar spent."

According to June, many far-out but useful ideas will emerge if you just encourage your team to come out with them. For example, usually if you ask for ideas for marketing a new brand of jeans for horse riding or for motor car driving or perhaps in a school or disco setting, conventional ideas will emerge. But if you encourage a team to seek a novel or "crazy context" they will create ideas like:

- *The TV symphony orchestra's director Ricardo Monteverdi is conducting, and the picture slowly slides from his white tie and tails downward, revealing that he wears new jeans, marked clearly, "Free-Style", the brand name invented by the team*
- *In a luxurious boardroom, all of the directors are wearing jeans, and yelling in chorus: "We want Free-Style!"*
- *Frankenstein's monster rises slowly up from the laboratory table wearing jeans and states in a somber voice: "Free-Style, I'll live"*

"However, crazy ideas are not enough." She continues: "As Creativity Director I have to manage the input of our people to guide the flow of ideas into effective implementation." June's secret as a STIMULATOR and successful innovative manager is her ability to work through creative teams. "As a manager you have to understand how important it is to be patient, to overcome the temptation to always present your own solutions to the problems before the team members have even had time to open their mouths. You'll never benefit from the whole potential of the team's creativity if you don't give them the chance to participate", June states.

After getting to know her better, we could appreciate the symbolic meaning of the question marks in her room, on her memos and even on some of the blouses she wore. It is simply a reminder to herself and her people that the most productive creative technique is to use catalytic questions whenever possible. "You'll often get the best solutions by formulating problems clearly and stimulating other people to come up with their answers", she declared. We found out that this questioning approach was also one of the main reasons for her success with customers.

PEARLS

June Hayward's further opportunities for success are dependent on her ability to recruit talented individuals and provide an environment in which they are able to work as really creative teams. She is able by her personal contribution to stimulate a spirit within the department characterized by excitement and enthusiasm for original, novel ideas as well as a high work motivation. Her presence continually spurs the team's efforts to produce unique and effective advertising campaigns for the agency's clients. A survey done by a local market research institute revealed that her colleagues described the culture of their agency as shown in Figure 3.2.

To be able to keep motivation high among the staff, June must continue to turn in a winning performance in the highly competitive advertising business. This will bring further rewarding opportunities to the team members and increased personal recognition. Her success as a manager is especially dependent on her ability to continue to invent new, attractive rewards and incentives for getting the right new people onto her teams and to stimulate senior team members to continue to work enthusiastically.

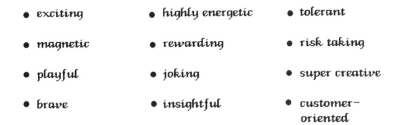

- exciting
- magnetic
- playful
- brave

- highly energetic
- rewarding
- joking
- insightful

- tolerant
- risk taking
- super creative
- customer-oriented

Figure 3.2 The Culture at June's Agency

STONES

Despite an overall sympathetic view of June's role profile as an innovative manager, we do have a few critical comments:

What concerns us is that as a Stimulator, June sometimes separates herself from the group and fails to enter into the play with her own ideas. She has a fine inquiring mind which formulates questions accurately and guides the listener's interest to the real focus of the problem. But she must also think about developing her own creative talent. Some, especially new team members, expect her to contribute her ideas in group sessions — even if just some encouraging examples. She must remember that she is their role model and the person with whom they identify. One of her colleagues remarked that June is a super delegator. "She gives freedom, challenges for creative approaches, but she should also think about how many tasks one can accomplish within our projects' time limits."

ASHES

Even the most original ideas fly away and are easily forgotten. Today's original ideal and unique solutions are routine tomorrow, as they are followed, imitated and used repeatedly. To stay innovative, the company must seek fresh views and approaches. But to do that the people should be stimulated, rewarded and continuously challenged. This requires that managers use a great deal of imagination. June's main problem and threat might be how she will be able to maintain her own originality in her management and leadership tasks. Marion Diamond, the noted brain researcher at the University of California, would probably give June some simple but effective advice: "Use it or lose it", pointing to the importance and the necessity for continuous use of the brain in creative exercises.

What about June's capacity to get things done? We are aware of the "too much creativity and too little profitable implementation" syndrome, but we believe that June has energy to push her projects and campaigns through, which will reflect on the bottom line.

Our message to June:

- *KEEP your inquiring mind. It helps you to find solutions and unique ideas with your teams and your customers*
- *KEEP your efforts to maintain creative teams working in the most inspiring atmosphere and environment*
- *KEEP fostering creative talent and encourage newcomers to act as enthusiastic team members*
- *DEVELOP the incentive system and look continuously for new means of remuneration*
- *DEVELOP managerial support within your company in order to be able to execute new ideas. You need supporters and protectors at the board of director level*
- *DEVELOP your own creativity; profit from the immense potential of your brain: "Use it or lose it"*
- *DEVELOP your knowledge and skill in the use of advanced creativity techniques like Synectics, Morphology, TKJ, Pool-writing and IMAGINE! They help you to find your productive path in creating imaginative solutions.*

Chapter 3

Self-Assessment:
Stimulator

HOW DO YOU RATE YOURSELF AS A "STIMULATOR"?

Please take a few minutes to rate yourself according to the following items.
Place one numerical rating in the left hand column and one in the right.

How do you rate yourself in the following activities? (Select numerical rating.)		How important is this to your managerial career? (Select numerical rating.)	
VERY GOOD 7.....6.....5.....4.....3.....2.....1	INEFFICIENT #	VERY IMPORTANT 7.....6.....5.....4.....3.....2.....1	NOT IMPORTANT #
a	Creating an environment where my people feel free to express their ideas	a	
b	Communicating by humour	b	
c	Maintaining rites, rituals and ceremonies	c	
d	Making clients feel that their suggestions and ideas are valued	d	
e	Twisting and shaking complacency	e	
f	Encouraging my subordinates to present wild, far-out ideas in meetings	f	
g	Visiting subordinates' home-ground to discuss improvements in their work	g	
h	Using catalytic questions	h	
i	Stimulating creative teamwork-ing in my organization	i	

Plot your ratings in the matrix:

I am inefficient (1–4)	I am very good (5–7)
IS VERY A IMPORTANT	IS VERY B IMPORTANT
IS NOT C IMPORTANT	IS NOT D IMPORTANT

MY TOP FIVE DEVELOPMENT CHALLENGES AS A "STIMULATOR":

1 _____

2 _____

3 _____

4 _____

5 _____

Chapter 4

Bridging the Gap Between Inspiration and Application: The Manager as a MASTER

The Master as an innovative manager is an expert in his/her field, and uses expertness as the source for continuous innovation. The Master is often an independent entrepreneur or an intrapreneur in an established company. His/her objective is a highly developed expert organization with an intellectual atmosphere where professional pride is a leading motivational force and career development has a high priority.

USE IMAGINATION AND CREATE ORDER!

The Master has a creative human drive to understand, to reason, to imagine and to create order[1]. The scientifically oriented Master's innovative work has roots in scientific research and discipline that helps a company to grasp opportunities in the highly competitive business world. The *creative* scientist is involved in basic research aimed at increasing our understanding of natural phenomena, experimenting with things, and adding new information to current theories and methodologies or providing the basis for totally new ones. However, the creative scientist does not always approach difficult problems by working logically and sequentially. As Arthur Fry[2] in his speech at AMA's New Product Conference recently emphasized: ". . . in fact, science advances by discovery, or the observation of surprises or anomalies that don't fit our current theories. And then the theory is always developed afterwards".

The Master is rather an *innovative* scientist, often in the role of an engineer who aims to create something concrete, to apply scientific understanding to some practical purpose. Creative scientists long ago formulated a theory of how atoms interact with each other. The innovative IBM scientists Gerd Binning and Heinrich Rohrer earned the Nobel Prize in Physics in 1986 for inventing the scanning tunnelling microscope, which creates images that allow us to see how individual atoms are arranged on surfaces[3].

The discoveries created by innovative scientists show the way to practical uses and the more mundane work, usually done by an engineering team, is the development of these discoveries into efficient devices and saleable products. Herbert A. Simon[4] suggests that *hard work and persistence represent a very large part of the ingredients that go into creative performance.* "We should not be surprised if we find that many creative people behave like workaholics", he emphasizes. Simon's review[5] of the managerial creativity process includes strong evidence of the need for managerial expertness derived from scientific research as well as management practice. His evidence shows that effective problem solving rests on knowledge that permits the expert to grasp situations intuitively and rapidly. The intuition is, according to Simon, the by-product of training and experience that has been stored as knowledge. Per Benterude[6] says that *intuitive thinking is a gateway to knowledge beyond logic.* He even goes so far as to argue that the future's most important managerial tool is more likely to be human intuition rather than the computer.

Innovativeness is a core concept in Research and New Product Development. A manager needs innovativeness to:

- *acquire and administer continuously new information*
- *create new knowledge to dispersed and utilized within the company*
- *master customer and supplier contacts*
- *apply discoveries imaginatively to new product and process development*
- *create breakthrough products*
- *acquire financial and material resources*
- *attract talented and creative individuals and teams*
- *master the management of creative individuals and teams*
- *master entre- and intrapreneuring*
- *create markets for new products*

DOUBLE YOUR MISTAKES

To function successfully as a Master you have to encourage imagination and still create order. The expert organization normally has an abundance of ideas which come from the imagination of the creative staff as well as from diverse outside sources. The Master encourages continuous ideation by accepting the fact that creative people often make mistakes. As Dorman Lesley refers to Dean Simonthon[7] at the University of California saying, *"Great geniuses make tons of mistakes. They have a kind of internal fortress that allows them to fail and just keep going."* The Master helps his people to build up this kind of fortress. But an abundance of ideas is only the starting point. It takes the innovative processes to develop the ideas into workable forms and further efforts are needed to bring the innovations successfully into the market.

The Master guides these processes by leaving enough space for non-conforming, creative thinking. Otherwise the process of guiding turns into a bureaucratic control with administrative procedures and forms resulting in "paper shuffling" instead of the essential dedication of time and energy to innovation.

DEVELOP YOUR PROFESSIONAL EXPERTISE

A Master's thinking is largely conditioned by a devotion to professionalism, which according to Corwing[8] exhibits certain general characteristics. Among these is expertise in a particular area of work where the complexity and the need for adaptability requires case-by-case decisions. The development of such expertise usually takes a lengthy period of training. By definition professionals act on a basis of service to others as well as a commitment to the values of their own community of colleagues. In practical commercial terms this often results in a thoughtful orientation to the needs of their company's clients. They exercise considerable autonomy in making work decisions. This, of course, requires a high standard of professional ethics which implies that it is the profession itself which sets the standard, rather than the employing institution. Characteristic of the Master is his/her pride in the ability to solve difficult problems alone, a tendency supported by a lifelong devotion to learning.

NETWORK

The development of innovations is at present highly dependent upon new knowledge. *Ingenious ways to acquire and use information sources and resources provide the essential venue for the practice of innovation.* John Kay[9] has created the concept of "organizational knowledge" resulting from easy and open access to information and giving more value than any individual knowledge in a company. To Kay the "architecture of a firm" means a network of relationships inside a company and between companies. The current trend to decentralize research and development activities and production in global companies has necessitated the development of a new kind of "architecture of a firm" — networking. The Master is the pioneer of *networking* in his/her organization. He/she has the ability to innovate and get other people to innovate in an information intensive environment. Ideas are often born out of intensive communication with others in the company — salespeople, production staff, researchers, designers. In the case of complex problems and technically highly advanced innovations, communication with the external world — customers, consumers, suppliers, inventors, scientists and research-ers in other institutions — is essential.

The intellectual "social network" may operate via traditional channels like technical conferences, laboratory meetings and buyer seminars. Some highly innovative companies like Sealed Air, the inventor of the ingenious "bubble packaging" (AirCap, Bubble-Lite, Poly Mask), have discovered many ways to contact customers to understand thoroughly their packaging problems. For example, Sealed Air's representatives are told to end some of their workdays on the packaging lines of their customers. This behaviour encourages creative discussions between representatives and customers. One of our executive friends told us that he occasionally starts a day having morning coffee with one of his key customer's directors to find out what new discoveries *they* have come up with lately. "A useful way to get up-to-date ideas", he says.

Especially in computer, telecommunication, banking and insurance companies the intellectual creative network is based on the use of new information technology. Telematics, as it is called by the EU Commission, is the combination of computer-based technologies and telecommunications and will make a significant contribution to the development of innovations within the EU markets. Establishing trans-European networks between companies, libraries and other information centres, such as universities, research institutions, and public organizations, provides an excellent opportunity for highly skilled professionals to keep abreast of innovative developments in their fields. The conventional modes of information acquisition and exchange are usually too time consuming and costly. Modern networks allow just-in-time access to learning and knowledge resources. Some of the telematic tools and systems such as information database systems and electronic mail are available for information acquisition and exchange. Others like computer-conferencing, audio- and videoconferencing and PC-videoconferencing are applicable for creative idea exchange and discussion. The use of expert systems and simulations via close links with key customers and suppliers through collaborative R&D belong to the Master's core capabilities.

Do not neglect the human social network. Regardless of Internet, "The real networking is still done face to face", as *Euro Business* magazine points out in their June 1995 edition. They offer some handy suggestions as to where one might "bump into" some of the big names. A few examples: Terry Barnevik, CEO, ABB—walking in England's Lake District; Silvio Berlusconi, CEO—Fininvest, wherever his soccer club, AC Milan is playing; Jorma Ollila, CEO—Nokia, any respectable sauna between Oslo and Omsk. (A common complaint is that women are effectively excluded from the deal-making process because they are rarely invited into the same sauna as men. The Finnish companies solve the problem with two saunas—the women rejoin the men for dinner. The authors can also testify that women occasionally engage in "sauna crashing". We've heard no complaints to date.)

Generating a workable networking system is by no means an easy task. The manager has to find the most valuable sectors and areas of collaboration, attract partnership in the network, motivate participation and find resources. Here the skills of the Creator are needed and, as we shall see, those of the Persuader.

HARNESS INDIVIDUAL ASSETS

This professional orientation leaves its mark on the managerial behaviour of the Master. He/she seeks to hire and find ways to support talents who enjoy working as experts within the organization. As a manager, the Master will respond to the needs of these talented people for challenging tasks that require intrinsic motivation and provide a sense of the joy of discovery.

To advance the organization into top-level technology or applied science and to achieve success as the "reformer" in the field, the Master's managerial style is supportive. This is evidenced by continuous recognition of co-workers' achievement, special awards, support for career development and encouraging the innovative projects of individuals and teams. He/she typically ranks the intellectual atmosphere higher than the "crass" business culture within an organization.

The Master as an innovative manager understands the danger that, although producing remarkable inventions and innovations requires a high degree of expertness, specialization of many experts, for example product development people, may cause them to value product improvement and new products as an end in itself. Whether it be functional, image improvement or of economic value, it is a product, rather than a user orientation, typical of many giant manufacturing organizations.

The Master is client oriented and tuned to their needs and preferences. This prevalent attitude helps him/her to overcome the difficulties which expert teams can encounter, especially when the team members represent various disciplines. Their specific expertise may make them unwilling to accept other members' approaches and ideas. In this situation the Master must act as arbiter and help them understand that satisfying customer needs and desires should be the real focus of their concentration.

* * *

3M — INNOVATION MACHINE

In November 1994 the company announced that 3M people had contributed 4100 ideas which helped the company to eliminate 1.3 billion pounds of pollutants and saved the company more than $710 million in 3M's *Pollution Prevention Pays*[13]. We became interested to know more about how management functions in 3M and found out that information was easily accessible because top management have openly described their management methods[14]; especially informative is the innovative home page of 3M on Internet[15].

The large number of suggestions is understandable considering 3M's size — more than 80,000 people operating in 45 business units in 49 countries around the world, launching 66,000 products of enormous variety and achieving annual sales of almost $15 billion. They achieve this by:

- *Visionary methods*: every business unit manager is expected to vision business opportunities 15 years ahead
- *Hunting for new products*: 30% of sales must come from products introduced within the past four years
- *Mastering teamwork*: mix information, people and expertise for lowering new product lead times
- *Allowing bootlegging*: technical personnel and researchers can use 15% of their time for experimenting with new ideas
- *Encouraging communication*: cross-functional, cross-hierarchical, cross-cultural, cross-technological, cross-tool communication is rewarded
- *Stimulating customers*: searching for customers' needs and problems and brainstorming with customers for getting new ideas is expected
- *Motivating creators and champions*: making the researchers' career ladder conform to the management ladder in terms of prestige, position and compensation
- *Providing support*: giving trust and facilitating change processes and tolerating failures especially when one is experimenting with original ideas and gaining new knowledge through making mistakes
- *Loyal lifers*: encouraging managers to stay in 3M and carry the torch of innovation
- *Nurturing innovative culture*: hiring entrepreneurial people and providing them with time, funding, facilities, teams, projects, and creative environment

* * *

JUMP SHIP

The Master's innovative achievements can take many forms. According to the traditional classification of Robertson in Minkes[10] they can be:

- continuous innovations, i.e. marginal changes, of which fluoride toothpaste and chemical fertilizers are good examples
- dynamically continuous innovations, such as electrically powered movers and computer aided design methods
- discontinuous innovations, such as television, computers, video recorders

Radical discontinuous innovations are of course the most attractive for the Masters because they hold the most potential for the future and when successful bring with them prestige and financial reward. But the work is the most risky and the absolute majority of discoveries in that category are failures in their implementation.

It must also be considered that not only is innovative work a complex and time-consuming process for those directly involved, radical innovations often disturb existing patterns of working and established organizational relationships. Nonetheless the innovative spirit seems to flourish among individuals and entrepreneurial organizations. Steven H. Kim[11] refers to a study of 58 major innovations drawn from Europe and America ranging from photography to fluorescent lighting and from computers to ballpoint pens, pointing out that among these innovations, at least 46 originated from individuals or organizations other than key companies in the mainstream industries.

Pryor and Shays[12] argue that a formal product development process is rarely an innovating force. "Many if not most successful innovations come from the 'wrong' places — mavericks with an obsession about something, individuals stumbling on new discoveries by accident, people finding new uses for products intended for different markets, and so on." They base their thesis on the research done by Brian Quinn who found after 25 years of studying IBM, General Electric, Polaroid and Xerox that not a single major product had come from the formal planning process.

Many Masters have found it difficult to work out the transition from their original ideas to innovations in the company where they have made their discoveries. They have to move elsewhere to pursue their interests. They "jump ship"! This provides an opportunity to build up a business of their own. Only a few companies can provide the high level of earning that the brightest "breakthrough innovators" are able to achieve as independent entrepreneurs. The ownership of the company and the status and freeedom it brings with it causes entrepreneuring to be attractive to many innovators.

Research shows[16] that a large proportion of those innovators who have left their companies and formed their own enterprises are successful.

TAKE A LEAP WITH A SAFETY NET BENEATH

A greater number of Masters as innovative managers can usually find no real reason to leave their established companies. They enjoy their interesting work, excellent working conditions, respect of their colleagues and real security. Consequently, they strive to behave like intra-corporate entrepreneurs, i.e. intrapreneurs within a company. The intrapreneur is an ambitious employee who invents a new product or service and strives to push it through within the company until it is launched onto the market. Intrapreneurs attempt to get the space, time and freedom to experiment, assess, test and modify their ideas. They are often motivated without any encouragement other than an opportunity provided[17]. However, the intrapreneurs' efforts will often be compensated in various ways, most often with incentive bonuses because they cannot work on a set time schedule. They often have to work extended hours and do all kinds of mundane tasks themselves. The intrapreneurs' main problem is usually how to get resources. The greater the degree of creativity, the more radical the innovation, the larger should be the investment of capital, people and time. If not available in the form of R&D money, or someone's "petty cash fund", they usually simply "bootleg" the resources. If the company does not allow "slack time", a certain amount of freely usable time for experimenting with new ideas, they use their own time for that purpose.

FOCUS ON LONG-TERM INVESTMENTS

Quinn and Mueller in Minkes[18] interviewed 200 research executives in the USA and concluded that they had to perform research as a leisurely process somehow abstracted from the "crass" commercial world. They were constrained to work almost casually on projects of tremendous competitive significance to the company. They explained the problem as a tendency of the operating management to favour quick returns on their investments. Adams[19] argues that the operating management usually wants a short-term improvement, "more for the buck" and ends up giving a short-term commitment of "bucks" to get to the desired end. "As the short-term wisdom has it, R&D comes out of profits (usually this quarter's profit)", says Adams. On the contrary, the innovative manager understands that the firm may have to invest considerable resources for the long term in order to improve the company's situation in the future.

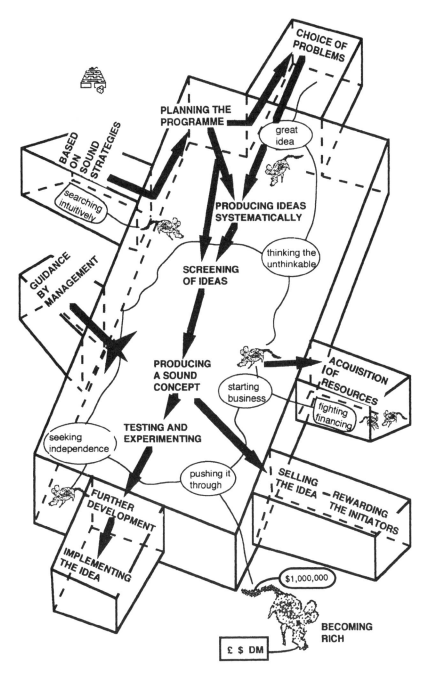

Figure 4.1 How do We Innovate — Through Normal Channels or Underground?

Improvements to products and services are possible with a short-term cash commitment, but the "star products" can only be created by investing time and money for the long term. The Master as an innovative manager urges top management to find the resources for long-term efforts even in a company where they are tightly controlled and restricted. If the resources are not available in the budget, he or she tries to find them from outside sources such as foundations or venture capital. The Master is in a privileged position if his CEO also happens to be a Master who understands the need to help other Masters overcome resistance within the organization and to support innovative efforts. It often happens that when the Master has successfully launched an innovation onto the market the CEO assigns him/her to be the manager of the new venture.

The Master may not readily understand that he cannot solve all the problems and make all important decisions by his own technical competence and special expertise. In most innovative companies particularly in the high-tech sector, it may take as many as a hundred innovative contributors to create a successful breakthrough. *Knowledge may also inhibit creativity, especially if the expert wears a mental straitjacket and is unwilling to admit that others can also come up with something remarkable in their own particular subject areas.* The manager must be on guard to prevent expert knowledge from becoming a weapon to strike with: a killer of the layman's idea-generation. Total professional orientation may also be an obstacle to innovativeness in the Master's organization especially if his/her self-image is that of a scientist rather than a business person. He or she may create great new ideas but may be uninterested or too impatient to work out commercial innovations from them.

The Master as an executive may prefer to organize the company's activities according to the model of independent entrepreneurial units which when led by aggressive and innovative experts may develop into autonomous competitive divisions. Although this situation may cause a hindrance to the necessary cooperation in marketing, product development and research, companies such as 3M and Citibank have deliberately fostered this type of competition. Our point of view is that the Master must take advantage of developments in diverse units by getting them also to cooperate in attaining corporate goals.

Our first profile manager, Max Hopper, is an innovative scientist. He was on the way to becoming an academic researcher until he became interested in business life. He had an urgent need to see his efforts implemented successfully in practice. The second profile manager, Lenty Tregubenko, is a Master in a more restricted area, but is perhaps even more persistent and hard working so as to be able to tolerate very difficult, even hostile working conditions and continuously changing environments. He maintains close contacts with other Masters in his field as a stimulus to innovativeness.

MAX HOPPER: A MASTER'S INTRAPRENEURIAL FLAIR

Max took part in our seminar on Corporate Innovativeness and he attracted our attention in the first "ice-breaker" exercise. Being an electrical engineer, he was elected by the seminar participants to supervise the design of a moveable steam train, using the seven members of his group. The start in the morning had been a bit stiff, perhaps because it was an open seminar and people had not known each other beforehand. So we decided to start with an exercise which gets people to loosen up. Max's train was a hit. He had organized the seven participants by giving to each of them a role description, such as: to act as a wheel, or an axle, or as an engine or a steampipe. And of course the whistle! He rehearsed them briefly, and the train started to move in a very amusing way. The atmosphere soon became very relaxed and responsive.

Max Hopper's interest in electronics goes back to his childhood in Australia. He was fascinated by all kinds of electrical toys, taking them apart to discover how they operated. He was a member of the "Edison Club" which was run by the physics teacher in the school. His classmates were exceptionally bright, and several of them later achieved high academic and professional status. Max considers that the "intellectual" atmosphere at the school greatly influenced his development.

Max was not considered by his fellow students to be a particularly sociable person. His younger brother, William, to the contrary, knew everyone in the small town near Melbourne where they lived. He sought the company of many of their neighbours and greeted everyone he met on the street in a friendly way. No wonder that he later found his career in Australian politics. Max, instead, would often avoid contacts, even crossing to the other side of the street if he recognized someone approaching. He liked to spend time alone, reading and experimenting with things. His only close contacts were with fellow students he worked with, creating something together.

Any kind of electrical apparatus became fair game for his inquiring mind and probing hands. His anxious mother often warned him that he would one day be the victim of electric shock, but this did not deter him. On one occasion, an elderly neighbour told William that she urgently needed the services of an electrician and had not been able to find one of the few in town to be available. Max gladly offered his help and proceeded to repair the electrical wiring and replaced the old switches and sockets. As he was only 17 at the time and had no licence, this was of course illegal, but at the time it seemed the best solution. "One day", Max told us, "I was returning home when I heard the fire engine approaching. Looking towards our neighbourhood there was smoke billowing into the air. I started to run towards the fire, thinking: my heaven, that's the house where I worked on those damn things. My shock and fright turned to joy when I saw that it was a neighbouring building that was burning. I wondered what people thought as they saw my smiling face."

During our discussions with Max we spoke of people who from a very early age were completely devoted to their work and who would eagerly seek contacts and aquaintances with older professionals, virtually begging them for the chance to assist or be helpful in some way. Max was that kind of youngster and usually was able to find a mentor who would share his knowledge and skills. Despite some rather risky experiments, Max fared better than the later-to-be-famous Nobels, father and son, who in their time literally blew a small Swedish village into the air with their unrefined dynamite, and had to escape to Russia.

Already as a young boy, Max had gained considerable skill as a laboratory technician, and when he graduated from high school it seemed a natural decision for him to study physics at Melbourne University. There he was actively engaged in research in the field of photoelectronics, an interest which continued into his professional life.

When his father, an engineer for a multinational firm, was asked to move to New Jersey, Max faced a difficult decision. He had recently finished his work for his PhD and had been offered a research fellowship at the university and, of course, opportunities which he envisioned in the US were also enticing.

Max's decision to remain in Melbourne was influenced by a close friend and colleague, Gary Anderson, who planned to start his own company specializing in solving technical problems of safe operation of electrical systems. The government had recently passed stricter safety regulations, and Gary judged the timing to be just right. Max accepted his offer of a partnership. The new partners' initial attempts to raise venture capital were discouraging, but through friends and aquaintances, and a few local businessmen who had faith in the project, they managed to raise nearly $500,000. In addition they applied for and received $200,000 as a federal R&D grant as well as local government credit guarantees.

Max and Gary invented a number of interesting products, not only directly applicable to electrical safety systems, but in related areas as well. One of the most successful was a means of connecting residential smoke detectors into a "safety series", a product that found a European market as well. This was later developed as a standard model for use in larger buildings such as stores and warehouses. Max enjoyed being in at the birth of a new enterprise and considered himself lucky to experience the fascinating early growth period of the business.

Though their business was flourishing, Max started to become restless. He had to devote too much time to solving problems which were not related to his line of research or real interests. Many of his evenings were spent going over research reports, or reading books and product descriptions written and produced by others. Lacking time for concentration on his own main interests, he felt frustrated. "My projects were too mechanical because we were working in the area of industrial wiring, with its sockets, screws, plugs and switches, and I'd been all through that too often before", Max told us. He realized that either he should go back to concentrating on his own special field and build a university career, or join a major company which had the resources to permit him to do both basic R&D and applicative work. "In a larger firm I would be surrounded by other scientists and engineers. The work load could likely be set on a more steady base and I could have more time and opportunity for further study and research activities", Max explained.

Max left the partnership and with his father's assistance found a position as assistant R&D manager in a multinational firm headquartered in New Jersey. His first assignment was to develop original safety features for the company's large industrial projects. At work, Max made the aquaintance of Terry Dougherty, chief of the company's "lucrative technologies" centre, and was intrigued by what he observed there. As Max continued, "A professional engineer might not be excited by the goods they produced, but the technologies and machines which were developed there — well, that was something special! You may remember me telling you that at the Institute of Technology in Melbourne I had been working in the area of photoelectronics and we had experimented with a zooming mechanism. After my first visit to Terry's center several ideas of how to apply a combination of these two concepts to Terry's electrical machinery had been churning over and over again in my mind. Even while I continued to work on my main projects my mind couldn't rid itself of the new challenge."

Lacking official permission to move to Terry's department, Max asked him if he could work there in his free time. He "bootlegged" material and soon presented Terry with a prototype of his first significant invention, FOCUS ONE. Terry enthusiastically organized money and material to support the idea and got permission for Max to move to his centre. After FOCUS ONE was put into production and had quickly found a worldwide market, Max was assigned as head of a unit to develop new products of this type. Over the next several years, his progress was rapid, and he was promoted to head the New Business Division. In later years, as vice-president of the company, he still maintained his responsibility for new business and application of technological advances. When the board of directors promoted Max to president, he had to enlarge his attention to overall strategic issues of the corporation.

DIAMONDS

Max Hopper is a MASTER, an expert in his field who combines genuine insight with experience and superior knowledge. His main interest is to find new solutions to challenging problems. His inner enthusiasm for research and new technologies drives him to a fanatical dedication to whatever intrapreneurial project he happens to work with or lead at the time. He has been able to create an intellectual atmosphere in his organization where professional pride and individual career development are fostered. Max is able to solve many problems through his own means, and this in turn motivates his colleagues to seek new and exciting solutions as well. Even though not a very sociable person by nature, as we have observed, Max can be quite funny and amusing in his own weird way. This often relieves tension and makes it easy to work with him. He constantly emphasizes the importance of top professional know-how, and presents continual challenges to his people. This demonstrates a keen understanding of his group.

* * *

A statement put by Max on his laboratory wall:

A Professional Engineer *is competent by virtue of his fundamental education and training to apply the* scientific method *and outlook to the solution of problems, and to assume personal responsibility for the* development *and* application *of engineering science and techniques, especially in research, designing and manufacturing, superintending and managing. His work is predominantly* intellectual *and varied, and not of a routine mental or physical character, but requires the exercise of* original thought *and, if necessary, the responsibility for supervising the technical and administrative work of others.*

(The definition developed and was accepted at the European and United States Engineering Conference.)

* * *

PEARLS

One of the reasons why Max was appointed as Director of New Business and later as president of the company was his ability to promote, recognize and reward professionalism and intrapreneuring, giving opportunities to his colleagues for career advancement and individual project work. He is aware of the need for a highly developed research and development capacity and an effective information centre to help him to reach the company's ambitious goals. Even though advancement in the higher level of technology remains his top priority, Max strongly promotes the commercialization of the ideas and products developed by his group, thus adding the practical side to the conceptual element. Although a talented engineer himself Max has learned to avoid one-sided emphasis on creative engineering. According to him designers should not dictate what a company has to sell. Marketing, service and sales people are closer to the customers. Listen to them!

Max Hopper's company has brand names which exemplify original and lasting, top-quality products. More than 400 R&D people and ten wholly owned production facilities support the company's innovative efforts. Future opportunities for Max are based on expertise in his own area, combined with an extraordinary creative imagination. He is prone to stimulate thinking with "absurd" questions: How can we radiate underwater coloured lighting for swimming pools, for underwater ballets, or for use in bathtubs and aquariums? Or how about lighting up Niagara Falls from within? Even an idea of how to light up a large punch-bowl from which a waiter with an illuminated dipper would serve drinks. But he consequently comes up with creative solutions to those problems with apparent ease. He has considered going further with the commercialization of these ideas by designating them with the brand name WATER SAPPHIRES and suggested the new venture be called THE PHANTASY ILLUMINATING COMPANY.

Even though some of his colleagues consider many of his ideas naive, Max's flights of fancy are sometimes real starting points for new businesses. His career path now lies in developing his ability to act as skipper. He knows what to do, but needs the efforts of his whole team to assist in navigating the company in uncharted seas. In this role he has grown to act more as a champion or sponsor for new intrapreneurs from among his large group of graduate engineers and researchers.

STONES

In some situations Max Hopper seems to hesitate too long. He is reluctant to admit that he doesn't know the answer to some difficult question. He told us that he often thinks that his subordinates consider him to be smarter than he really is. That causes him difficulty to ask questions or to get advice when he is working in unfamiliar areas. We were agreed, though, that fear of being overrated is a common phenomenon among those who advance to high positions. We reminded him of Professor Hans Zetterberg's observation, that once you reach high status in your career, you'll never get rid of it! It follows you everywhere and for your whole life.

ASHES

Max believes that only the "elite" of the company are able to cope with the complex methods and processes which research-based innovation requires. He searches for intrapreneurs only among the "smart circles" of the company.

The threat to Max and to his company lies in his own management style. He seems to be unwilling to utilize the whole company's creative resources. Emphasizing expert knowledge exclusively weakens generations of "floor-level" suggestions and efforts to improve products. When chairing meetings Max often emphasizes his own expertise in the matter in question and is unwilling to listen to the different opinions or may even attack ideas, questions and opinions which do not suit his thinking. This attitude can inhibit creativity and change in his organization.

The company surely produces unique and interesting new products, but the problem seems to lie in a weak adaptation to production. According to our observations, the company must undergo in the next few years a painful process of restructuring operations in order to raise productivity and cut waste.

Max should consider that the company also needs imagination and expertise in various areas. Administration, maintenance, human resource planning and worker protection as well as increased concentration on individual initiative in each person's own job responsibilities are all areas needing attention. Even though progress in these areas does not appear as dramatic to company stockholders, it is essential to the health of the organization. If Max will welcome ideas and suggestions wherever they come from, new ideas, new business concepts and intrapreneurs will pop up all over the company. The Master should give them training, support, resources, time to experiment with their ideas and encourage them to act in close contact with customers. Give them new opportunities for intrapreneuring after failures, because many of them will fail as always happens with development and implementation of new ideas. The future of any engineering firm depends on its people's ability to create new ideas, to come up with better products and processes and smarter designs which provide original solutions for customers' unsatisfied needs.

Our message to Max:

- *KEEP developing and utilizing your own expertise. Using your brain's capacity will continue to provide the most cost-effective and unique solutions*
- *KEEP working with your teams, supporting them and assisting their efforts to find new opportunities together*
- *LEARN to delegate and to give others responsibility. Encourage autonomy among your staff. Demonstrate your confidence and trust in your people*
- *LEARN to take advantage of the creative talent of the whole staff and to invest in the neglected areas of the company's activities*
- *LEARN to act as the master of the transformation process. That's what will be most required in the future*
- *LEARN to listen not only to your innovative researchers and engineers, but also to your marketing, service, sales and production people*

LENTY TREGUBENKO: A MASTER'S ENTREPRENEURIAL DRIVE

We arrived in Leningrad on Sunday morning, having sailed overnight from Helsinki. There was no sight of, or word from, Mr Tregubenko as we came ashore, so we decided to ride into the city and look around. As we passed through the dock area, we noticed a large quantity of heavy and light trucks, buses, construction equipment as well as large wooden crates, all marked for shipment to Cuba. At this time in the mid 1970s, it seemed an impressive lot.

After about a twenty minutes' ride, we arrived at the Hotel Astoria, a large non-descript building with a slightly run-down look, although it was reputed to be one of the best tourist accommodations in the city. We went into the dining room, a large, plain-looking area, with tables with dinner settings on clean white cloths, and in one corner a small platform where, we were told, an orchestra played nightly.

As we drank some not-too-bad coffee, while waiting to be served the "second breakfast" we'd ordered, we overheard an interesting conversation: a gentleman approached our waitress and asked for a glass of mineral water. She replied that she couldn't bring it to him unless he sat at a table and ordered a meal, but that if he went up to his room they would send it to him there. He replied that he wasn't a guest in the hotel, and was informed that if he would go to the desk and register, and then go up to his room, the water would be sent to him. This seemed to us a rather roundabout way of getting a glass of water, even for the Soviet Union.

As we left the hotel and walked out into the square, facing us was the magnificent old St Isaac's Cathedral, now a museum. There was a long line of people waiting to buy tickets to enter, and not wanting to endure the long wait, we asked the elderly ticket taker if we could just look inside for a moment, adding the obvious that we were foreign tourists. She left for a moment to speak with someone, then returned and told us to enter. The interior was breathtaking, with tall columns of the Russian malachite, fine paintings and elaborate lapis lazuli and marble work.

Upon leaving the cathedral we saw Tom, the ship's photographer, signalling to us from across the square. He told us that shortly after we had left, as he was leaving the dock area, a "Mr Tregubenko" had spoken to him, asking if he knew us. It seems that he'd tried to meet the ship, but was denied access to the dock area. Questioning several people, including Tom, he had sent a short note to let us know where to meet him later in the day.

We'd come to know about Tregubenko through our friend and neighbour in Milan. Renato Sacchi was the Export Sales Director for a large Italian motorcycle manufacturer. Through his business connections, he'd established a correspondence with Tregubenko, who was considered to be one of the foremost Soviet experts in the field of small motors for both land and marine use. His writings and research were noted in the Soviet encyclopedias and his articles were published in trade journals throughout Europe and in the USA. Through his extensive correspondence with Renato and others in the industry, he'd been supplied with a flow of printed material pertaining to his professional interests. This access to foreign developments had enabled him to accumulate an exceptional knowledge in his field.

With Tom's description to guide us, we met Mr Tregubenko, and after sending off a greeting card to Renato, we set out to explore the beautiful city of Leningrad. Lenty, as we were soon to call him, had turned out to be a rather small, wiry and energetic man of indeterminate age, perhaps fiftyish. His open friendliness and exuberant spirit immediately endeared him to us. As we headed for the Leningrad subway, which ran from the main station on Nevsky Prospect to the end of the main trunk line, Lenty was a fount of information, both personal and political/historical. He explained that several of the above-ground subway stations are old converted churches. Each underground station is very much like the lobby of a grand theatre, complete with marble floors, columns and crystal chandeliers. One of the most beautiful is the Pushkin station, with a statue of the great Russian poet and dramatist on the platform.

Despite heavy rain, we went next to the Pushkin museum, located in the great man's former home. We saw many fascinating souvenirs of the poet's personal life, even bills for his vain and extravagant wife's clothing. Attentive visitors shuffled about, all of us wearing cloth slippers over our shoes to protect the shiny, waxed floors. Lenty acting as our voluble guide was asked by one group to kindly lower his voice. "Culture" was evidently taken very seriously in the Soviet Union.

JBE continues:

As Lenty and I trudged through the continuing downpour to his apartment, he related details of his life: born into a family of humble origins, his teachers had early recognized his talent for mathematics and science. As the Soviet system provided educational opportunities for promising students, he completed his elementary studies and was admitted to the University of Leningrad where he earned a degree in Electrical Engineering. His warm and open nature, which we found to be typical of many Russians whom we were to meet, combined with a very lively and penetrating intellect, helped him to get a good job in an industrial plant soon after graduation.

We arrived at Lenty's apartment house, which appeared to be the same design, as well as age, of the several adjacent pre-war buildings. Entering, the stairs were chipped, dirty, with the paint and plaster on the walls peeling and cracked. A bare bulb hanging by a wire was the only light. I was shocked to learn that the building had been completed only six months previously. Apparently the materials used in the paint and plaster are of such poor quality they deteriorate immediately. This undoubtedly explained the reason for the city's general look of disrepair, despite the marvellous architecture of many of the buildings.

Entering into the apartment where Lenty lived, he showed me into his own room — one of three in the entire flat, which he shared with two other families. As he busied himself making tea, he continued to tell me about his life. I knew from our mutual friend Renato that he had been in Siberian exile, and hoped he might tell me of the circumstances. Early in the beginning of his professional life, Lenty had begun to make contacts with foreign engineers through the many technical publications he avidly read, and using a postbox number, he had carried on correspondence with a number of foreign professionals in various technical fields. He produced prototypes of his motorcycles and small power boat engines in a musty cellar which he found for his small team, consisting of himself and a few technicians. His first customers were neighbours who were interested in trying out his "handmade" machines.

However, the Soviet officials were suspicious of his activities and they did not allow the promising small enterprise to grow. Lenty soon understood that developing small power machines was one thing, producing and selling them was another. But he was tough. He kept pursuing the development and experimental work. He had no typewriter, and the copy machine in his organization was kept locked up. Direct-dial long distance phone calls were strictly prohibited. So Lenty worked nights to handwrite several copies of his research work, which he secretly got carried to his correspondents in the US and England. As he was permitted a postbox, he received some foreign post, mostly technical journals sent to him in response to his urgent requests.

Due to his propensity to express his freewheeling opinions quite openly, he had attracted the attention of the KGB. After a meeting with Mike Dougal, an American engineer he had corresponded with, the KGB — which had been following his movements — arrested him on a charge of espionage. He was tried and sentenced to *an indeterminate exile in Siberia, in a region where a large industrial plant was under construction. As he was a trained electrical engineer instead of being assigned manual labour, he was given the job of supervising the electrical installation in the plant. This afforded him somewhat better treatment than the others. Also being of robust constitution and a sportsman, he was able to withstand the rigours of the life and climate. His team worked long hours but were motivated because of the better treatment than others in exile. They were able to create workable systems with the most basic materials and tools imaginable, in some cases producing the machines almost from scratch.*

For five years he was kept at the job, forced to remain and work without pay. As the Soviet hierarchy gradually changed, he applied for a review of his case, which was in due time granted, and he was adjudged innocent. Though not allowed to leave, he was put on a salary of 500 rubles per month, at the time considered to be very good pay. After completion of the project in another two years, he was then permitted to return to Leningrad. His wife had died of TB during his exile, and other than a brother living in Kiev, he had no remaining close personal ties. Working independently out of the small room he had found upon his return, Lenty began to concentrate on small power boats and outboard motors, and as we knew, had gradually established himself as an authority in the field.

Looking about his new apartment which he'd just recently been assigned as a "privileged person", I saw that every available bit of wall space was filled with bookcases containing English and American publications in addition to his Russian collection. He said his favourite author was Aldous Huxley and he had many of Huxley's books with the notable exception of Brave New World. *He explained that he had given his copy to a friend, and I promised to replace it. I noticed also copies of Henry Miller's* Tropics. *His opinion: "Very scandalous, but very interesting!" On his desk were copies of US government printing office publications on the flights of the US astronauts, generally available to the public.*

On our way back to the centre of town, we stopped off in a bookstore where I wanted to buy a set of Russian/English dictionaries: the approximately $3 price for the set was a stunning indication of the emphasis placed on education — and propaganda. Obviously my clothes and accent marked me as an American, and we were approached by several young Russians who wanted to talk about the United States. Among them were a chemist and a student engineer who were particularly eager for information. Though we spoke mainly in Russian, they spoke very acceptable English which they had learned in their schools, so they claimed, in just a few semesters. Their serious approach to the study of the language was very impressive.

Lenty told me that he felt there was a natural affinity between the Russian and the American people and that he could foresee a breakdown of some of the existing barriers to trade, commerce and cultural exchange. Moreover he saw himself as a potential mediator in the process, and said he hoped that at some time in the future he could use his extended contacts to become a consultant to foreigners seeking entry into the Soviet system with their products and services. As his thoughts coincided closely with my own, we gave mutual assurances that we would keep our correspondence going. Perhaps certain clients who attended our communication and creativity seminars could possibly be interested in his services, if his predictions of the future turned out to be true.

DIAMONDS

Lenty Tregubenko is an inventor-entrepreneur kind of manager. He has an intrinsic need to invent solutions to the practical problems he observes. His interest and expertise in motorcycles has led him to develop interesting technical solutions in small engine and design technology. He enjoys getting his hands dirty and is committed to metal, screws and oil, but understands as well that to develop something really interesting and important requires that you also commit yourself to research and development matters. That's why he has always made efforts to keep his foreign contacts alive even at the risk of his civil position.

When he returned to Leningrad he accepted a job offer to design small motors in a military equipment plant where his energy and expertness in creative problem solving found an outlet. In this period he experienced for the first time a climate of freedom and he eagerly made contacts to give and receive information and discuss solutions with colleagues. But as he was basically an entrepreneur, he missed the more informal way of doing business. He was more interested in doing right things than doing the things right as his job required, and for him the right things were designing and building small civilian motorcycle motors and outboard motors. He dreamed of a small enterprise of his own like some of his foreign friends had. Finally, Perestroika opened new opportunities and Lenty searched for ways to start his own business. However, he soon realized that even a small technical operation needs to have a good resource base, which he lacked. Again his entrepreneurial talent helped him to find new opportunities.

Lenty, now in his late sixties, has become a respected consultant and trade representative in Russia. He runs a small consultancy group which now employs experts in several fields. The company's mission is to tackle the constraints and problems when starting a client's business in Russia. Lenty is able to convince his customers to start their businesses even when many observers are discouraged by the turmoil and chaos there.

PEARLS

Since the onset of Glasnost and Perestroika in the mid 1980s, he has helped several Italian and German companies to make the right connections. He is presently engaged in steering a medium-sized American producer of educational films through the Russian bureaucracy. He has realized his ambition to become, in his own way, a catalyst in the accommodation between the ex-Soviet Union and the Western world.

With inexhaustible energy and a gradually developing mature patience he is now becoming an effective negotiator for agreements between his foreign clients and their Russian counterparts.

At our invitation, Lenty was recently a guest speaker at one of our seminars, offering some practical advice on how foreign companies could best enter into partnership with Russian companies or state-owned entities. Among his chief recommendations were:

1. *Despite all present problems, Russia has a huge potential being the largest country in the world. To make progress in Russia, above all one has to have patience! It takes time to open up solid lines of communication before one can expect concrete results. Don't transpose your own negotiating time frame to the Russian context. The market economy there is regulated by endless norms, requests for permission and reporting formalities. But even more, the Russian officials change the rules whenever it serves their interests. Personal relationships are extremely important and our company can help you to build up the contacts.*

2. *Even after gaining a foothold in the Russian market, continuing advice from specialists is needed. This is particularly important in coping with the complicated and often incomprehensible tax system. A guide will be needed to lead you through the maze.*

3. *The Russians can generally be relied upon to go through with their side of an agreement. That's the good news. The bad news is that it may be a painfully slow process by Western standards, as the Russians are much slower to enter into agreements. They see the process as a procession in stages, i.e. initial contact, preliminary negotiations, sometimes with an endless succession of meetings before a letter of intent is accomplished and a final agreement is reached.*

4. *By all means use an intermediary who knows his/her way through what is still a "Soviet" system. It is virtually impossible to make the right contacts and carry through to an agreement without one.*

5. *He echoes President Yeltsin's recent remarks to a group of Western business men, advising them to start now. "Get in on the ground floor. We want your help and cooperation."*

With a well-disciplined expertness combined with a real love for human contact, Lenty has finally — somewhat late in life — discovered his path. And he never forgot his special interests which he now can pursue in his free time. For the first time last year he travelled outside Russia and after our seminar he participated in a power-boat regatta held in Stockholm. Lenty, in his newly acquired colourful boating costume, was a popular figure during the festivities.

STONES

Lenty as a Master and an entrepreneur has been able to produce innovations successfully. However, as Greiner has shown, entrepreneurs' energies are often mainly directed at product or service development. An entrepreneur enjoys organizing things through informal and frequent contacts and long hours of work. But this kind of activity leads to crisis when managerial competence is urgently needed. He seems to have difficulties understanding that the managerial problems cannot be solved merely by his technical competence.

During negotiations Lenty's somewhat impetuous nature makes him want to get to the high hurdles before he has been able to build up a sufficient basis of perceived benefits and mutual trust with new clients. Although humanly very empathetic, his highly emotional nature often brings him into conflict with others who may not share his very definite views.

ASHES

As a patriotic Russian, Lenty Tregubenko is torn between love for his country and a complete distrust of all forms of bureaucracy. He is pessimistic about the possibility of the present system acquiring enough flexibility to accommodate the market-oriented changes necessary. This distrust leads him to continue to work without sufficient administrative back-up in his own small organization, and he has lacked support in some critical negotiation situations. This is also because, like many entrepreneurs, Lenty is apt to think that no other person in his organization could take his place in a given situation. His inability or unwillingness to delegate caused one of his promising young associates to leave.

Our message to Lenty:

- *KEEP your spirit and love of your fellow man, your joy in human contacts*
- *KEEP your inquiring mind, which looks constantly for new ways to open up new opportunities for clients*
- *KEEP your entrepreneurial bent which helps you to maintain the ability to take risks, to work under conditions of high uncertainty and unpredictability and to remain willing to change your course of action*
- *LEARN to take an interest in, and to become a mentor for, younger colleagues. Train them to grow up to the forefront of their expert area and learn to take pleasure in their success, rather than seeking the "bright lights and trumpets" for yourself alone. This is the sign of a mature person*
- *LEARN to accept the fact that your colleagues may have even better knowledge in some of their areas than you have. That's why you must encourage them to find solutions to their problems independently*

Chapter 4

Self-Assessment: Master

HOW DO YOU RATE YOURSELF AS A "MASTER"?

Please take a few minutes to rate yourself according to the following items.
Place one numerical rating in the left hand column and one in the right.

How do you rate yourself in the following activities? (Select numerical rating.)			How important is this to your managerial career? (Select numerical rating.)		
VERY GOOD INEFFICIENT 7.....6.....5.....4.....3.....2.....1 #			VERY IMPORTANT NOT IMPORTANT 7.....6.....5.....4.....3.....2.....1 #		
a	Being a life-long learner		a		
b	Dedicating my time and energy to innovation		b		
c	Keeping abreast of continuous discoveries in my field		c		
d	Encouraging my people to create, invent, experiment and innovate		d		
e	Accepting real risk when experimenting with new things		e		
f	Supporting champions who dedicate themselves to innovations		f		
g	Developing my subordinates' professional knowledge and skills		g		
h	Placing high priority in the corporate value scale on professional pride and career development		h		
i	Creating an environment favourable to intellectual discussions and debates in my organization		i		

Plot your ratings in the matrix:

I am inefficient (1–4)	I am very good (5–7)
IS VERY IMPORTANT A	IS VERY IMPORTANT B
IS NOT IMPORTANT C	IS NOT IMPORTANT D

MY TOP FIVE DEVELOPMENT CHALLENGES AS A "MASTER":

1 _____

2 _____

3 _____

4 _____

5 _____

Chapter 5

Empowering People: The Manager as a Consultor

> The Consultor sponsors, supports, promotes and coaches the innovative efforts of his/her staff, uses various means of sponsoring and rewarding and creates a rich and cosy working atmosphere. He/she is particularly effective in problem-solving situations which require advice and close support.

The traditional approaches of promoting creativity and innovativeness in companies stress particularly the importance of individual input. A highly creative person is granted mythical corporate status, and magic is expected, Matherly and Goldsmith[1] note. Many executives and consultants believe that a company's most effective way to innovativeness is to conduct careful talent screening and to search for creative individuals. Recruiting them and giving them the opportunity and freedom to use their talents guarantees the creative results. While this may work in some cases like searching for breakthrough ideas in high-technology areas, even there the management has to secure an appropriate working environment and conditions for their talented people.

The main criticism concerning this approach stems from the fact that every organization is a cooperative system and therefore limits individual freedom of action. It is common experience that *many creative individuals encounter difficulties in getting approval of their original thoughts and encouragement and support for their innovative efforts.* As a consequence, the practical results of individual-based creativity training are often limited.

Cooperation and participation provide benefits especially when problems prove difficult to solve. The joint expertise of many fields may be necessary to arrive at the required innovative results. Cooperation is also essential to increase the efficiency of continuous ideation, taking advantage of group pressure and mutual encouragement and motivation among group members. This is especially needed when the management has to guide a transformation process within the organization, for example in the management of quality. The management usually has to work out change operations in all sectors and at all levels. It is not enough to get a few geniuses or experts to produce plans and solve quality problems. The whole staff (why not also customers' representatives?) must be involved and committed to the problem-solving and ideation process. Quality belongs to everyone! Consequently, management has to incorporate quality concepts into every aspect of the operations. It must be remembered that quality includes the quality of the client relationship as well. This means that continued feedback from customers remains the ultimate control.

Innovativeness is a core concept in Management of Quality. A manager needs innovativeness to:

- *incorporate quality concepts as institutional goals into every aspect of a company's operations*
- *get especially customers' and suppliers' input for quality improvement*
- *maintain a high level of quality without impacting negatively on the bottom line. Quality gurus have always maintained that "Quality is free"*
- *organize a high degree of cooperation between units and at all levels*
- *organize training and continuous learning to become an institutional priority*
- *gain mastery of teamwork*
- *create a climate where quality improvements, quality work, innovations and self-improvement are recognized and fostered*

Employees of the twenty-first century will be much better educated than today. They will have easy access to enormous, rich information sources via new communication channels locally, nationally and even globally. Hierarchical levels will not be so clearly differentiated in terms of knowledge and working skills. Subordinates will often be more advanced than their bosses in specific skills like computing and "surfing in communication channels". They simply will have more opportunity to acquire and practise modern technologies than their ever busy managers. With open access to information it will not be possible to run a hierarchy-based work system. Innovative companies will truly realize that their employees are their most important assets.

Not surprisingly, the importance of reformulating human resource (HR) strategies to emphasize training, teamwork, cooperation and participation was one of the key recommendations of the MIT study of competitiveness in eight US industries[2]. An impressive example of the execution of this kind of HR strategy can be found at Premier Industrial Corporation, Cleveland, Ohio. CEO Mandel, interviewed by Richard Osborne[3], described the company's "Profit Improvement Program" as a basic step in the rewarding, top-creative environment. "We employ 5400 people and can have 5000 suggestions a year", said Mr Mandel.

COACHING STRATEGIES

If you ask the people in your organization what they consider to be ideal leadership conditions to encourage ideas and innovations, their answers will probably be:

- giving opportunities and challenges
- consulting in difficulties
- support, encouragement and proper rewards

GIVE OPPORTUNITIES

Not all people in companies need or want to exert all their energies to produce radical innovations. But you as an innovative manager can allow and encourage them to provide important contributions in problem-solving situations which concern them. Most workers willingly participate in programmes to provide continuous incremental quality improvements on their jobs. *Empowerment brings good results.* According to Bowen and Lawler III[4] a survey done by the Center for Effective Organizations at the University of South California shows that Fortune 1000 companies' empowerment programmes had a positive impact on a number of performance indicators such as productivity, quality, profitability and workers' satisfaction. "When skillfully done empowerment of people and total quality management programs can go hand in hand supporting each other", say Bowen and Lawler III.

In many companies the management has been able to collect thousands of ideas and suggestions through empowerment of people. For example, Du Pont in one Pennsylvania plant organized into self-directed teams, letting their employees find their own solutions to problems. They were supported

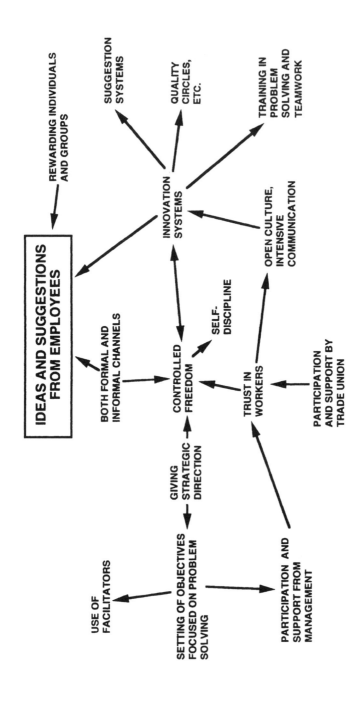

Figure 5.1 Getting People Involved is a Complex Matter, with Many Different Forces Acting in Different Directions. (Printed by Permission of IMA)

by the managers who functioned as facilitators. Fortune[5] reports their past four years' production as being up by 35%.

At Ford Motor Company employees were asked for their ideas for improvements on the prototypes of vehicles. More than three out of four suggestions proved practical, and were incorporated into the products or processes[6]. McDonnel Douglas Astronautics Company reports that employee-suggested changes have saved more than $2.5 million yearly since 1985[7]. Kodak managed an impressive turnaround of its "Black and White" film division by supporting the B&W people to become empowered problem solvers. Team Zebra, as it was called, brainstormed huge inventory savings. In the United States there are an estimated 3000 formal suggestion systems operating in any given year. Survey results of APC (the American Productivity Center) have shown that employee involvement practices are increasing especially in service companies[8].

Though individual-based suggestion schemes are effective, there are many situations and conditions where idea-generation in teams better suits a particular purpose:

- the problem-solving task is very complex and its solution will demand heterogenic expertness
- the problem involves many departments and functions. This is often the case in quality management
- the problem-solving task requires coordination of various skills and crafts
- the proposed solution calls for profound changes in the organization and you anticipate strong resistance from the staff
- you want a huge amount of ideas to be generated in the long-lasting sessions, for example when planning new or renewed strategy
- you want to train people in teamwork
- people need to be initiated into the problem-solving process
- you want customers, suppliers and dealers to generate ideas and invent solutions for your company

The Consultor may wish to promote participative creativity training and activate a working team to use creativity techniques such as brainstorming or a brainwriting pool. The method employed will depend on the specific objectives one wants to achieve as well as the nature of the problem to be solved, the resources, time and the experience level of group members. But even more important, the Consultor may promote creativity and innovativeness among his/her staff by organizing innovative systems. The available options include group suggestion systems, quality circles, work design teams and idea competitions. Whichever system is chosen, the commitment of the supervisors and senior managers, as well as training of leaders and participants, is essential. Sufficient resources including time, financing and efficient team management are necessary prerequisites for successful execution.

Peter Senge[9] emphasizes the importance of *creative team learning*. He identifies three critical dimensions. First, there is the need to think insightfully about complex issues. Teams must learn how to tap the potential for many minds to be more intelligent than one mind. Second, there is the need for innovative, coordinated action. Third, team learning involves how to deal creatively with the powerful forces opposing productive dialogue and discussion in working teams. Above all, the discipline of team learning requires practice, a continual movement between rehearsal and performance. The capacity to support innovative teams is one of the essential characteristics of the Consultor.

CONSULT IN DIFFICULTIES

Even the most experienced staff encounter obstacles on the way to innovations. If you also rank high in the Master role dimension, you can be effective as a Consultor in problem-solving situations where specific knowledge is sought. Often people do not need direct advice, rather an empathetic manager to discuss their problems with. "A good counselor is interested in what others have to say, not just what he or she wants to hear, takes the other seriously and is willing to spend time . . .", says Tom Peters[10]. Creative input can be stimulated by giving all participants assurance that their suggestions are valued and will be considered. In this way they will acquire self-confidence and self-discipline to contribute. During discussion, one's own thoughts will be developed and clarified. For others it may be important to know that their solutions are valued. It provides them with the self-confidence they need to stimulate their own creativity.

The top innovative companies emphasize high performance and excellence. Good is not good enough. The Consultor coaches his/her people to do the right things right. When a traditional boss controls his or her subordinates' actions and demands obedience the development of independence and initiative is hindered. The Consultor by *empowering people creates extraordinary self-confidence by giving people opportunities to cope with demanding tasks and challenges*. They may need advice on how to gather and use resources, recruit staff or find solutions to conflicts. Skilful managers are able to suggest ways of dealing with these practical questions and achieve a high degree of mutual satisfaction.

GIVE SUPPORT

Creative people in organizations need strong support from their managers, especially if their criticism, suggestions and far-out ideas are seen as harmful and disturbing to others' routine work. The Consultor helps people over the organizational barriers and acts as a conflict arbitrator. It is important to support innovators' efforts even if they do not follow formal work rules. Creative and innovative people expect the Consultor to:

- organize some free time for experimenting with ideas
- provide feedback on their creative performance
- provide proper resources; places to think and experiment, materials and equipment, assistance or when needed, a team to work with
- provide access to needed information sources and relevant contacts if they are not able to provide these by themselves
- provide opportunities for continuous internal and external training
- encourage a stimulating and supportive environment by backing and legitimizing their efforts
- give proper rewards
- not interfere with their work if they don't want it and if they are able to work out innovative solutions independently

R. Whitfield argues[11] that encouragement or discouragement is the main factor affecting the whole atmosphere in which the innovator works. "The most significant element of this environment is the attitude of individuals — immediate colleagues and the boss — whose example, personal support and encouragement are crucial to the development of novel and useful ideas." We may enlarge upon this approach by emphasizing that an innovative manager has a substantial influence upon the innovative climate of his/her company. *Innovative climate* can be defined as a composition of individual beliefs and attitudes favourable to the encouraging, sustaining and flourishing of the innovativeness of an organization[12].

Judith Kamm[13] surveyed the innovative climate among scientists and engineers in the pharmaceuticals and semiconductor industries and compared their subjective evaluation of the climate with the mean scores of idea-generation, idea-use and idea-acceptance. She concluded that "satisfying the favourable climate conditions is *necessary* but not sufficient for a high level of idea generation or discovery". This means that as a manager you must take into account other factors as well (innovative systems, innovation strategies) but you always have to satisfy the environmental demands. Sidney Parnes has recommended that we have to plan and construct environmental "freeways" to encourage creative functioning. This implies that both the socio-psychological and physical atmosphere should support creative action. The famous Hallmark Innovation Center in Kansas City was planned according to this principle. Its whole atmosphere and architectural arrangements are designed to encourage collaboration, to nurture ideas and encourage the free flow of information.

The same kind of informality and ease in the relationships between the management and staff and staff–customer communication are also to be found in the Digital Corporation, Citibank offices and SAS hotels. Moreover, quality improvements can only exist in an environment of *open* communication where employees and clients are encouraged to discuss quality problems and make suggestions on how to solve them.

The support function in encouraging innovativeness may be structured formally by the management. An outstanding example is the Office of Innovation Network (OIN) at Eastman Kodak[14]. Kodak has instituted the role of "innovation facilitator" to help make the connection between idea-generators and potential sponsors (our Consultors). When a person creates and submits a promising idea, a facilitator contracts experts and sponsors to help formulate and develop the idea further. The idea-generator keeps the rights to his/her idea. The facilitator merely guides the implementation. Kodak receives about nine suggestions for every ten employees! About 40% of the personnel actually submit suggestions in a given year. The average is raised by a group of enthusiastic suggestors.

Empowerment of people does not only mean giving them more freedom and responsibility but also distributing information, knowledge, rewards and power within an organization. Bowen and Lawler III[15] indicate this with their equation:

Empowerment=Power × Information × Knowledge × Rewards

According to them any company which aims to get results by empowering people has to accommodate their policies, practices and structures to this end.

The Consultor as an innovative manager has in the terms of French and Raven[16] a kind of "personal" or "referent" power stemming from his/her personal attributes, a kind of charisma. He or she may also share the Expert role. The Consultor favours the empowerment of people as the approach to creativity and innovativeness.

Our profile manager, William McPherson, acts like the coach of a team. He makes very high demands on the team members, but also provides adequate resources, guides, supports and encourages their efforts. With his optimistic and enthusiastic attitude toward people, he contributes to a stimulating working environment that results in high initiative and productivity.

WILLIAM McPHERSON: A CONSULTOR COACHING FOR QUALITY

Letters, mailboxes and mailbags have always intrigued people's minds. Professor Kurt Lewin, who escaped from Nazi Germany and continued his memorable research in the United States, tells a story about people's behaviour when they intend to post a letter. They write a letter, put it into their pocket, but forget it is there until walking along the street when they happen to see a red mailbox. The mailbox reminds them of their original intention and the interrupted behaviour will be completed. They will post the letter. This typical incident nicely symbolizes Kurt Lewin's scientific work, a part of which describes people's behaviour when an important task is interrupted, but at a later time one returns to finalize the work.

While going to school in a big English city, William McPherson worked in the local post office. Perhaps this work experience stimulated his ambition to become a plant manager in the future. However, his post career was interrupted when he entered university to study engineering.

His studies were not yet completed when he left college to work as an information officer in a local transportation firm. After serving some hectic years in that company, he met the Industrial Engineering Manager of the Royal Mail who asked if William might be interested in a newly formed position of Manager of Information Services. This incident apparently reminded William of his previous ambition and he returned to continue his post career.

He soon realized that his interrupted studies in information science at college were insufficient for him to pursue his ambitious goals or even to keep up with the day-to-day business demands. After seeking advice about the various options for advanced study, he chose the International Management Centre's MBA course. It was actually in our seminar on "Entrepreneurship and Intrapreneurship" that we met him for the first time. He told us that he had been challenged by the method of "Action Learning" developed by Reg Revan, one of the founders of IMC, particularly as it combined practical work experience with theoretical and scientific studies. As he explained, "I couldn't think of interrupting my work for a long period, being quite new in the job, but I urgently needed to get up-to-date information and to broaden my managerial knowledge base by studying while I continued to work." William's main project was a study concerning "Process Innovations in the Postal Services". Innovations were to continue to be his greatest challenge throughout his career.

William was also a genuine "people person". Though not a particularly high achiever in college, he was very popular among the students and the faculty. He could often be found in the cafeteria, where he had simply forgotten to attend his scheduled lecture, surrounded by his fellow students earnestly discussing a variety of topics. He was elected class president and represented the school at inter-college events. His friends recall that he already had a particular charisma which attracted people to him. He was a tall man, over six feet, played an excellent defence on the college's soccer team and was, of course, the team's captain. Later, he maintained his interest in the game and played in the city's semi-pro team, also becoming a member of the team's board of directors. We could understand that his public sports figure *contributed to his popularity with the post staff and it surprised no one when he was eventually appointed as the Regional General Manager.*

DIAMONDS

William McPherson is a chatty, sociable person, whose relaxed, informal behaviour encourages open discussion. Even strangers soon find themselves involved in familiar discussion with him. He dislikes pompous behaviour, calling people who act so "archaic monoliths". He's not afraid of losing his authority or lowering his prestige by getting his hands dirty with manual work around the plant, and if he sees some interesting new piece of equipment and wants to know how it works, he'll pitch right in.

One of his friends, Jim Wilson, told us a typical story which characterizes William's personality. Jim had been invited to join William and his wife who were on a short holiday at a village inn, and they had arranged that Jim would phone at 9 am Sunday to confirm their meeting. Jim called as planned, and was quite surprised to hear a familiar voice answer, "Country Inn, good morning, William McPherson speaking." "How on earth is this possible?", asked Jim. The response: "Well, the inn-keeper put on a real bash last night to celebrate his son's graduation, and it went on till quite late. When I came down this morning, there was no one at the desk, so I've been sitting here and answering the phone." William as usual had downplayed this in his low-key manner, not making a big deal of it. But this small incident, like many others told among the personnel, strengthened the human side of his image and this helped him to gain cooperation when starting the laborious transformation process in his organization.

The truth was that the plant was far from being a modern mechanized mail processing facility when William McPherson was appointed manager. The sorting centre was run more like a military organization. Every morning the "Director-Commander in Chief" called his senior managers to plan "today's assault on the huge mountain of mail". The management team planned the tactics for the next work period and gave their orders to the superintendents, which were then passed on to the supervisors, who ordered the workers to "attack". The supervisors were very much the traditional bulldog kind of bosses. They worked hard themselves each day and strictly saw to it that the work of their subordinates was done. The level of the workers' morale was low, however, with a high rate of absenteeism and less than desired productivity and quality.

According to our discussions with William, the bosses often held lengthy meetings to discuss problems at the plant, often without results. Actually, the former director was aware of the need to encourage worker's involvement and used the traditional suggestion box. As the supervisors either ignored the ideas suggested or neglected them for long periods of time, the idea stream soon dried up. It seemed obvious that the suggestions were not really wanted by management.

William himself was quite the opposite kind of manager. For good reason we call him a Consultor — a manager who acts like the coach of the team. With his expertise he is able to offer advice and help when the people need it. He describes managerial excellence by saying that a good manager needs the ability to envision the next move while his staff is working with the present one. "In any team sport, this ability often differentiates the super talent from the mediocre player", he explained. This reminded us of what the Canadian hockey superstar Wayne Gretzky said in an interview. When asked about the secret of his superior talent, he answered simply that perhaps he is more able than other players to imagine the moves of the puck; where the puck will be next, he will be there.

PEARLS

When William took over, there were already serious threats in the competitive business environment. The private sector was offering its services in more flexible ways attracting many of the best customers with competitive alternatives like telecommunications and private overnight delivery services. As delivery time was a critical factor, William realized that he must modernize his plant in order to compete and especially to solve present quality problems in order to regain customers' confidence.

Understanding that plant work itself is not very fascinating, William was particularly concerned with the workers' motivation. He was aware that some of the productivity problems in the auto industry had been solved by implementing new socio-techniques like "work-unit processing", which replaced the old automobile assembly line procedure in Volvo's Kalmar plant in Sweden. Though aware that such procedures could not be implemented in a mail processing plant, William still wanted something equivalent. "Perhaps we could introduce some teamwork-based process to improve quality and productivity", he reasoned.

We received a call inviting us to have lunch with him and the plant's Industrial Engineering Manager. He presented a plan to start a quality-circle system, and asked us to act as consultants to implement it in his plant. We agreed to study the plan, and subsequently rejected the quality-circle approach in favour of a plan for "WORK DESIGN TEAMS" (WDT) in the plant. We pointed out that there was a need to get not only the first line supervisors but also the middle management involved and committed to the work improvement designs.

"The best way to get ideas and suggestions implemented in practice is to involve management in the design-team work from the beginning", we argued. We also suggested that to gain their trust and avoid the earlier bitter opposition of the union they should be involved from the outset. In addition we wanted to "tap" into the project the informal staff communication channels. This would encourage and guide the employees to more open discussions and bring forth ideas for positive change in the working systems. William accepted the plan, and we are starting our second year's association with him.

WILLIAM'S GROUND RULES FOR WORK DESIGN TEAMS

1. Find work problems — "One per day"
2. Transmit them to be listed
3. Rank them — set priorities
4. Start with the easy ones — set targets
5. Follow the WDT scheme* — still be flexible
6. No rank — a facilitator guides the process
7. Everyone participates — no one dominates
8. Create solutions — use your imagination
9. Respect your colleagues — listen to them
10. Develop ideas to innovations!

*Similar methods as used in quality circles: fishbone diagram, brainstorming, statistical analysis, etc.

William's opportunity to create a bright future for the plant lies in his ability to support the transformation process with his own hearty involvement and commitment. This process was aided by his ability to act as a "Change Master" as Rosabeth Kanter might call him. With his optimistic and enthusiastic attitude toward people, there is growing evidence to show that he is starting to build more productive teams with greater initiative. "Increasingly self-directed, rather than watched every nit-picking minute: more imaginative, thoughtful and diverse in their skills and less likely to grab chances to do nothing", as journalist Jack McArthur has described the sought-after behaviour. "If problems are caused by ordinary people, who shall solve them?", William asks. "The same ordinary people", is his answer.

STONES

Though William's practice of making contact directly with people at all levels has encouraged a more open communication, it has also revealed a serious flaw in his managerial style. His tendency to take personal hands-on action at the source of any problem has caused serious unrest among his closest co-workers. Senior managers as well as supervisors who formerly exercised decision-making power feel that their status and authority is diminished and that this causes confusion in the ranks. It is true that the new "team approach" occasioned a lot of open criticism. The WDT process opened the floodgates of long-suppressed thoughts and opinions of the workers, and the start must have been very trying for the managers and supervisors. But when we advised William to plan a new kind of organization which would involve the managers in the team-dynamic process, though accepting the idea in principle, he has been slow to implement it.

ASHES

William McPherson is surely quite capable of guiding "his ship" to clear water. But because his major concern is people and staff and industrial operations, perhaps he is too concentrated on improving the inner processes. William should become more involved with customer relations which would permit him to resolve many problems at the plant which are often the result of the excessive demands made by the customers. While it might be difficult to change customer attitudes and expectations, there are many innovations possible that would make the postal service more flexible and attractive to clients.

William has understood the concept of empowerment of people in a too restricted way. He should balance the need of giving individual freedom and opportunities to people to independently design their work processes and his tendency to put hands on in the teams' problem-solving sessions. William should give overall guidance to the team and then let them go ahead. "Empowerment of people without a shared sense of long-term direction can lead to anarchy", say Hamel and Prahaled. William actually should be wholeheartedly committed to the process of change and concentrate on pulling the essential threads of the process together. In doing so, it is useful to keep in mind Nayak's and Ketteringham's conclusion[17] when they researched 13 famous breakthrough innovations: "A manager cannot create the creative team. Like saboteurs, creative people hatch their plots and form their own little cells. A manager can't control it; he can only help."

Our message to William:

- KEEP your efforts to get everyone involved and committed to the development of the processes and work in the plant
- KEEP your ability to communicate easily and naturally with everyone in the company
- KEEP your attitude and interest in all areas of work in the plant
- KEEP your ability to motivate people to a self-directed way of working. Encourage high initiative, but keep them on track to honour their commitments to time, resources and results
- LEARN how to create and maintain "people power" within the company while building the trust and cooperation of the managers and supervisors
- LEARN to give long-term direction when empowering people
- LEARN to intensify customer and supplier relationships
- THINK AND THANK people, but also respect your managers' and supervisors' authority
- LEARN the "helicopter thinking" model, the ability to raise your sight above daily routines in order to see what is going on from a broader perspective

Chapter 5

Self-Assessment: Consultor

HOW DO YOU RATE YOURSELF AS A "CONSULTOR"?

Please take a few minutes to rate yourself according to the following items.
Place one numerical rating in the left hand column and one in the right.

How do you rate yourself in the following activities? (Select numerical rating.)		How important is this to your managerial career? (Select numerical rating.)	
VERY GOOD 7.....6.....5.....4.....3.....2.....1 INEFFICIENT	#	**VERY IMPORTANT** 7.....6.....5.....4.....3.....2.....1 NOT IMPORTANT	#
a	Having genuine interest in my subordinates' needs and problems	a	
b	Being comfortable with the "nuts and bolts" of our business	b	
c	Encouraging my subordinates to come to me to discuss their ideas in confidence	c	
d	Promoting creativity training and use of creativity methods in our organization	d	
e	Motivating my subordinates to self-directed ways of working	e	
f	Providing genuine feedback on their creative performance	f	
g	Providing adequate resources to innovative individuals and teams	g	
h	Encouraging high initiative at all levels and in all sectors	h	
i	Being able to build successful teams	i	

Plot your ratings in the matrix:

I am inefficient (1–4)		I am very good (5–7)	
IS VERY IMPORTANT	A	IS VERY IMPORTANT	B
IS NOT IMPORTANT	C	IS NOT IMPORTANT	D

MY TOP FIVE DEVELOPMENT CHALLENGES AS A "CONSULTOR":

1 _____

2 _____

3 _____

4 _____

5 _____

Chapter 6

Rethinking Innovative Strategy: The Manager as a Course-keeper

The Course-keeper acts as direction giver to the company's overall operations. He/she provides special input in institutionalizing the innovation process and manages strategy development as a continuous mutual learning exercise.

Many newly appointed managing directors are apt to misunderstand their role in regard to their organizations' creativity and innovativeness. They have never learned the type of creative thinking needed in the strategic planning and implementation process. This is perhaps due to their background, primarily analytic and pragmatic, and the fact that many executives who have got to the top management level still devote themselves to solving short-range problems in their own narrow functional areas of expertise. Innovative activity at all levels must be encouraged. This requires dedication on the part of top management and specific attention to creation of an atmosphere conducive to risk taking. Though often accepted in principle it is rare to see this applied in practice.

The essence of success at the top management level is flexibility and innovativeness in diverse areas, a multiplicity of skills. "Individuals with several strains of experience are likely to uncover more creative solutions to nontechnical problems (to which strategy problems belong) than people who have always been in, say production", says Steven S. Brandt[1].

Goldsmith et al.[2] have taken notice of the importance of top management innovativeness in their article concerning the two faces of creativity: "While creativity has long been assumed to be of value in such areas as marketing and product development, there is a growing feeling that its impact on the strategic planning process makes creativity desirable at the highest level of the firm." Tudor Richards[3] emphasizes very strongly the importance of the creative role of the CEOs by pointing out that: "*Ultimately the chief strategist and the chief innovator in any organization is one and the same individual — Chief Executive.*"

MANAGEMENT UNDER CHAOS

The corporate management should be able to create visions and anticipate and adapt the organization to the fast changing social, political and economic development and to technological and market needs. Companies operating worldwide must create and implement innovative competitive strategies. Rather than just talking about the future, planners should actually try to envision clearly how the future could and should be. "To accomplish this, strategy planners must become more imaginative and creative", emphasize Wheatley et al.[4]. How is it possible to envision or plan the future of a company in the present day conditions of high environmental complexity and uncertainty? Could one perhaps envision or produce a long-term plan for a company in present day Russia? Social scientists[5] describe the condition of enormous complexity of any system as a *chaos* and insist that this kind of system is capable of creating a complex new order in a self-organizing and regulating manner. Ralph Stacey[6] recommends that the management group should:

- handle strategic issue agenda: a dynamic unwritten list of issues, aspirations and challenges
- rely on their experience-based intuition and ability to detect analogies between one set of ambiguous circumstances and another
- provoke strategy development by setting openly ambiguous challenges and presenting half-formed issues for others to develop, instead of trying to set clear long-term objectives
- develop a new strategic direction through a self-organizing process of political interaction (among interest groups) and complex learning

"New strategic directions emerge when the attitudes and behaviour of managers create an atmosphere favourable to individual initiative and policy, as to the learning in groups", says Stacey.

INSTITUTIONALIZING THE INNOVATION PROCESS

It is meaningful to differentiate between the concepts of "the *innovative strategy*" and "the *strategy for innovativeness*" in the company. McPherson[7] has given importance to the need for institutionalizing the innovation process. According to him, the goal of the organization must be defined so that seeking innovation is an axiom. The whole action policy has to reflect this aim. John Heap[8] supports this kind of thinking by pointing out that "Innovation and design must be part of the general management remit, treated with the same importance as other issues and subject to the same control processes. Only then can they become a part of the true corporate strategy." *The strategy for innovativeness is a deliberate and targeted activity for accelerating ideas and implementing them into innovations in all or selected action spheres, functions and levels of the company.* Thus the role of top management is both to create innovative strategies and the strategy for innovativeness.

Innovativeness is a core concept in Strategy Development. A manager needs innovativeness to:

- *envision the future*
- *design scenarios*
- *act as direction giver to a company's overall operations*
- *handle strategic issue agenda*
- *provoke strategy development*
- *design the strategy of innovativeness*
- *institutionalize the innovation process*
- *run management meetings innovatively*
- *handle crisis and chaos*

ORIGINATE VISIONS!

George Bernard Shaw said that we need men who can dream of things that never were, and ask why not. J. Quincy Hunsicker[9] has defined vision as the ability of an enterprise's top manager to construct and evaluate creatively the implications for the enterprise of scenarios for the future. Bill Gates, the CEO of Microsoft, has a famous vision for the next decades — a vision which he calls "Information at Your Fingertips". Microsoft is producing creative solutions for the emerging needs to have easy and flexible access to all kinds of information from various sources such as E-mail, CD-ROM, interactive TV and pocket, wallet or wristwatch PCs.

As a Course-keeper you may envision the future by using many methods:

Dreaming: your visions may be manifested through dreams, daydreaming, fantasies, deep relaxation or meditation. These processes may end up by accident with sudden insights. Many entrepreneurs have experienced this kind of vision when faced with a challenge requiring a breakthrough. Imagining vividly great personal advantages which the idea will bring seems to release creative energy.

Scanning: searching the environment (customer field, competitor's activities, societal trends, emerging technologies) in order to find some interesting future opportunities such as market trends, gaps and emerging service needs. If you also score high in the Master's role you may acquire your visions by scientific analysis and experimentation, reading periodicals and research reports, searching relevant information from databases or taking part in conferences and exhibitions. Perhaps you may act like futurologists, who originate far-sighted views about societal and environmental matters. They love to read such periodicals as *Future* or *Trends* and may belong to the "Futurologist Society".

Discussing: reflective communication with your management group, senior managers, scientists, engineers, market experts, futurologists or perhaps just intelligent people whom you know to be capable of envisioning. Why not take part in executive clubs and meetings where you have a chance to meet and listen to gurus? Especially useful are discussions with executives from other industrial sectors than your own because you may discover interesting visions through analogies with other fields.

The thoughtful and deliberate construction of a supportive network inside the company and externally to include stakeholders such as key customers, suppliers and industrial associations is a great help.

SCAN THE FUTURE

Experience demonstrates that speculation about the future is valuable primarily for its creative thought-provoking effect on strategy planners rather than for any statement of predictive accuracy. The corporate economist may be able to predict for example the demand and price level trends in the metal industry worldwide within the limits of certain probability values but we have seen how often they miss the mark.

There is an abundance of statistical and forecasting information available produced by the experts in Prognos, INSEAD, Battelle Institute, American Management Association and many national institutions. The problem is that companies usually have too much information available for forecasting rather than too little. We are reminded that Chester Karras has stated that for every expert there is an equal and opposite expert!

The future of companies is very much dependent on a multitude of trends and factors which may drastically effect the market development in a certain sector. For example, the future of the automotive industry is dependent on consumers' life and work patterns, telecommunication developments, public infrastructure investments, other means of transportation, fuel prices, impact of new technologies, ecological aspects, economy of nations, population trends and political decisions, just to catalogue a few.

Prediction is an extremely complex and difficult process for many companies. It was Nihles Bohr, the father of Atomic Physics, who observed that prediction is very difficult, especially about the future. Because of that, innovative companies use suitable means such as the "Scenario Method" to handle the complexity of the future. Scenarios usually consist of parallel descriptions of a few hypothetical trends, situations and processes of the future and include a carefully designed sketch of probable changes within some agreed upon time period. *Writing scenarios is a real creative exercise.*

David A. Aaker[10] emphasizes the importance of scenarios in the realization of a company's new assets and skills for business success. He refers to studies which describe cases in which innovator firms have not been able to sustain their leading position. Management has not been aware of new assets and skills needed to counteract the competitors' new moves. A great deal of creativity is demanded of corporate strategists who have to generate "master strategies" based on the scenarios. Imaginative thinking is also needed when management try to predict disruptive events which may cause radical deviations from the scenarios. Two interesting examples of scenarios designed for the automotive industry are to be found in the reference list to this chapter[11].

GUIDE THE PROCESS

Even though visions are perhaps most often created by CEOs, the innovative strategies are more often the mindwork of creative teams, for example the board of directors or the management team assisted by staff members and/ or by a consultant. In top innovative companies such as ABB, strategies are intensively reviewed with key customers in order to create and maintain a long-lasting partnership with them. The CEO as a Course-keeper plans, starts, stimulates and guides the process by which the strategic insights and options are generated.

THINK BIG

The first major issue deals with the shareholders' objectives. Their representatives define broad goals concerning profit and risk levels, market measures, leadership or follower expectations and in some corporations also statements of the position in the context of innovativeness: market pioneer, first-mover, trendsetter or creative copycat. In acquisitions and mergers one of the biggest issues affecting shareholders is profitability. For example, when the globally operating elevator company Kone acquired several unprofitable companies which were equally large or larger than itself, the main objective was to turn them into profitable subsidiaries. From the point of view of Kone's management, they wanted to gain growth and footing in new continents; to be there where the growing markets are.

When working with your management team generate "the start chart": shareholders' expectations and objectives, current big problems, great challenges and opportunities, and big on-going projects. Add to the chart the results of analyses of information about emerging technologies and innovations, breakthrough trends and influential driving forces. Changes in the external business environment such as critical market changes, emerging new competitors and trade channel developments also have their place.

IMPLEMENT CREATIVE SWOT

Thinking about and writing down strengths, weaknesses, opportunities and threats is merely the first step. Stimulate your team to think how you could further utilize the opportunities and accrue incremental benefits from the present strengths. Or, how could you effectively reduce and eliminate weaknesses and threats and turn them into opportunities? Too often the SWOT is just nicely written down without putting enough energy into creative thinking.

WRITE THE SUMMIT REPORT

Producing a lot of information and analysing the complex internal and external environment create confusion. The Course-keeper is able to transform that confusion into order by writing a short summary in which all essential issues are gathered and presented (visions, conclusions of scenarios, big issues, SWOT, results of analyses). The summit report is a stimulating start for the next phase.

Leave Creative Slack

Imagine that your company's environmental condition is chaotic. (Perhaps it is, even without imagination.) Write an open-ended strategic agenda which could include challenging and even conflicting, ambiguous issues, questions and problems to be further discussed and reflected upon. What might be your people's future, aspirations, ambitions and explanations of opportunities and trends?

IMAGINE SUCCESS CONCEPT

This phase is perhaps the most creative one. The Course-keeper has to stimulate team members to imagine how their company can compete to win. Ask them to imagine their products and services as pioneer products, knock-offs, creative copycats, impossible to replicate, or their marketing as a kind of model marketing in their company's business field. Ask participants to refrain from "censoring" their thoughts. As they think about the organization and its functions ask them to imagine the world's most admirable organizations and how they operate. Create analogical conclusions for the company's operations. Stimulate the team to imagine their company to be the best in the world in the year 2010. Many of Fortune's most admired corporations such as Merck and Wal-Mart have long stated as their objective to be the best in their business and they have been able to gain that position. Kone expressed their intention to be "The Best in Town" and have been able to create a very successful core concept of maintenance and modernization in the elevator business.

DESIGN THE STRATEGY

The actual design of strategy includes many stages where innovativeness is needed throughout the organization. The formulation of visions, a company's mission, basic values and designing business ideas demand a high degree of imaginative thinking. Actually when solving problems concerning strategic matters the Course-keeper skilfully combines creative and analytical thinking. The strategy design process requires profound analysis of facts, and when drawing conclusions and presenting recommendations based on accumulated data, imaginative thinking is needed as well.

DO NOT NEGLECT THE STRATEGY FOR INNOVATIVENESS

This process starts by defining the desired goals which are to be reached through innovativeness. It continues by developing plans of how to get there. Indeed, many failures in trying to gain a higher level of organizational innovativeness are caused by imprecise objectives or by failure to define objectives at all. Such a vague statement as "We intend to reach a well-spring of ideas everywhere in our company" hardly leads to any significant results. We have to give strategic directions when igniting innovativeness. The clear formulation of objectives is necessary because it focuses the search for information and idea-generation on critical issues. *The common problem in many creative organizations is the dispersion of interest and attention in too many directions.* Objectives indicate where to allocate resources. However, in strategy formulation it is a mistake to appreciate only "high level intellectual creativity" such as R&D. Implementation of ideas into business practices often requires far more innovative activities at different levels of the company. For example, the ingenious Post-it notes (prototypes of which were a result of a complex research and engineering process) received serious attention at the senior management level in 3M only after managers saw that their secretaries used the experimental notes in various ways for several purposes. Many competitive, innovative products are virtually alike. Highly creative and competent sales representatives make the difference.

When formulating the strategy for innovativeness you must answer the following questions:

- What ultimate goals do we want to achieve by increased innovativeness? (increase in growth, improved quality, improved profitability, increase in the proportion of new products to sales or annual turnover). These goals can be presented in precise numbers. Alan MacDonald's "Newtonian law" is that in Citibank half of all revenues come from products and services that did not exist five years earlier. Quite a target for product development if we bear in mind that other great innovators, such as Rubbermaid and 3M, have set only 30% as their goal
- In which special areas and functions of the company do we want to take advantage of new ideas and innovations? (R&D, product development, production, marketing, administration, logistics)
- What are the main target groups? (top-management, senior managers, middle management, experts, the entire organization)
- What purposes should innovative activities mainly serve? (multiplicity of ideas, incremental improvements, breakthrough ideas, process innovations, promotion of ideas, commercialization of ideas, implementation of ideas)
- How will the objectives be reached? (by promoting individual and/or team creativity, developing innovative management behaviour, learning creativity techniques, promoting innovative systems, encouraging innovative climate)

An important function of the Course-keeper as an innovative manager is to insure that the efforts are fundamentally directed towards managing a process of planned change toward higher innovativeness in a turbulent environment.

DEVELOP COLLECTIVE LEARNING

Even the most innovative strategy will not work if people in the organization are not committed and involved in the implementation process. Strategic thinking at present in most innovative companies is understood as a continuous process of change which actually is based on the idea of a *learning organization.* Instead of following a sequence of strategic planning, documenting and then implementing, innovative companies look at strategic management as an integrated process. Innovative companies are able to recruit high quality experts who can solve technical, commercial and financial problems, often working in teams. However, without the guidelines and framework of sound strategies and continuous development of "human resources as the most important asset", one may expect only modest returns. There is a risk especially in conditions of recession if the management concentrates its attention primarily on cost reduction and improvement of short-term financial results and neglects long-term strategies.

Argyris and Schon[12] are often mentioned for their theory of "single loop" and "double loop" learning. In the context of innovation, single loop learning can be described as improving present concepts, i.e. incremental improvements, innovations in strategies based on existing insights, principles and norms. Double loop learning in the same context may be described as generating "genuine" innovations based on new insights. In principle, single loop and double loop learning can happen in a loose context or even in the absence of corporate strategy (for example, innovations by bootlegging).

Swieringa and Wierdsma[13] have added the concept of "triple loop learning" which has a special relevance to strategic management. They call conventional strategy development a "blueprint method" by which a specific committee of managers, staff members and consultants design a new or renewed strategy complete with visions, mission, business ideas, structures and systems. The implementation requires a continual process of communication by which management tries to convince the employees of the relevance of the strategy.

Triple loop learning means learning multilaterally and collectively. "The essential principles on which the organization is founded come into discussion. . . . It means the development of new principles . . . what kind of organization we wish to be, the contribution we want to make, the role we choose to play and what values we consider important. . . . Learning is a constantly repeated, cyclic process of doing, reflecting, thinking and deciding", say the authors. Although in principle we accept their viewpoint, we believe that top management has the main responsibility to innovate the strategic framework, and has a great influence on how strategic planning, renewal and implementing will be performed in the organization. And this itself is an innovative exercise.

The management of "new stream businesses", especially based on breakthrough innovations, is a strategic area where usually only top management has all relevant information available and can distribute the resources necessary for innovative activities. It is not the question of nuts and bolts. For example, the investments on R&D can go up to 8–12% of sales in top innovative companies. We know of a typical example of innovation failure in the field of sports equipment. A revolutionary product was brought to market by a division manager without direct communication with the CEO, who was the only one in the company who knew about pending international regulations which presented obstacles to the use of that product. James Bandrowski[14] is right when he says that, "Creativity without direction is like a runaway horse–wasted energy. Saddling it up ensures productive, innovative thinking. This requires some structure and focus for the thought process and, ultimately, wise decisions." In many cases breakthrough innovations can be developed and implemented on the market only via acquisitions, strategic alliances, joint venture collaboration on key design projects or with available venture capital. This collaborative relationship is very complex, time demanding and expensive to implement; a strategic area of top management responsibility requiring an especially creative input.

Even though strategic planning is an important factor in securing the successful future of the company, there always exists real need for flexible, "unplanned" operations. Art Fry[15] argues that the future is only 80% predictable. Twenty per cent of it is a surprise. Warren Bennis, when interviewed by *Fortune*[16] in December 1991, said, "I have never experienced a time when the environment was so complex and unpredictable as it is now", when thinking back on his 40 years of consulting experience.

Finding the delicate balance between concentration on strategy and attention to mundane affairs can be difficult. The more the Course-keeper works with strategic planning the greater the risk of neglecting the everyday business reality. The hard lesson of the past learned from excessive planning periods was the alienation of the top managers from grass-root matters. Many had to learn again "hands-on" management, to get closer to the staff, especially at the floor level, and to customers and suppliers.

RUN MANAGEMENT MEETINGS INNOVATIVELY

Strategies have value for your business only if they are implemented and followed through. The main instrument of implementing strategy is the management meeting. Meetings are means of giving information, coordinating efforts and controlling activities. The agenda may swing from ideation and problem solving to decision making and implementation. To act as a successful Course-keeper the skill to manage meetings innovatively is a must.

Our profile manager, Jari Silta, is an example of a manager who developed from a functional manager into a Course-keeper, the chief strategist of the corporation.

JARI SILTA: A COURSE-KEEPER INSTITUTIONALIZING THE INNOVATION PROCESS

Mr Jari Silta celebrated his 50th birthday at home in Helsinki, greeting the flow of guests in the beautiful garden behind his comfortable wooden house. He is chief executive of one of Scandinavia's leading forest industry companies and is well known in business circles. Still it was surprising to see the variety of people celebrating this event. Politicians and diplomats, leading businessmen, scientists and sportsmen. Even the President of the Republic of Finland, Urho Kekkonen, had dropped in to pay his respects to a close and influential friend.

As we knew, President Kekkonen respected Jari's ability to promote new ideas, many of which were linked to progressive social programmes. They shared many interests together, fishing, hunting and sport, which held a place close to the President's heart. As a hardened cross-country skier, Jari was in especially good physical and mental condition which he claimed he needed to tolerate the long-lasting, heavy business negotiations with his customers — at that time mostly Soviet counterparts.

These meetings usually lasted into the early hours of the morning and then continued again at noon, sometimes personally led by the charismatic President himself. There were endless toasts of friendship, applause, story-telling and singing of Russian and Finnish folk songs. Dinner was served in the best Russian style, spiced with an imaginative coalition of champagne and caviar, Russian vodka and salmon, all contributing to a heightened atmosphere. As he could speak fluent Russian and had a solid baritone voice, Jari was a central figure at these gatherings. His warm temperament, combined with extraordinary will-power, endeared him to the Russians he dealt with. They in fact nicknamed him "walking folklore".

After finishing his university studies, he had started a diplomatic career, serving in the Finnish Consulate in Leningrad. His mother, a temperamental Russian beauty, had taught him to speak the language, and he was able to study linguistics and Russian literature while at his post.

Jari's father, born in the middle of Finland, was a personnel manager in a forest industry company. A cautious man, who some even considered a bit slow. This mixture in Jari's genetic origins perhaps explains his somewhat split personality: sometimes he is a very extroverted, open person who enjoys wild scenes with his friends. At other times he is a serious, quite cautious person who has learned to control his temperament with deliberation and diplomacy.

After a few years Jari found the diplomatic career unsuitable because, as he explained, "I felt constrained in the social atmosphere of diplomatic circles. I realized that I would prefer to devote my time and energies to more creative activities in a much more dynamic environment". Also he had lacked the particular status-consciousness that was necessary to become a top diplomatic personage.

While at the consulate, an interesting opportunity appeared when Jari met the director of a Finnish forest industry company at a trade show in Leningrad, and was invited to accept a job as manager of a centralized function coordinating services between Finnish plants and their Soviet and other foreign counterparts. In addition to Jari's talent for languages — besides Russian he was fluent in Swedish, German, English and French — the job urgently required diplomatic skills to develop and maintain long-term business relationships. Jari accepted and began an often difficult but steady progress up through managerial rank until his appointment as managing director of the company.

DIAMONDS

Jari Silta has learned to concentrate his creative talents on the strategic aspects of the company. "Earlier I made many mistakes, getting involved with all kinds of operational problems which the staff actually should have handled themselves", he explained to us. "I see now that when one is overly involved in short-term daily matters, there is a risk of losing the sight and vision of long-term business objectives. I've tried to learn to balance these aspects of leadership." Fortunately one of his major strengths has been his capacity to treat mistakes as stepping stones, rather than blocks.

Like so many other managers he started to run the business by clinging to the same management principles instituted by his predecessor. The efficiency of "existing" operations was the major determinant of business success. Jari implemented cost-effective operational methods and procedures throughout the organization. Productivity, profit, quality, service and cost effectiveness were the key concerns of his initial strategy. He ran endless meetings with his division directors to discuss urgent and difficult matters of quarterly bottom line results, production issues, key personnel turnover and quality policies.

To be able to achieve company objectives, Jari had imposed strict controls, standardizing operations in all plants and sites. Corporate headquarters required financial and other administrative managers to compile reports concerning operative issues and problems. Time and space for developing innovative strategic plans was hardly left. At least this had a positive effect on the short-term profit picture in the conventional lines of business. As Jari describes it, "Our business philosophy was a matter of replication. We wanted things to be accomplished in a certain predetermined manner, with very little flexibility or tolerance of local variation."

As the economy grew and the level of customer expectations kept pace, strong competitors entered into the game and were quicker to adapt to the clients' changing needs and preferences. The slumbering giants of the forest industry started to awaken to the new reality — their own overcapacity in a highly competitive market.

Jari also had to cope with difficulties within the organization. He had built up a hierarchical top-down organization where strategy formulation and control, planning and decision making were highly centralized.

The local directors started to demand more room for independent decision making. They pointed out that many of the strategic assumptions produced in headquarters'

ivory tower were wrong, particularly predictions of interest rates and competitors'
actions. They also complained that it took too much of their time to compile
operational data for headquarters, which in any event was soon out of date.

Jari tried hard to resolve an on-going conflict with Mats, one of his best local
managers from Ontario, who heatedly argued that the present strategic planning
system failed to take into account the local timber market and competitive conditions.
According to Mats, all business is local. New territories are changeable, unknown
and very difficult to predict and corporate strategy should give more consideration to
the ideas of local managers. "To work effectively the business structure has to be a
real creative exercise between us and not only at headquarters", Mats emphasized.
"You may hammer out a megamerger deal at the corporate headquarters in a couple
of months, but the real joint ventures can easily take years to even begin to work
together smoothly." This opinion was shared by many other local managers and the
atmosphere at the yearly strategy meeting at headquarters was very tense.

After Jari presented the yearly results, pointing out accumulated losses in several
new businesses and explaining the reasons for failure, he waited for some strong
reactions. He was, of course, carefully prepared to defend the replication strategy.
But surprisingly enough before any of the managers had time to comment, Mats had
walked up to the overhead projector and placed an acetate which read, simply:

How did Robinson Crusoe survive?

This gesture left everyone momentarily confused. Everyone looked in stunned
silence. As Jari later explained, "Thinking afterwards, it was fortunate that I had
suppressed my irritation at this naive comment in our serious meeting. In retrospect
I admit that he was justified in calling our attention to the need for survival in the
demanding and hostile environment. This could only be accomplished by close
teamwork with Mats and the other local managers and giving them more power to
run their own show. I had to admit that strict centralized control was taking us in
the wrong direction, and all we were doing was increasing our speed."

Jari acknowledged that even though the principles in the strategic plan were
sound they often were not followed. "We were so wrapped up in our business
operations that we didn't have energy to re-examine and modify our thinking. I
wanted us to move fast, grow fast internationally and take opportunities wherever
we found them", Jari explained. However, he was criticized as being overly cautious
even as he preached expansion.

Operational problems, financing, modernizing, restructuring and trying to get
rid of unrelated loss-making subsidiaries caused the pressures to mount. "I tried to
solve these problems by working, literally, a twenty-four hour day with my
headquarter group. We postponed the necessary long-term strategic development,
reasoning that new factors would be considered at the next planning stage."

"Even then I realized that there was not enough time for that. Our competitors
were reacting too quickly. It became clear to me that in the light of fast changing

business conditions the plans formulated by our headquarters were simply inadequate."

Jari was finally ready to admit that it was time to bring the local managers into the planning process. They had been agitating for a louder voice and had actually been giving a great deal of thought to solving their daily operational problems, if they could only get headquarters to loosen its grip. Once they were taken into the long-term strategic planning process as well, they eagerly accepted the "discovery-driven planning" which Jari had learned from the works of Ian C. McMillan of the Wharton School[17].

For the first time, the energies of the entire organization started to be directed in the way that Jari had envisioned. The participative planning followed by a serious effort to communicate and implement the strategy in practice gradually began to effect a release of the company's creative resources.

Jari's growing talent as a corporate strategist has taken years of dedication and hard work and many mistakes along the way, while learning the essentials. Now the globally operating company continuously undergoes re-examination of its strategy by the board of directors to whom Jari briefs on clearly focused items and carefully thought-out initiatives.

PEARLS

Jari is now better able to negotiate and cooperate with his partners and staff. He continues to keep in touch with daily matters but he understands that his main duty is to guide the implementation of his vision of the future of the corporation.

As a CEO he is more of a scanner than a dreamer, more pragmatic than visionary. He constantly searches the business environment for relevant trends, customer activities and new technologies and services. He has a proactive mindset that can identify and grasp new opportunities which he personally pursues with his accustomed drive. "Don't overlook small signals of future trends", he likes to point out in his frequent messages to the company. "You don't always need a large volume of quantifiable data to justify entering into a new market or starting a new business." He tells about one of his golfing partners, a director of a chain of department stores, whose market research is sometimes very simple and direct. During a visit to Germany in the late 1970s, he was surprised to see many bio-shops in the cities. "I went into a shop in Frankfurt, and asked the saleslady how business was going, and the lady replied 'very well indeed' ", the director related. "My gut feeling was that this would continue to be a major health trend." Returning to his home country, he advised his managers to start bio-shops, which now flourish in many of their stores.

By nature, Jari is an avid conversationalist, eager to take part in discussions with executives in the clubs and meetings he frequents. Here he meets others who are trying to turn their visions into reality. The new generation of professional managers does not find the late-hours business meetings in restaurants and night clubs so attractive. Jari likes to joke that during Kekkonen's time, to trade successfully with the Finns, there were three basic rules: take saunas, drink vodka and play late. Today's formula still includes the sauna, but now you drink wine and play golf. Jari is still trying to progress beyond the duffer stage in golf, but he does already find it useful for doing business. It took some time for him to take the game seriously, but as he began to realize the amount of concentration required to play even acceptably, his respect for the sport increased. "Still, I think it's the social aspect people enjoy most. Golf has a special charm for me", Jari explains, "because it gives me the opportunity to build personal relationships. I find it to be an ideal setting where I can learn about a potential client's personality and interests. It also gives me the opportunity to test my own projections of future trends with knowledgeable people not only in business but also in government."

Jari's special potential as a CEO is his ability to create bright visions of the future for his company, and turn these visions into practical insights for innovative strategic planning.

STONES

Mats used to call Jari a "planocrat". Jari still loves written documents and plans, though where he formerly produced them with a small headquarters group, they now result from the input of the entire organization. It seems that his greatest joy is improving organizational systems and this gives him a feeling of greater control over the future of his company's operations.

The problem with Jari is that it is difficult to get him to discuss strategies on a continuous basis outside of the scheduled strategic planning meetings. Jari's style of management is to preset strict boundaries, but his managers often wish to express their insights and are sometimes brought up short by comments such as: "This question should be handled when starting the next strategic plan", or "We should not expand our discussion to strategic matters now."

There is a danger that the managers will be reluctant to present their new ideas, which might have value, when again asked to do so. They find it difficult during the "on-going strategy phase" to gain approval for radical suggestions, although some of the ideas could be very profitable if promptly implemented. It is obvious that Jari still avoids risks and breakthrough changes because he feels that they could disturb the implementation of plans and the effectiveness of existing systems. The fact is that even though Jari may encourage the expression of new ideas, he seldom is committed wholeheartedly to implement them. He tends to avoid decisions on complex matters, even promising ones, by postponing action. There always is the risk that the really entrepreneurial and innovative people will become frustrated and jump ship.

ASHES

Jari Silta is hardly a great risk-taking manager. He is reluctant to accept new emerging business opportunities recommended by others. He probably became overcautious when the company experienced failures during the previous phase of rapid expansion. We recommended that in order to estimate real risks Jari should start scenario projects to forecast uncertainties and discontinuities in the business environment. He should not just concentrate on collecting huge piles of current data because, as Eric Clemoms[18] has concluded, "Discontinuities affect the way that current data become meaningless as predictors of future sales, competitor actions and customer demand, and then as determinants of strategy." He has started to orientate more to the future, with several teams working to forecast worldwide trends and discontinuities in the forest and related industries.

Our message to Jari:

- *KEEP your attitude and ability as an innovative corporate strategist. It is the key characteristic of any CEO-achiever in the business world*
- *KEEP your interest and vision of the future by scanning continuously the business environment and interacting with your professional colleagues*
- *KEEP close touch with your own people's and your customers' needs. That is necessary for the successful implementation of your strategic plans*
- *KEEP searching for new business opportunities. Profit from them*
- *LEARN to involve your management team in a continuing process of rethinking strategy. It will spark their creative input*
- *LEARN to create an atmosphere where disagreement and diverse views and opinions are accepted. Increase your ability and willingness to take risks*
- *LEARN to support not only experimentation but also the implementation of new ideas*
- *LEARN to lead your organization through tough times. Help them to tolerate the "slow down" periods*
- *LEARN to support the real creative and innovative people on your staff. Listen to their ideas and suggestions especially in strategic issues. They are your entrepreneurs of the future*

Chapter 6

Self-Assessment: Course-keeper

HOW DO YOU RATE YOURSELF AS
A "COURSE-KEEPER"?

Please take a few minutes to rate yourself according to the following items.
Place one numerical rating in the left hand column and one in the right.

How do you rate yourself in the following activities? (Select numerical rating.)		How important is this to your managerial career? (Select numerical rating.)	
VERY GOOD 7.....6.....5.....4.....3.....2.....1 INEFFICIENT #		VERY IMPORTANT 7.....6.....5.....4.....3.....2.....1 NOT IMPORTANT #	
a	Seeking to understand the conditions which will affect our company/industry over the next ten years	a	
b	Scanning constantly new market trends, emerging technologies and environmental changes	b	
c	Dedicating myself energetically to new business development	c	
d	Championing new ideas and values	d	
e	Inspiring others to rethink our strategic directions	e	
f	Challenging the whole organization to strive to attain our company's visions	f	
g	Creating an atmosphere conducive to risk taking	g	
h	Running management meetings innovatively	h	
i	Managing strategy development as a continuous mutual learning exercise	i	

Plot your ratings in the matrix:

I am inefficient (1–4)	I am very good (5–7)
IS VERY IMPORTANT A	IS VERY IMPORTANT B
IS NOT IMPORTANT C	IS NOT IMPORTANT D

MY TOP FIVE DEVELOPMENT CHALLENGES AS A "COURSE-KEEPER":

1 _____

2 _____

3 _____

4 _____

5 _____

Chapter 7

Gaining Willing Consent: The Manager as a Persuader

The Persuader understands that creativity and decisiveness in selling an idea or innovation is as important as the creativity needed to invent something really new. By persuasive communication, he/she is not only able to convince doubtful listeners to willingly accept his/her suggestions, he/she is also able to gain support for further development and implementation of ideas, innovations and plans.

The authors' work experience with many companies like Philip Morris, Ford, General Motors, ICI, Citibank and others has proven true the maxim that numerous refusals to accept ideas and innovations are caused by the innovator's failure to plan an effective selling strategy. Many managers value the processes of idea-generation and development more than planning how to sell the ideas generated. They seem to think that really good ideas and inventions sell themselves. Others fail to recognize the fact that, in reality, selling is "both art and science", a skill which is an essential part of persuasive communication, a type of language which, through study and practice, can be developed to a high level.

Some fundamental errors which are often observed:

- lack of a detailed plan for the selling of an idea or innovation
- confused presentation
- hurried or rushed presentation
- concentrating on the speaker's rather than listeners' viewpoint
- a presentation style which evokes conflicts
- inadequate facts and arguments in the presentation
- "know-all" attitude when presenting
- ignoring objections
- belittling opposing ideas

Creativity and innovativeness is a core concept in Persuasive Communication. A manager needs innovativeness to:

- *understand other people's needs and objectives*
- *plan an effective presentation of his/her ideas*
- *imagine listeners' viewpoints and possible counterarguments*
- *reduce negative emotions in any negotiation situation*
- *overcome objections*
- *gain willing consent*

In competitive business life, ideas, suggestions and proposals compete with each other within an organization. This is natural, because the development and implementation of new ideas not only costs money, it also takes time and resources. There are situations where a champion of major change, sometimes single-handed, faces the task of selling the message on a daily basis. Many top managers who have followed this route say that they seriously underestimated this portion of their task.

Most of a manager's working life consists of communicating with other people to gain acceptance of his/her ideas and proposals. In our hi-tech era it would seem that computers and other sophisticated means of communications might make these personal skills less important. But the opposite seems to be true. A recent poll of top managers in American corporations asked what was the main quality they looked for in young graduates who applied for positions in their company. A significant majority gave the answer: *The ability to express oneself clearly and forcefully, and to convince others to accept their ideas.* Technical skills were taken for granted. The interpersonal skills were the ones which were sought after.

It was interesting to hear the comments of those selected as the year's top non-commissioned officers in the US military. When asked for their own appraisal of why they had been selected, they replied in essence: "The ability to communicate!"

When selling an idea we often need not only other people's support but also their time, money and other resources. We tell the person or the group about the merits of our ideas and above all we try to show how they can benefit by accepting our idea. "But", you may say, "we know this." The pendulum has swung from the concept of winner–loser, the zero-sum game, to the "win–win" approach. In the past two decades practically everything written about selling and negotiation has supported win–win.

Unfortunately, the "how" is often missing. We may go into a selling situation with the best of intentions and find that we finish up in a rigid, controversial position which we either defend emotionally, or use as a base for attack. Often the end result is that even if we manage to get our way, the price in damaged relationships is high.

Let's take a look at some of the "hows" by examining the framework of SAI, a method of communication called "The Listener's Viewpoint." This system has won worldwide acceptance and is presently being taught in 13 languages.

THE LISTENER'S VIEWPOINT

The Listener's Viewpoint is based on the idea that whatever our individual, national or racial differences, all of us share a common human element — a common denominator. Translated into practical terms, this means that the person with whom we are negotiating wants to be satisfied about certain points before they can willingly accept our new idea, plan or proposal. Let's identify these points. Whether they are in India, Scandinavia or one of the Mediterranean countries, if a group of managers is requested to identify the major steps in a "complete sale", the cardinal points are always:

1. Establish human rapport.
2. Understand the Listener's needs.
3. Show the benefits of the idea or proposal.
4. Establish credibility with a clear and believable explanation of the idea. Show where the benefits come from.
5. Gain commitment.

SAI provides a formal setting for the sequential process of thought-flow that takes place in the Listener's mind and identifies the points on which the person or team to whom we are presenting wants to be satisfied before they give their willing acceptance.

The Listener's Viewpoint provides us with a framework which we can use to build the communication process and appeal to our Listener from his or her point of view when presenting our idea.

Figure 7.1 The Listener's Viewpoint. (Printed by Permission of SAI® ViewPoint Training, Madison, Wisconsin)

CONSIDER THE LISTENER'S VIEWPOINT

Lord Israel Sieff of Marks and Spencer once argued that the future of business depends on a quick, imaginative study of what people (i.e. customers) need. Determining these needs is essential when trying to sell a new idea, product or service.

Communication between people is fundamentally creative, resulting in a synthesis of new insight, argues Bleicher[1]. Management teams consist of different people who have differing needs, interests and opinions which depend not only on their position and background but also on their personalities. They may also have varying interpretations of the needs of customers when something new is being proposed. If these interpretations were simply based on rational, conscious arguments and criteria, it would be relatively simple to sell Listeners your idea. Unfortunately, emotional and often unconscious motives come into play and the combination of heightened emotions and possible opposition to the new proposal can inhibit a team's ability to arrive at a favourable conclusion. Even in cases where you find emotional and perhaps "wrong" counterarguments against your proposal it is necessary to consider the Listener's viewpoint: what does he or she really want to achieve?

SHOW HOW THE BENEFITS OUTWEIGH THE LOSSES

When we present a new idea to a Listener we quite often meet resistance caused by their anticipation of costs or risks if the idea is implemented, or simply because of habit, the natural reluctance to change. How can we achieve willing cooperation from our Listener, rather than opposition or conflict? We suggest that you keep in mind a basic principle: *People act for their own benefit, and to avoid loss!* When you ask a person to accept a proposal which is new, difficult or unfamiliar, he/she will react willingly only if the result of the mental weighing process which goes on in his/her mind shows that the benefits clearly outweigh the losses.

When you as a manager want to get your colleagues to accept your idea of implementing a new technological solution, you should have information available which clearly shows how the proposed system meets the most important criteria of efficiency, user friendliness and cost effectiveness. Your

Listeners will surely think about losses such as additional costs and problems arising from change. Putting pressure on them by criticizing their existing operations or by insisting on your way will be counter productive, since they will resist if they see insufficient reason for change. You can add to the credibility of your presentation by presenting the potential benefits in relation to present losses and by using clear demonstrations, perhaps audio-visuals, tables, computer graphics, charts or a written proposal. Judith Brown Kamm[2] recommends written justification to communicate new ideas to management. "Rather than stifling innovation, such formality can actually enhance the likelihood that an idea will be given a fair evaluation", says Kamm.

REDUCE THE NEGATIVE EMOTIONS

In any negotiation where our new idea is markedly different from the Listener's present action we must expect to encounter obstacles. If you present to the management team the idea of replacing an old supplier by a new one, the production manager may object to your proposal in a very heated manner. When he poses obstacles, they will always contain some degree of negative emotion. Pressure will only serve to heighten the level of these emotions. Your Listener, suffering an awareness of loss, will have difficulty in listening to reasoned argument. His/her preference for the old supplier may be based on a good personal relationship or have some specific advantages. Continuing with reasoned arguments *at that moment* will only increase the tension.

The indispensable *first step in the resolution of any obstacle is to reduce the emotional level to a point where reasoned discussion can be resumed.* Control your own emotions and listen to what the other party has to say. Indicate that you do not intend to use pressure. Show that your purpose is to listen and to understand. It is important for us not to *agree* with the Listener's action as expressed by the obstacle. We are merely sympathizing with his/her feelings and encouraging him/her to express himself further. This gives us more time to think, to improve our analysis of the problem and to select the arguments which will be effective in overcoming the obstacle. We also encourage our Listener to fully express his/her feelings, thereby creating an outlet for negative emotions and satisfying the need for attention. This is an effective way of bringing the negotiation back to the level of reason.

The Persuader must understand that ideas which are in opposition to his/her own may often contain ideas for productive and profitable further development. As Judith Brown Kamm concludes: "If general management does not intervene, the sum of initiating-plans can become a 'meaningless catalogue'." The Persuader's own interest requires that his or her ideas will be listened to by others. It is the continuing task of top management to evaluate these ideas, always searching for a possible breakthrough.

PATRICIA SCHALLER: A TALENTED COMMUNICATOR

"POKS !!!" — "That has to be one of the most beautiful sounds in the world", said Jack, as the waiter popped the cork on a bottle of champagne at the restaurant of the Bayreuth Festspielhouse. Still under the spell of Wagner's music, we were sitting at a table with Patricia Schaller, an old friend of Jack's. Against all the odds, she had managed to purchase tickets to a performance of Die Meistersinger. We had been trying to find tickets to any of the festival performances since early in the year, but had always been told that everything was sold out almost a year in advance, and that the demand for tickets stretched years ahead. Finally, recalling that Patricia had a wide circle of friends and colleagues in the music world, was herself Artistic Director of the Aspen Festival, and was a near genius at achieving the impossible, we called upon her for help.

After a couple of weeks Patricia called to say that not only had she found the tickets, but would actually be able to attend herself. So here we were. The weather, earlier cold and rainy, had turned sunny; the champagne, cooled to perfection, and our marvellous companion, made it seem the best of all possible worlds. As Patricia commented on the various aspects of the performance, from the singers to the conductor and the stage sets, her striking appearance and passionate gestures were a centre of attraction. Time ran out quickly and we had to hurry to our seats for the last act.

Later, after the performance, when Patricia had left to return to Berlin, I asked Jack to tell me more about her musical career. I knew that she had been born in Germany of Italian and German–Jewish parents, and that after her father, an avid yachtsman, had disappeared on a voyage to Australia, her mother, fearing the Nazis, had moved to America with her young daughter. There, living with their relatives in New Jersey, the child had shown an early love and talent for music. The mother, a talented amateur musician herself, had encouraged Patricia's musical studies and gave her piano lessons. Whenever the family budget permitted she had taken her to hear the magnificent performances of Flagstad and Melchior at the Metropolitan Opera House.

During Patricia's high school days, as her voice matured into a brilliant mezzo-soprano, she began to dream of a serious musical career. She obtained a scholarship at the Julliard, and though her main stage experience was in conservatory opera class performances, her voice and musical talent were sufficiently impressive to gain a debut performance as Carmen at the New York City Opera. This was the start of a very successful career in many of the world's major opera houses, though the Metropolitan always eluded her grasp, for political reasons, she claimed.

In post-war Germany and Austria, as the vitality of musical life began to return to the opera theatres, Patricia returned to her native country to sing in Stuttgart and Munich as well as in Vienna. At the urging of the Musical Director at the Vienna Opera, she studied the soprano roles in Wagner's Flying Dutchman *and* Lohengrin. *For some time she had been secretly planning to make the change to the soprano repertoire, and was delighted to be given the opportunity. She sang as a soprano with some success for several years, but was never completely at her ease in the higher tessitura. This, together with the brutal rehearsal and performance schedule demanded by the theatres, caused permanent damage to her voice.*

No longer a performer, her continuing love for the theatre made her turn her attention to stage direction and production of both opera and drama. Her reputation as an exceptional actress as well as a singer helped her to enter the closed world of theatrical production. She first became an assistant at the Academy of Music and Drama and was then given the opportunity to stage her own production of Madam Butterfly. *The first performance was received splendidly, and the second, after the indisposed German tenor had to be substituted for a hurriedly obtained Italian "Pinkerton", was vocally even better, though linguistically a bit confused. The tenor sang happily in his own native language while the rest of the cast sang of course in German. Patricia was later to describe the performance as "musical minestrone".*

During this period, while she gained experience as an artistic director, her early piano studies were also put to good use. Her ability both to rehearse the cast and accompany them gained the attention of several influential musical directors, and contributed to an all-round artistic development rare in the world of the theatre.

DIAMONDS

Patricia's childhood was by no means easy. The tragic loss of her father and her subsequent emigration to America placed a heavy burden upon her mother, who had great difficulty during the early years in a new country. Patricia, though, had inherited her father's independence and love of adventure, and it was she who often had to organize the necessities of life, persuading various relatives to provide help.

Money for her early vocal studies was earned by her staging "Fun Concerts" for various social clubs. Her friends would then take up a "music collection". Later, as her natural talent as an entertainer grew, she was able to earn sufficient money to support herself by performing in hotels and night-clubs, accompaying herself at the piano, and doing imitations of well-known popular singers. This experience was useful in developing her sense of timing and contact with an audience that served her well throughout her career.

In considering her early persuasive and creative talent, it is clear that she had an unusual ability to get her way with an audience, not only by means of her musical talent, but also through her extraordinary emotional appeal. She demonstrated a real sense of persuasive communication when she obtained her first job in a hotel bar by pointing out to the owner that if he would hire her to play and sing light music, he would be able to attract people into his lounge during the usually slow mid-day hours, either to eat lunch or to have a drink or two. His trust in her ability was well repaid. Wearing an old-fashioned dress and hat, with her charming gestures and small talk, singing songs that touched an emotional chord in her audiences, she attracted warm and appreciative listeners.

This innate acting ability and courage to confront any situation also had its amusing side. She relates one occasion when she was going to a cafe on a cold winter's day. She bought a cup of coffee and a bar of chocolate at the counter, and since the cafe was crowded, she chose to sit at a table with a distinguished looking gentleman. As they both sat, silently drinking their coffee, Patricia opened the chocolate bar on the table and took a piece. The man, looking at her, reached over and took another piece from the bar. Patricia was somewhat taken aback, but said nothing. Moments later the gentleman was called to the telephone and disappeared, leaving his coffee and an untouched sandwich on the table. By this time, Patricia had decided to repay his impudent behaviour and, reaching over, picked up the sandwich and bit a large chunk out of the corner. Upon returning, the man looked at Patricia in a slightly puzzled way, but without saying a word took the sandwich and finished it. The incident ended there, but later, when Patricia opened her handbag at home, she found the bar of chocolate that she had bought. Hearing Patricia tell this story, punctuated with gales of laughter, is in itself a delight. Some time later, after a particularly rousing performance of Carmen, there was a knock at the door of her dressing room and the same gentleman entered to present her with a beautiful long-stemmed rose and a bar of chocolate.

Patricia's main characteristic is her own decisiveness and ability to convince others to do what she wants them to do. Even before she had obtained any formal authority in the theatre, she could usually influence others to act by creating a vision of what was to be done and inspiring them to join in her perception. Later she developed into a manager who—as John Nicholls describes this type of managerial behaviour—could PACE her influence on other people's environment, with a special blend of Perception, Articulation, Conviction and Empathy; the very special talent of being able to remove people's doubts and direct their energies towards positive goals.

In the authors' conversation with our friend Anna Kontek[3], a brilliant stage designer, we discussed the subject of the management skills every stage designer should have in order to create an ideal production. Anna pointed out that he/she should first of all have a Creator's capability to imagine the scene's events and to visualize each act when reading a libretto and listening to the music. He/she should be a Master in order to solve complex engineering problems in an ingenious and practical manner. By being a Stimulator the designer can inspire all the project's participants. Above all, the characteristics of a Persuader are needed in order to convince others to accept new and sometimes radical ideas. The applause of the audience when the stage curtains open is the reward for everyone involved in creating the setting in which the action and music take place.

PEARLS

As Patricia started to work as a production manager in various theatres, she added a very logical and rational approach to problems to her intense emotional appeal. She learned to carefully anticipate objections beforehand and plan a persuasive strategy, supported with clear evidence for her way of reasoning. A typical example of this was the strategy she adopted when she was asked to assist in planning the next season of the San Carlo Opera Association, as well as to assume responsibility for a major production. She knew that the Opera Association was in debt from the past season's lack of financial control and that a combination of temporary recession and lack of government support for the Arts was biting deeply into the funds available for the new season.

Quite naturally, in such a situation the management wanted to have a season of "popular" operas, such as La Traviata, Carmen, and Tosca; operas which were certain crowd-pleasers and which could be guaranteed to fill the theatre with long lines of customers at the box office. But Patricia's thoughts went way beyond this type of "playing it safe". She had ambitious plans for a production of Alban Berg's Wozzeck, an opera which, though standard fare in some European opera houses, was seldom given in America.

In the subsequent management meeting, there was a furor seldom seen at meetings of the socially elite members of the board. One of the influential ladies pronounced Wozzeck to be "An effete poetical work of no merit whatsoever, and certain to be a disaster in the present financial crisis." Patricia, prepared for this opposition, presented her case: "I understand your viewpoint, particularly as a new production is very costly. I also know that you doubt that this production could be profitable in its first season, and that it would require a continuity of performance before it could begin to repay the costs. For this reason I've been in contact with other potential partners, and can say with certainty that the Edinburgh Festival would be interested in using our production next summer. Also, considering the world-class cast that I've selected, both San Francisco and Dallas have expressed an eagerness to participate." She described what followed: "My presentation was followed by an absolutely stunned silence, then everyone started to talk at once. But in the end, approval was given."

Patricia's success as a talented artistic director, and also as a future general manager of an important theatre, is assured. She is able to coordinate the efforts of the many groups necessary to put together a theatrical production: principal singers, chorus and orchestra members, stage technicians and the "spear carriers", unpaid extras who make up the crowds necessary in the grander spectacles. Of special value is her easy contact with the "prima donna" conductors, whose friendship and respect is a carry-over from her own performances under their musical direction. All of this is combined in an extensive overall knowledge of the gigantic machinery needed to produce a modern operatic spectacle.

STONES

Patricia risks being too enthusiastic with her ideas and may insist upon her way even when the counterarguments are valid. Winning a victory in the communication conflict may become the goal itself rather than discovering the best available solution to the problem: an all-or-nothing mentality can come to dominate the thinking of the Persuader. She may fear "losing face" when her idea is not accepted. With her forceful personality Patricia can put listeners into a mental state of conflict and dissonance and they may relinquish their objections because they seek a peaceful compromise, not because her proposal is the best one.

In her presence, it is difficult to be aware of weaknesses which could compromise her future. Her ability to persuade others to do what she wants them to do is overpowering. But we must also take a closer look at the negative side of this creative Persuader's talent. Patricia must always have her own way. Her skill in imagining what the other person wants sometimes leads her into what others can easily view as manipulation, i.e. holding out a vision that is either unrealistic or very difficult to achieve. One of her leading singers told us that whenever he had a meeting with her, even though he quite seriously intended to refuse a role that he thought was not suitable for him, he was eventually brought round by a combination of emotional and rational appeal. In his own words, "I get angry with myself, and also with her, because I permit myself to be persuaded and seem to have no defence. I wish there was a vaccination against this kind of infection."

As we try to see this from an objective point of view, an exceptional talent to persuade can result in the creation of difficult feelings among staff; feelings which often remain latent, causing resentment among those who consider that they are not privileged to be counted in the circle of favourites. The occasional negative consequences of overpersuasion must therefore be taken into account.

ASHES

Patricia's insistence on having her own way may create too many conflicts within an organization, and hamper her future progress. It is certainly possible to accept that a creative Persuader will often upset the emotional tranquillity of those around him/her, but most of us are inclined to seek a state of mental equilibrium in which our beliefs, attitudes and values can be in balance. Patricia's artistic fanaticism leads her into situations where the conflict between her artistic goals and theatre management can only be resolved in her favour. She resolves management-related issues by confrontation, saying "Art knows no compromise."

Patricia must also come to understand that not all of the people involved in a production are necessarily motivated by her own high artistic goals. It may be possible to gain cooperation from performers and the various artistic directors by holding out the vision of a splendid performance which will enhance their reputations. But to the stagehands, computer operators and others who receive no public recognition, success must be translated into their terms; job security, additional overtime pay and smoothly running operations that make their job easier.

We are reminded of a story about the first performance of Bizet's opera, Carmen. *After the performance a friend asked one of the orchestra musicians, "How was the opera?" The musician replied, "Boring—all the music does is go 'blump-blimp, blump-blimp'", demonstrating by plucking the strings of his bass violin. "But I must say the audience seems to be very enthusiastic, I don't know why." The next night the friend went to see the performance and afterwards told the musician, "You know something, while you are going 'blump-blimp', there's a guy up on the stage singing 'To-re-a-dor, en ga-a-a-rde.'"*

This is what we must remember. While the star is up on the stage singing about the Toreador, there are an awful lot of people who are doing their "blimp-blumps" and without them there would be no performance.

Our message to Patricia:

- *KEEP your ability to understand other people's needs and desires. You will grow to become a well-liked and empathetic manager*
- *KEEP your talent to persuade and convince others to accept your good ideas and suggestions: you will be an exceptional Idea Salesperson*
- *KEEP your skills at balancing the emotional and the rational sides of your argument*
- *KEEP your ability to know what you really want as a manager, and to formulate strategy to achieve those goals*
- *KEEP influencing people by using the PACE strategy: your own personal blend of Perception, Articulation, Conviction and Empathy*
- *KEEP your ability to motivate the many people you work with: artists, musicians, technicians, and your ability to integrate their efforts into magnificent performances*
- *LEARN to perceive the negative consequences of overpersuasion and to realize that it is your long-term credibility that is at stake*
- *LEARN to handle conflict, and as a creative manager learn to accept that sometimes, better solutions are found when you give way to the other person and end up working out ideas together*
- *LEARN to continually develop your negotiation strategy and to build common ground between negotiation partners by first discussing minor issues that can easily be agreed upon. Then you can embark on major issues on a basis of trust, which will help in reaching final agreement.*

Chapter 7

Self-Assessment:
Persuader

HOW DO YOU RATE YOURSELF AS A "PERSUADER"?

Please take a few minutes to rate yourself according to the following items.
Place one numerical rating in the left hand column and one in the right.

How do you rate yourself in the following activities? (Select numerical rating.)			How important is this to your managerial career? (Select numerical rating.)		
VERY GOOD INEFFICIENT 7.....6.....5.....4.....3.....2.....1		#	VERY IMPORTANT NOT IMPORTANT 7.....6.....5.....4.....3.....2.....1		#
a	Communicating visions to my staff		a		
b	Creating enthusiastic followers		b		
c	Challenging people in discussions of new ideas		c		
d	Discovering quickly needs and wants of new prospective clients		d		
e	Encouraging members in creative discussions during management meetings		e		
f	Mastering communications media when presenting my great ideas		f		
g	Wandering around to meet inspiring people to stimulate creative thoughts		g		
h	Reducing negative emotions and calming down aggressive behaviour in meetings and negotiations		h		
i	Getting other people to willingly support my ideas		i		

Plot your ratings in the matrix:

I am inefficient (1–4)		I am very good (5–7)	
IS VERY IMPORTANT	A	IS VERY IMPORTANT	B
IS NOT IMPORTANT	C	IS NOT IMPORTANT	D

MY TOP FIVE DEVELOPMENT CHALLENGES AS A "PERSUADER":

1 _____

2 _____

3 _____

4 _____

5 _____

Chapter 8

Maintaining Excellence: The Manager as a Leader

> The Leader influences employees so that they channel their innovative efforts into pursuing organizational goals. The Leader motivates and develops people by setting mutually agreed-upon objectives, showing confidence in and respect for people, giving them real responsibility, encouraging them to join in the process of idea-generation and providing support for the implementation of ideas.

So far we have not examined the question of non-innovative managers. The role behaviour of non-innovative managers seems in most dimensions to be in contrast to the behaviour of Leaders. Robert E. Levinson[1] contrasts the bureaucrats and Leaders in the organization and views bureaucracy as an antonym for leadership. Because the concept of the bureaucrat is ambiguous we prefer to speak about non-innovative managers. They are first of all *thought-freezers*. They take sceptical attitudes towards their employees and their ability to create bright ideas and innovations. In their view, it is the task of management and experts to develop ideas and innovations, the job of subordinates is no more than implementation. They justify their stand by stating that workers do not have the knowledge and skills that are required to engage in problem solving. Workers' suggestions are usually too costly or unrealistic to be implemented. They even may deprecate the necessity for creativity and innovativeness in their company by emphasizing the usefulness of tested systems, rules and methods. Such sceptical attitudes kill creativity and innovativeness in the organization and top-creative individuals may soon depart.

In some organizations managers who personally score high in the Creator's role are non-innovative in their management style. They kill idea-generation by their people with their own idea-egoism. But as Murakami and Nishiwaki say, "If the president is always right the level of creation will rise no further than that of the president's creativity."

Non-innovative managers act like *controllers*. They base operations and activities on permanent orders, regulations and prescribed norms. Above all they believe that the company should consolidate on earlier success and maintain its position in the market. Caution, safety and a risk-avoiding mentality are characteristics of their behaviour. They closely follow the well-known maxim: "Never surprise a vice-president." They avoid bringing ideas as unexpected or unrequested suggestions to their superiors. As 'Mangham's Muffler' has it: "When communicating to superiors new news is bad news."[2]

The controller's management style attracts conformists into the organization. His staff are committed to the status quo, avoid taking risks and are afraid of change. Standard operating procedures leave little time and space for creativity.

Non-innovative managers are *hard-handed*. They concentrate on daily activities, work diligently, appreciate routines and handle people like subordinates, controlling them. They like hard working drudges and argue that workers produce their best results under continuous daily pressure. Behind their negative view of innovation lies the fear that innovations cause disturbances in normal working practices. They strive for short-term profit and discourage builders of the company's future by knocking out proposals for long-term innovative development. Subordinates' willingness to generate ideas and make suggestions is stymied by the effective use of "killer phrases". The company slides into routines.

In contrast to the bureaucratic non-innovative managers, innovative managers are Leaders who ignite creativity in their organizations by their own style and example. They achieve the goals of the company by energizing the efforts of the whole organization. "Successful Leaders realize they must get extraordinary performance from ordinary people", states W.T. Buchanan[3].

Innovativeness is a core concept in Leadership. A manager needs innovativeness to:

- *communicate visions*
- *formulate credos — statements of winning performance*
- *motivate people to extraordinary performances*

- *encourage and support innovative efforts*
- *find ways to develop core capabilities*
- *adopt an appropriate management style in different situations*

COMMUNICATE VISIONS

Think about the great leaders of the past, such as Abraham Lincoln, Mahatma Gandhi and Winston Churchill. What they had in common was a dream which they were able to communicate to their people. Lincoln dreamed about the unity of the United States, Gandhi about an independent, peaceful India, Churchill about victory in war. Because they were able to communicate strongly the vision of a promising future and the path to that future, they gave hope to the masses of people who followed them. John Reed took over as chairman of Citibank a decade ago. He visioned Citibank building up its branch network worldwide and gaining a significant foothold in emerging markets. Reed is *remembered* for his determination to stick with that vision even in the most difficult times. During his leadership Citibank has grown to be arguably the world's only truly global bank[4].

John Nicholls[5] calls this ability "meta-leadership". "Leaders exert influence on individuals by linking them to their environment through 'visioning' which creates the psychological ground for common action, releasing latent energy and/or channelling enthusiastic followers." Leaders have the ability to think creatively but in addition they possess a kind of missionary skill. As *they communicate their visions in a fascinating way, they get enthusiastic audiences and committed followers who are willing to build the path to the promising future.*

Clifford Jr and Cavanagh[6] have used the descriptive word "credo" to explain a set of fundamental beliefs, concise statements of the values of winning performance. Credos vividly set forth the company's guiding principles including the company's mission, success visions and expressed values.

As a matter of corporate practice, executives and managers articulate credos in the company's visions and statements. The corporate visions communicate promising future aspects of the company and are able to lift spirits and spark enthusiasm among staff. The credos of innovativeness may be, for example:

- ingenious ways to create and maintain superior quality
- creative ways to find solutions to customers' problems and satisfy their needs
- innovative professionalism, idea-rich people, leading experts, distinguished researchers and engineers, all of whom together are able to achieve technological leadership

- innovative marketing which brings growth and market leadership on a worldwide scale

MOTIVATE PEOPLE

Messages from management are not enough to maintain innovative behaviour. A Leader must behave consistently in ways which will support credos. People's efforts to solve problems creatively or to create innovations are based on their motivation and willingness to achieve something original, new and usable. Without Leaders people might merely be motivated to come up with solutions which only serve their own short- or long-term objectives. The Leader has the essential skill of forming a bridge between these individual goals and the company's objectives by motivating people to seek both personal success and company success, and to realize that the two are intertwined.

Actually, many very creative people are self-motivated to find something new and they are excited when they find creative solutions to complex problems. Leaders are able to channel this motivation to serve the company's objectives and to develop successful innovators from among the creative people. Innovators need challenging tasks and responsibility and proper financial rewards, as well as recognition and time to experiment. According to McClelland[7] *Innovative people have a built-in need for high achievement*:

1. They have a preference for performing tasks over which they have sole responsibility, to enable them to identify closely with the successful outcomes of their actions. Involve your people in creative problem solving and implementation of ideas so that they can see the results in practice!
2. They are moderate risk takers, and to maximize their chances of success they set themselves moderate goals. This does not mean to say that they avoid challenging situations, but simply that their goals are within an attainable range. Encourage risk taking but set the objectives of innovation together with your staff so that people accept high but nonetheless attainable objectives. (W. T. Buchanan[8] refers to studies which show that the most effective goals are those with a 50% probability of success. Goals that are impossible to attain or goals that are certain to be attained do not motivate.)
3. They need continual feedback, since it is only from the awareness of success that satisfaction can be derived. Engage yourself wholeheartedly in the projects of your people but do not interfere unnecessarily with their work.
4. Their respect for people is clearly discernible when management devotes itself to creating a favourable environment for innovativeness.

SUPPORT INNOVATIVE EFFORTS

The Leader is often cast in the role of sponsor. He/she acts as supporter, facilitator and coach by providing the resources and support needed to get innovative jobs done. This includes the provision of time, money, access to information sources, supplies and equipment. The Leader also uses his/her authority to legitimize the innovative efforts, whether these are individual, teamwork, or an innovation project. Leaders often organize and support innovative activities and programmes within their companies. One notable example of an innovative programme is 3M's Pathfinder Project which was founded in 1978 with "the main objective to stimulate innovative thinking and action for guiding new products, services and ideas through the critical stages of their introduction"[9]. Since 1978 several hundreds of successful projects have been initiated. Each project is organized as teamwork consisting of the innovator, a marketing specialist and a technical or lab specialist.

Other examples include Federal Express which grants awards of up to $25,000 to employees who come up with ideas and innovations. Federal Express also delivers annual Five Star awards to the most creative and innovative managers of the year. Since 1985, Domino's Pizza Distribution Corporation has very successfully sponsored the Domino's Olympics, a company-wide incentive programme consisting of competitions in delivery and service, measured by customer satisfaction and cost effectiveness. The Sensor Systems Division at Vaisala has achieved impressive results by lean manufacturing methods. The number of instruments delivered has grown significantly while average order lead times have been cut in half and on-time shipment performance has continuously been above 95%. One consequence is that there has been a significant increase in profitability. Vaisala relies on multiskilled workers and teams, and also on teamwork with suppliers at every step of the production chain. Management's ability to get workers' commitment and to be ready to perform a variety of tasks has been essential. "Once you establish the Continuous Improvement Process among the personnel, it will never end. The lean manufacturing concept, which emphasizes the importance of multiskilled teams, participative management and system throughout, supports continuous improvement of processes", says Mr Tuominen, Production Director, Vaisala[10]. Leaders are able to make operational innovativeness exciting and rewarding and to generate innovative actions and results through their people.

DEVELOP CORE CAPABILITIES

Companies must excel in refreshing their own special expertise to be able to stay ahead in the ever changing competitive business environment. Lorriman and Kenjo[11] claim in their analysis of "Japan's winning margins" that "One of the extraordinary aspects of Japanese management is the very high proportion of time (20–30 percent) managers and directors devote to developing and training their subordinates." Their Western counterparts have also learned that companies must continually upgrade the knowledge and skills of their workforce in order to be able to add value for customers whose needs and expectations are more complex than ever. Top innovative companies train their staff in disciplines and technologies which will be current in developing products even ten years into the future.

As has already been pointed out, while the Leader's role is essential to promoting creativity and innovativeness in the company, successful innovativeness is dependent on many additional factors. Depending upon the business environment Leaders must often perform strong supporting roles as Creators and Masters, as well as being devoted to the continuous development of the core capabilities of their people.

ROBERT HARTMAN: A LEADER GETTING EXCELLENT RESULTS FROM AVERAGE PEOPLE

Robert Hartman's secretary knocked on the door and entered our conference room. She walked over to him and handed him a note which he read quickly. Addressing the group he spoke quietly: "Gentlemen, please meet with me in my office immediately after the end of the seminar." Then, nodding to us, he said: "Please continue."

We had been invited to take the group through our seminar: "How to sell your innovative ideas within your own organization". As the newly appointed managing director of one of the car divisions of an American giant, Robert had asked us to do a creativity analysis of the organization. The profile that had emerged showed that the group was bound by its conservative tradition. Upper level management, while paying lip service to innovation, had in practice discouraged taking any risks that might jeopardize bottom line results. Year-end bonuses and public praise were usually accumulated by those who played it safe and maintained the status quo.

It was 22 November 1973, and the message that Robert's secretary had handed to him was the announcement that the Arabs had imposed an oil embargo on the Western world. It appeared that the era of the gas guzzlers was to end, "Not with a bang, but with a whimper."

Fortunately the company had a solid base in the smaller and medium range of cars, but the upper level and the top-of-the-line models which brought the real profits to the dealer organization, and which also represented the latest state-of-the-art technology, could pose a real problem. Dealer stocks were high, and immediate action was required.

By Monday morning at 8 am Robert had gathered together a representative group of area and district managers, as well as the key staff sales personnel, for a *brainstorming session. The group members were astonished that Robert was present and very active in this meeting, but as he explained, "I'm convinced that the way in which we handle this crisis situation will have a great effect upon company dealer relationships for years to come."*

The first problem they tackled was: "Let's start with ourselves. How could we help our own thinking and attitude?" Then they went on to brainstorm specific ideas. This resulted in several hundred ideas, including many wild suggestions. During the next two days they settled upon almost a hundred of these ideas, all useful in developing a practical and positive approach to helping dealers to continue selling larger cars in the months to follow. There was real practical value in the suggestions, which ranged from a visit to every dealer in the network by the responsible district manager to discuss the dealer's specific situation and the conditions he faced at first hand, to immediate training reinforcement for all sales personnel. A positive publicity campaign to counter over-reaction by the news media was also undertaken.

Asking dealers to recall what positive actions they had taken in previous recessions, a programme was drawn up to make every employee a salesperson, with prizes for the best contributors. Dealers were also encouraged to take part in any local shows, to hold exhibitions in shopping centres, and above all, not to lose heart. The advantages of superior comfort, safety and the ability to transport large loads over long distances still remained with their models.

Perhaps the most important result was the effect on dealer morale, to see immediate positive action by the company in acknowledging that they had a responsibility to offer guidance and leadership in working through the difficult period ahead. In this crisis, Robert was able to get extraordinary performance from his people who strongly supported his initiatives.

SOME YEARS LATER

Robert took a hefty swing at the golf ball, and after separating from the clump of earth that accompanied it, the ball soared down the fairway and landed in the bushes. "As usual", he exclaimed, "maybe I should stop using this game to vent my frustrations." Later when we were comfortably ensconced in the 19th hole at the Starnberg golf course, Robert explained to us the background to his "frustrations". A year earlier Robert had been appointed managing director of his company's European operations. His personal leadership style had developed to the point that he felt quite at ease with the philosophy of Mitbestimmung *(co-determination) wherein a workers' council sits on the board of directors of the company and shares its decision-making power.*

As for the members of management, he remained somewhat less than happy, sensing that most of them were resistant to any kind of radical change. Their basic approach was essentially to keep things moving along with only incremental improvement—"Don't rock the boat." Towards their subordinates they were supportive, but in their paternalistic manner, this was conditional upon absolute obedience.

As Robert continued, "I'm really beginning to appreciate what old John D. Rockefeller meant when he said that he'd pay more for the ability to handle people than for any other executive talent."

"The company instituted quality improvement systems several years ago and some progress has been made. Our quality improved, but so has that of our competitors, and our quality only comes at the cost of unending inspection and supervision of our employees. I was visiting friends in Sarasota, Florida, several years ago and went to hear a short seminar on Quality given by W. Edwards Deming, then in his nineties but still giving us hell! His point was that truly concentrating on quality will reduce costs. He claimed that following the carrot and stick method, offering incentive pay and meting out punishment to the laggards leads only to fear, resentment and destructive rivalry within the organization.

I don't mean to sound pessimistic. Our workers are well educated and competent. We have a high degree of independence and a market share that still makes us profitable, even though we still carry the burden of our past success. For years the entire German auto industry bucked the trend. During the last decade 400,000 jobs in the auto industry were eliminated in other countries belonging to the European Union. In Germany, to meet export demand, 80,000 additional jobs were created. Until recently, we've been so wedded to traditional methods that instead of doing our utmost to improve productivity and lower costs, we have a production cost base which is nearly 30% above that of our major competitors. Our workers have the highest pay in the world, combined with the shortest working week. This means that we need radical change in other areas that we can control. We must evaluate each step in our entire operation, not only in production but in management as well. If you need a name for it, call it re-engineering, but its what effective managers have always done."

"There is an enormous amount of untapped talent, particularly among the younger members of our organization. But they are so hemmed in by the layers of vertical management structure that it's difficult to get their ideas implemented. I believe I've started to gain their confidence that they will at least be listened to. We've had some great "creativity" meetings and they are excited about the idea of moving into horizontal process groups and building teams with multi-competent members. It's the wave of the future, but as Toffler has been telling us for years, the future is here now. My job is to see that we participate in it."

It's important to reach out to our suppliers, giving them a much greater feeling of partnership. Traditionally the relationship has been antagonistic. We've tried to exert maximum pressures to keep prices down, using a combination of threats and bullying. They in turn do their outmost to keep turning the spiral upwards.

I think you'll be interested in an actual case where we were able to reverse the process to the great benefit of both parties. We had been forewarned that one of our vehicle transport suppliers was about to make a demand for a price increase in the

6–8% range. As we account for about half of their volume, that means over 20,000 vehicles per year, so we're talking about real money. Instead of digging in our heels to resist any increase, and in fact counter with our demand to reduce their price, we took the initiative saying, "let us come into your organization and prove that we can help you save more than you would gain by a price increase to us." They were a little taken aback, but agreed to our proposal. We negotiated a deal on the following terms:

- *We would form consulting teams to help them in potential areas of improvement*
- *They would also form teams to work with our people*
- *As work progressed, their management was to keep 'hands off'*
- *If their working groups approved of our suggested changes, the changes would be instituted*
- *Any changes suggested would not result in loss of jobs in their organization*

The areas selected for potential improvement were:

- *Internal transport; transport within the company confines, between warehouses, long haul and short haul and material handling*
- *Accounting; to include forms, average billing times, phones and faxes and time flow between performing services and receiving payments*
- *Overall organizational efficiency, including use of all buildings and installations on the premises."*

Robert continues, "They were very sceptical that we could improve their practices, but as agreed, the teams were formed and they projected a four-week period for the work. When our consulting teams started work, our people began to ask questions of those actually doing the production. Why do you use this method? What would you change in the way this is done?, and perhaps the most important question that companies rarely ask themselves: Is this operation really necessary at all? They were astonished at the flow of good ideas from their counterparts who were full of suggestions and very quick to respond. They really opened up when they realized that their suggestions were wanted and would be seriously considered for implementation. They said that no one had ever asked for their opinions before. By the end of the first week, decisions for major change had been made to include:

- *Internal transport: the compound which is approximately 1.5×2 kilometres in size accommodated a put-through of about 45,000 vehicles per year, from nine different automobile manufacturers. It consists of a railroad arrival station, storage areas and cleaning and washing area. With the new flow charts developed, it was estimated that over 141,000 kilometres of vehicle transport could be eliminated per year; over 3ks of needless movement per vehicle within the compound*

- *Accounting: billing systems which had been different for each of the nine clients were reduced from nine to five. This alone permitted a reduction of 25% of the forms used. By asking how much time was devoted to each client, it was ascertained that the most administrative time was devoted to the client with the lowest volume of vehicle transport. Re-examination of the work flow of the two account clerks and their assistants resulted in the release of one assistant to perform other work within the company. By the company's own estimate the accounting load could be reduced by approximately 30% on a yearly basis. Savings in phone, fax and data search efforts were not quantified, but we agreed that the savings would be considerable. An additional benefit was that bills could be sent out earlier, four to five days on average, and (presumably) payment would be received earlier*
- *Organizational set up: with the projected quicker movement of material, and the shortened delivery period, management re-examined their intention to construct another compound and decided that the existing facilities would serve their needs for another four to five years*

Needless to say, we have a very satisfied partner and we are convinced that we have a model for improving our relationship with other suppliers. An unexpected spin-off is that whereas we had to persuade our own people to participate in this first project, they are now enthusiastic volunteers for the next opportunity.

DIAMONDS

Robert Hartman, as a mature executive now in his mid fifties is beginning to be able to bring his value system and his actions into a consistent pattern. As he himself expresses it: "There was always an internal struggle between my own drive and ambition and the realization that my aggressive leadership style was exactly what prevented my subordinates from developing. Time and time again I would 'take over' in situations that they could probably have handled just as well, or even better than myself."

Robert has always believed that an organization's health and future growth depends on giving talented subordinates a "long leash" and encouraging them to take risks. He recalled with a wry smile that when we did the creativity profile for his organization some years ago, even though he'd been in his job for only a short while, his subordinates had already noted a disparity between his professed philosophy and his day-to-day behaviour. Robert in fact had asked at the time, with some heat, "How the hell does one learn to balance subordinates' human needs with company needs and objectives?"

Kari suggested at the time that some introspection on his part, that is, an analysis of his own leadership style, could be a useful first step, and in fact provided him with material to do just that. Kari also said that a study of Situational Management techniques, e.g. Reddin's writings on Managerial Effectiveness, could help in the development of a flexible and varied approach. As a leader, Robert must foster enthusiastic followers who can use their own imagination when problem solving and act accordingly. Of particular significance in Robert's own growth was his determination to open up the lines of communication with his own staff, and encourage them to do the same down the line. He later admitted that as he undertook the painful process of change he was acutely aware that his own behaviour would determine the success or failure of this effort. He told us that the concept of confronting issues without threatening the individual—which is part of the philosophical base of SAI—had been of enormous help to him. It had been a key concept in encouraging open and candid feedback from his close subordinates.

Robert has also taken the initiative of adding conversational German to his existing knowledge of that language which enables him to read it. Three times a week he comes to his office at 6 am for two hours of intensive supervised drill, and during the day while he practices "management by walking around" he takes every opportunity to speak German with workers on the shop floor, or when having lunch with them in the cafeteria.

Robert also regularly attends the monthly meetings of the Foreign Chamber of Commerce in Germany, where top managers from the various foreign companies present in Germany meet to discuss common problems and plans for the future. This has given him a wide circle of friends and acquaintances from different nationalities who appreciate his desire to integrate into the European business community.

PEARLS

Robert Hartman has brought considerable managerial talent and leadership skill to his present job in Germany. He will need all of it. The presence on his board of directors of several powerful, older managers who essentially resist the innovative changes he is bringing about must be dealt with. For the first time in years, however, there is a new spirit among key persons which reaches down as far as supervisory level. Several talented younger people have been attracted to upper level staff positions and the feeling of excitement is palpable. With the reuniting of Germany, Robert is visibly excited about the new business ventures that have already been put into high gear, and takes every opportunity to speak of his vision of a new common market with 330 million consumers. Those who know him either in a work or social context see him as a natural leader who is bound to progress to a position of multinational influence.

STONES

Robert is facing possibly the greatest challenge of his career. According to company policy, tenure of his present job is of short duration, possibly only another two or three years. As in the past, the company still harbours the residual feeling which he himself expressed as: "Managing Directors come and go. We remain. This too shall pass." Looking at the previous successful survival of the company, people are not aware that the environment of their industry has changed. Unless Robert can develop a loyal cadre of true believers, there is danger that no lasting organizational change will take place. The new generation of high achievers who possess intrinsic self-motivation has to be ready to take over.

ASHES

Robert has been successful in opening up lines of communication and establishing an atmosphere of trust with his people. He has been less successful in coping with the feedback he sometimes receives. His "take over" tendencies are still sometimes in evidence and he admits to being occasionally shocked when subordinates take him at his word and level with him about how they feel when he moves in on what they consider to be their territory. He must understand and accept the fact that the dominant characteristics of strong Leaders can in themselves be antagonistic to innovativeness and independent risk taking by subordinates. A very small percentage of top managers are able to consistently translate their genuine concern for the well-being and growth of their subordinates into the kind of supportive behaviour that actually encourages innovation and risk taking down the line.

Our message to Robert:

- KEEP your open mind and drive for personal achievement
- KEEP and develop your growing ability to handle open, frank feedback from your own people
- KEEP your commitment to the conviction that subordinates must be permitted to make their own decisions and accept the responsibility. This will permit you to leave your own imprint behind as you continue to move up the line
- KEEP your flexibility and interest in operating in a multinational and multicultural atmosphere
- LEARN to accept the fact that some of your key subordinates share the same drives and need for achievement that have made you successful
- LEARN to live with the dichotomy of your own position — that for the good of the organization you must quite often postpone your own fulfilment. Growing pains do not end with adolescence

Chapter 8

Self-Assessment: Leader

HOW DO YOU RATE YOURSELF AS A "LEADER"?

Please take a few minutes to rate yourself according to the following items. Place one numerical rating in the left hand column and one in the right.

How do you rate yourself in the following activities? (Select numerical rating.)		How important is this to your managerial career? (Select numerical rating.)	
VERY GOOD INEFFICIENT 7.....6.....5.....4.....3.....2.....1 #		VERY IMPORTANT NOT IMPORTANT 7.....6.....5.....4.....3.....2.....1 #	
a	Inspiring people to follow my dreams and visions	a	
b	Winning authority among people	b	
c	Getting other people to accept willingly my plans and projects	c	
d	Setting high standards for myself and for my subordinates	d	
e	Getting excellent results from average people	e	
f	Giving deserved credit to my people	f	
g	Being flexible in my management style: patient and supportive when needed, forceful when necessary	g	
h	Maintaining high consistency between my convictions and my behaviour	h	
i	Devoting wholehearted support to our personnel's continuous learning and self-development	i	

Plot your ratings in the matrix:

I am inefficient (1–4)		I am very good (5–7)	
IS VERY IMPORTANT	A	IS VERY IMPORTANT	B
IS NOT IMPORTANT	C	IS NOT IMPORTANT	D

MY TOP FIVE DEVELOPMENT CHALLENGES AS A "LEADER":

1 _____

2 _____

3 _____

4 _____

5 _____

Chapter 9

Innovation or Resignation: How to Destroy a Company's Innovativeness

Most companies operate through their established businesses and have designed hierarchical organizations in order to secure stability, predictability and a smooth operation. Top management, in planning and business meetings with their senior and middle managers, sets periodic business targets and establishes the key tasks for their managers. Top management controls how job descriptions have been followed and whether targets have been achieved. If managers accomplish their tasks and meet their targets they are praised and rewarded.

Over time, managers will tend towards cautiously staying within their operational limits, minimizing risks and avoiding spontaneous innovative actions. Accordingly, they will neither encourage nor praise creativity among their own people.

Naturally, modern management in many established companies understands the necessity of innovation in order to survive. But as Pryor and Shays[1] demonstrate, the response of conventional management is to try to keep innovators under firm control as much as possible. Management tries to regulate the idea-generation and implementation process by nominating special units (an R&D department, a new product development unit, task forces) or by forming organizations such as new ventures, spin-offs and strategic alliances to carry out this job. "The company has pinned a badge on the group's chests and designated them the innovating force", say Pryor and Shays.

While this kind of solution may provide some innovative performance, the use of the main creative human resource, the whole group of employees, is unfortunately neglected. But even worse than this, management operating under the constraints of short-term profit requirements, shareholders' expectations and strictly enforced planning and control systems may actively resist any creative and innovative actions. We often hear complaints about the management of publicly owned companies that most investors are only interested in short-term results and dividend payouts and are not really interested in long-term innovations. Management tends to believe that it is safer and more profitable to run the business the way they have always done. They are actually driven by short-term indicators such as sales, market share and ROI or ROE (return on equity). Many managers in our seminars have argued that it is more profitable to make minor product improvements and modifications such as change of brand name, colours, models, design, style or packaging than to create new products. Our answer is: "Yes, in the short term, but look ahead!"

Furthermore, the question is not only about product innovations but also about how we run our businesses. Many companies have operated in the strong belief that advantages such as locating stores or service points close to customers would continue to produce profit. In spite of this, competitors' innovative logistical or information transfer systems have undermined these advantages.

While top innovative companies invest huge sums in research (for example, Merck spends about $1bn and Pilkington some £40m a year), and the overall level of costs in companies has increased, investors are starting to enquire more pointedly whether research really provides value for money. The article in the *Financial Times* entitled "R&D placed under the microscope"[2] gives a warning of the danger of "short-termism" and describes cost control measures to guarantee value for money spent.

Carol Kennedy[3] in her article about Ciba Geigy gives a typical example of the resistance which occurs when a company embarks on radical innovative change. She explains that middle management emerged as the main source of resistance and suspicion. They felt threatened and insecure because they derived their sense of security from hierarchical positions, and suddenly that structure was being eroded. Jan Carlzon experienced similar resistance from middle management when he radically changed the culture of SAS in the mid 1980s. By their very nature innovations often result in organizational change and discomfort and consequently meet resistance from management. It is much more tempting for many managers to suggest increased investment in advertising campaigns and sales promotions which give fast payoffs rather than contribute to complex and risky innovation programmes.

INACTION: PROTECTING THE STATUS QUO

The authors' interview with Mats.

We were a bit uncertain before our interview with Mats whether he would be willing to talk about the critical issues in Jari Silta's managerial behaviour. We were in fact surprised at the freedom with which he expressed his views and proved to be a rich source of information about the way in which the company was managed. Later, we were able to sympathize with his motives, since he was not actually expressing criticism of Jari, as much as of the "power-game players in headquarters".

Let's hear what Mats has to say: "You surely remember that corporate board meeting where I bitterly criticized the 'replication strategy'. At that time, Jari had just been appointed President of the Corporation, and we could understand that he was keen to maintain the successful business strategy followed by his predecessor. What Jari didn't then understand was that it was the power game at top level that actually determined strategy. Some of the most influential decision makers actually followed short-term objectives and their main interests were achieving quick profits and solving the most acute problems without investing in further development. I think their short-sightedness was also based on the fact that some of them were due to retire soon and held a considerable number of company shares, which resulted in their restricted set of personal objectives for the future. They wanted to keep the company operating as it was and strongly opposed any essential change."

"You know of course many stories about companies that incur incredible losses when they try to enter unknown territory such as new markets or alliances. I personally think that many such failures could be avoided if top management would adopt a more open, flexible approach.

Looking at things from the headquarters point of view, it is natural that they would prefer all aspects of the company to be standardized and centralized, everything homogenized. That would make life in headquarters much easier and more problem-free. But you can't standardize customers or the competition, or the community in which we live. These things will always differ, have their own characteristics, and grow according to their own dynamics.

I could clearly see that the people at headquarters lacked the expertise and even the interest to try and cope with future local needs. For example, how could they see what is happening in the wooden home building market from the point of view of a newly acquired firm in a provincial rural village thousands of miles from headquarters? They would send us the direct marketing campaign material suitable for downtown yuppies who buy city condominiums. Our prospects, actually wealthy farmers, who drive Volvos or Saabs and who intend to build new, modern farmhouses would laugh out loud reading that stuff. Clearly, headquarters had lost touch with our customers. The only contact we had was through papers and statistics.

So they required us to fill out and return endless piles of reports and analyses — perhaps only satisfying the *computer-bred numerologists*, as Robert Levinson calls them. Then, if necessary, they could always blame us by pointing to bare figures and charts. The worst thing was that compiling all these reports and sitting in meetings at headquarters actually took time away from attending to our business or creating something really new and profitable. New local trends that we foresee here cannot be predicted from historical statistics. I read what CEO Yoshio Maruta, chairman of the Kao corporation, once said: 'Yesterday's successful formula is often today's obsolete dogma!'

Many of us local managers were both interested and willing to try out innovative operations and new ideas. Our suggestions were killed simply by their being put into the interminable queue of projects and headquarters committees. Every significant initiative was in danger of being crushed in the process of documentation, evaluation and review at senior management level. The result was not a promising cultivated business seedling but a carefully polished naked skeleton, a compromise of debates and discussions. I suppose senior managers simply wanted to avoid any real risk which could threaten their safety and comfort.

Even today, I'm still alarmed when I hear such talk as, 'Do you have it in your budget'?, or 'That's not in line with our present strategy'. I, personally, was viewed with suspicion and even hatred at headquarters, because I made it quite clear that I thought the best place for their antiquated strategy was the garbage can. Actually, I was not so worried about myself as I was for Jari, because I'd already made plans to jump ship and start my own business.

The corporate game-players aggressively defended the old strategy by pointing out that the overall financial results were still satisfactory. They produced graphs, histograms, polygons, to say nothing of correlations and regressions from the corporation's past. But we, as local managers, were worried about our own future in an ever more competitive environment.

The corporate game-players thought that our corporate performance was steady, but the fact that we had been doing things in the same way for years had made us blind to a world of thousands of new opportunities. I think many of us, at least the most ambitious and creative among us, were bored and fed up running the business without new and demanding challenges.

I know that Jari learned quite quickly to understand our point of view. We local managers were, as someone described us, *a knowledgeable but angry organization*. We knew how things were, and how they should be, but they would not listen to us — with the exception of Jari who, from the time of that memorable meeting at headquarters, started to turn things around. The bureaucratic structure of our organization prevented any real progress. The really important decisions were all made in headquarters and it was difficult even to get information, to say nothing of new ideas, passed up through the many layers of the hierarchy."

Mats continued: "Jari took important steps forward when he instituted our SBUs (strategic business units). They could have been an excellent means of encouraging innovation but unfortunately they were actually used more for controlling our performance and allocating tasks than as a tool for improving initiatives within our corporation."

"True, in theory we had an open company culture, but when people presented their proposals and initiatives they became frustrated by the wait for a decision. I am convinced that top management had no desire to listen to our ideas, and this caused both general scepticism and lower morale in the ranks. We realized that, as local managers, we had little influence over matters — even those that affected us personally. And as company restrictions made it impossible for us to reward our most capable colleagues, some of them left to take up other jobs."

CREATIVITY KILLERS

A conversation with William McPherson.

We knew that William had a lot of experience with managers and supervisors whom we might term "creativity killers", and he proved more than willing to talk to us on this subject.

J & K: What would you consider to be the typical characteristics of non-innovative managers?

WILLIAM: Let me start by asking what you, as knowledgeable outsiders, would look for to differentiate these beings from innovative managers. Their appearance? Their clothes? Their work place, fittings, cars, homes? I, personally, would listen to managers talking and observe their interaction with other people. Beware if you hear a lot of negative expressions, such as "No, by no means", "hardly", "costly", "in vain", "troublesome", "never has worked before", "costs too much", "not in the budget" and so on. You are aware of this, of course. But have you also observed that often the best way to kill people's creativity is to remain silent, to say nothing? Give no feedback when someone enthusiastically expresses his or her "great idea". To say nothing in this situation makes the speaker feel foolish and may cause him or her to give needless explanations or even become apologetic. This is, unfortunately, the way that many managers kill their people's excitement and enthusiasm for new ideas.

J & K: Yes, we see your point. Silence is even worse than saying "no", because in the latter case the creative person would start to develop his idea further, or develop stronger arguments, and the interaction would stimulate some progress.

WILLIAM: Sure. I think a typical personality trait of many non-innovative managers is excessive scepticism. This has grown as a result of the overemphasis on rationalism in present-day management education. They have learned to calculate, evaluate, and criticize everything. I believe that this sceptical attitude that prevails among many managers concerning their people's skills and abilities to solve problems actually kills the creativity and initiative within their own organization.

J & K: We have sometimes encountered this scepticism concerning innovativeness in general as well. There are still a lot of executives and managers who are very sceptical or indifferent to the needs of education and training to develop this area within their companies. Some may claim, "Yes we do try to recruit creative people. Just let them work in their own way. That's all you need to do about the development of creativity in our company." Others say, "All you need to do is to make plans, give clear orders to your people and make sure that they work hard."

WILLIAM: That's right. Earlier I had quite a few supervisors who accomplished a great deal by working hard themselves every day and checking that their people also performed their daily activities according to the rules and regulations. Well, don't creative people also take time to think what and how things could be done in more effective ways? It is true that a rigid management style can yield results, but the risks of short-sightedness are great.

J & K: Do you think that non-innovative managers make no plans for the future?

WILLIAM: No, by no means that. I think that many non-innovative managers are actually very interested in planning. They might have a high opinion of written plans and interpret these in the form of strict administrative instructions and iron-clad orders. It is just that they are not willing to "exceed the limits" or deviate from established practices.

J & K: This "planocratic" attitude makes it very difficult to gain approval for radical innovative suggestions for renewal, although these could perhaps be very profitable if implemented. Managers feel that change could upset their plans, structures and systems and damage their careers. Profit is, of course, what companies are created for. But the real difference between innovative and non-innovative managers is the understanding of the "time vs. risk" element. In most companies, managers are rewarded according to the short-term profit they generate, and non-innovative managers are not interested in changes which might risk the immediate balance sheets even to gain better results in the longer term. Here we have a clear difference between the short and the long distance runners.

J & K: This is why an athlete like Paavo Nurmi, the "Flying Finn", perhaps the greatest long distance runner of all time, was so exciting to watch. He won nine gold medals and three silver medals in Olympic competitions, and established 31 outdoor world records and 29 world records on indoor tracks. He was able to judge the right balance between speed and endurance — two indispensable qualities that Innovative Managers also need.

Chapter 10

Management Makes the Difference!

Economists have concluded[1] that innovations and increased information account for 60% of the competitive improvement in the economy of any country, while only 40% derives from direct investments (in new production facilities or sources of raw materials). In their comparative study of leading economies in the Far East and Europe, Botkin et al.[2] at Harvard Business School have shown that the differences in the growth of productivity are explained by differing levels of capital investment in education, creativity and innovation, and also by different management practices. Numerous studies also indicate that innovative companies succeed better than non-innovative ones[3] and original, high-profile products and services sell better, provided that customers' quality requirements are met[4]. *A high level of innovativeness seems to create significant results regardless of the function or area concerned.* For example, there are many studies referred to by Martha Gephart[5] which show that firms with innovative and inter-related human resource practices have higher levels of productivity and better financial performance than those that do not follow such practices. "A firm needs to be innovative to gain the competitive edge necessary to survive and grow", say Groenhaug and Kaufman[6].

One can perhaps consider it a measure of validity that the top companies in the categories on the Fortune 500 list — Rubbermaid, 3M, Intel, Microsoft and Motorola — have also, in recent years, been ranked among the most innovative companies in the US. The ability to survive economic down-swings is characteristic of companies which have a high level of innovativeness. In Europe, ABB, Siemens, Philips, LM Ericsson and Nokia get the highest rankings for innovativeness in the product and technology sector[7]. The same is true for Japanese companies such as Sony, Honda, Toyota and Mitsubishi.

Typical of, and common to, top innovative companies is that the basis of their innovation policy is strategic management which both emphasizes and favours innovative activity. As evidenced through visions and strategies, the managing director is the champion of innovativeness in these companies[8]. Directors must act as Stimulators, carefully listening to their colleagues, staff, customers and suppliers. They must come out from behind their oak doors and become sensitive to the input of those who are vitally concerned with the company's well-being. A winning strategy is formulated by the entire organization.

In appraising the innovative success of Merck and Wal-Mart, *Fortune* magazine[9] highlights the importance of the management function. Merck's managing director Roy Vagelos has, according to *Fortune*, been able to mix academic initiative with business administration in such a way that Merck gives the impression of being a university campus rather than a factory. The founder and long-time director of Wal-Mart, the late Sam Walton, managed to set up a highly creative, decentralized, flexible chain of discount stores which has always been able to do everything a little bit better and to time its moves more accurately than its competitors in the retail business. The Japanese companies mentioned above, on the other hand, have been praised for the ability of their directors to develop the companies through innovative, incremental changes.

IGNITE YOUR SALES — ACT AS A TRENDSETTER

Innovations are a significant strategic asset. Companies have to innovate to be able to adapt to the fast-changing competition and social, political and economic developments. They must be able to cope with market demands and expectations and be able to embrace the new possibilities offered by the latest technology. Some companies have made a conscious effort to become wide-scale innovators. 3M boasts an impressive catalogue of more than 60,000 products. Procter & Gamble innovate across multiple markets and market over 160 brands in nearly 140 countries. Others aim at being innovators in meeting the needs of a specialized and very profitable market (for example, Merck in the pharmaceutical business, Apple Computer among personal computer users, Vaisala in meteorological systems).

A majority of retailers are dependent on new products and actively search for items which could satisfy consumers' needs and preferences. People usually think that there is an abundance of new consumer products being launched onto the market — more than retailers really need. However, most of them actually are only improved or "copycat" products, new designs or slightly altered product versions. It may be surprising to hear what David A. Glass, the president and CEO of Wal-Mart, said when interviewed by the *Journal of Product Innovation Management*[10]. He claims, speaking about the

United States, that "One of the real problems we have with satisfying the consumer today is an absence of new products", and he continued "There is nothing really new on the market these days. Truly innovative new products have been rare the last few years." He points to Nintendo as the last example of a really new consumer product.

Companies will meet new problems in consumer market megatrends. Typical of these in the industrialized countries are the aging of populations, high unemployment, poverty, environmental problems, growing insecurity in large cities (criminality, violence, terrorism) and the restlessness of youth.

Other changes and trends cause difficulties for companies, especially retailers who have been operating in the traditional manner. At the turn of the century more than a billion people will be connected to computer networks. The number of teleworkers is increasing rapidly and consumers are more mobile than ever. They will change their jobs, titles, organizations, shopping habits and even their country of residence. New media behaviour and changing shopping habits will reshape advertising and retailing. On-line market research, advertising and shopping are increasing. Customers will surf the super information highways to discover a new and exciting choice of products.

Consumers will be segmented into ever more categories and niches. Their lifestyles and preferences will become increasingly difficult to predict. Think about a company operating in the food sector. Health consciousness, green values, new exotic flavours and ethnic preferences as well as the desire for variety, ease of preparation and price consciousness are factors which vary according to consumer sectors. Local manufacturers will be affected by the increasing power of global brands, growing R&D costs, concentration of food retailing and new EU directives. To be able to compete successfully, companies will have to move fast and innovatively.

* * *

CITIBANK — A TRENDSETTER

"If there is one characteristic common to today's diverse and complex financial marketplace, that characteristic is change. Change is the force that Citicorp uses to differentiate itself in the marketplace by developing innovative financial solutions rather than simply adapting old methods to new products."[11] The continuous change in financial markets is a kind of two-edged sword: it constantly brings new challenges and opportunities but it also causes major risks to financial institutions. Citibank's top management has strongly emphasized innovation. "Our hallmark is our energy and innovation", says Citibank's chairman and CEO John Reed[12]. Citibank is committed to innovation in all sectors of banking, especially in banking technology. Reed himself, a great innovator, graduated from MIT with an engineering degree. Top executives have generally been characterized as "manuscripters of breakthrough changes". Citibank seeks recruits who have the imagination and the drive to keep the bank one jump ahead of its competitors. Flexibility, renewal and heavy investment in management development and skills training are the key factors. As a very large corporation Citibank can offer excellent opportunities for career development and the innovativeness and professionalism displayed by their management and staff around the world is generally acknowledged. Citibank made a most impressive showing in *Euromoney* magazine's 1994 Awards for Excellence winning 18 categories, more than twice as many as the closest commercial or investment banking institution[13].

Citibank aims to generate top-innovative products backed up by state-of-the-art technology and quality service tailored to individual needs. The essence of Citibanking is a customer experience which is relationship based rather than one which is product driven. Innovative product and service offerings reinforce the value of the Citibanking experience[14].

A continuous stream of innovations are a great risk to a corporation if it is unable to master change. Citibank went through very troubled times at the end of the 1980s. Top management produced a successful turnaround in a couple of years by emphasizing performance, value, balance and predictability. In 1994, Citibank earned its record \$3.4bn profit[15]. From our viewpoint, Citibank has demonstrated an exceptional capacity to master change, with great innovations backed up by performance excellence!

The size and scope of their activities make it possible for Citibank to act as the innovation trendsetter in world banking. Citibank is one of the world's largest financial organizations serving over 90 countries and territories around the world and employing more than 80,000 people. They are the world's largest bankcard and chargecard issuer, with almost 50 million cards in circulation. Since 1990, the total number of bankcards and Diners Club cards in force has grown by almost 45%. Citibank has pioneered Photocard (which bears the cardholder's photo digitally imprinted on the card[16]) worldwide. Furthermore, Citibank has been innovative in differentiating the cards it offers into various customer segments, such as "Choice" (for the price sensitive), "Classic" (for the security minded) and "Preferred" (for those seeking higher credit). In Germany Citibank has approached several million new prospects through a co-branding agreement with the Deutsche Bundesbahn (German national railway)[17]. We recently received a brochure by mail describing the new Citibank Bahncard. The original Bahncard, a highly successful effort by German railways to increase public use of the rail system, is issued to clients upon payment of a fee which depends on their age and the class of service desired. The card entitles the holder to a 50% discount on rail transportation throughout Germany, and must be renewed annually. The newly designed Citibank Bahncard offers a combination of the previous Bahncard features plus a selection of different options available to the cardholder through application to Citibank. One version permits payment for rail tickets with the card itself, while another offers the complete range of Visa credit card services. The card carries the bearer's photo and is replaced free of charge if lost. With the credit card business in Germany dominated by powerful and long-established competitors, Citibank has once again demonstrated its innovative approach to the design and marketing of new products.

* * *

SHARPEN YOUR COMPETITIVE EDGE

Competition is one of the main forces compelling companies to innovate. For example, in the financial services sector a stable situation prevailed in many countries as late as the 1960s and also in many industrial sectors up to the 1970s. As one Citibank executive has been quoted[18]: "We all followed the '3-6-3 rule' — pay 3% for deposit money, lend it out at 6%, and be on the golf course by 3 pm!" The calm was shattered by government action which brought about deregulation in the financial business. New competitors such as insurance companies and regional banks entered the market. Companies were now able to borrow from very different sources. The traditional financial giants had to wake up. With Citibank in the vanguard, they started to innovate strongly. Customers appreciated these new innovative services and turned to the innovators. According to Robert Buzzel[19] one of the main criteria used to evaluate banks was "a pattern of innovative, useful financial ideas".

Companies innovate in order to maintain competitive capability. Increased competition is especially true for companies that operate on global markets. The flexible mobility of capital and ever changing technology have been the important driving forces of competition. Capital, ideas, information, skills and workforces know no boundaries. Competition prevails between products and between virtual corporations. European, as well as North American, integration and the worldwide ideological preference for more open markets have reduced the capability of companies which operate only on their domestic markets. Without innovations it is impossible for them to maintain their competitive edge in situations where they no longer hold a monopoly or oligopoly position. Competition is intensified by deregulation and privatization. The recession has left overcapacity in many industrial sectors. The competitive situation requires that companies allocate resources to product development, improvement of production and distribution processes, and creative marketing. Companies need to be more flexible in order to be able to cope with fast changing markets which are cut into ever smaller segments, each of them having different preferences for models, brands and designs. Innovation is the tool for survival. Time is critical. That is why many innovation activities have to be conducted in parallel — no longer in a sequential fashion.

REORIENTATE YOUR OPERATIONS

Production-centred, centralized organizations have been forced to make fundamental readjustments towards customer-centred, decentralized, marketing-oriented operation (Ciba Geigy, railway companies). Reorientation is also on the agenda at numerous public organizations (e.g. the European PTTs, hospitals, universities, culture houses) and associations (e.g. trade unions and national sports associations). Recession has enhanced creative activity, although at present it seems to be directed more towards cutting costs than increasing flexibility.

In order to regain innovativeness in large established companies top managers have either used structural means such as internal ventures, strategic alliances, mergers and acquisitions or initiated internal process developments, total quality management and re-engineering. Ghoshal and Bartlett[20] emphasize strongly that *without breaking down hierarchies and bureaucracy corporations risk failing to reach a top level of innovativeness*. They present ABB as a model company, which decentralized its entire global organization into 1300 separate operating units within a matrix structure. Consequently, at ABB there is only one layer between the top ranks and the business units. This ingenious reorganization process has ignited innovations in ABB. It has also decentralized R&D and product development activities, moving them closer to the customers. This solution keeps staff more market oriented and encourages innovation.

Today many innovations result from successful, intensive cooperation between the company's personnel and customers. Several years ago one of the authors was asked to assist in a development project which aimed at eliciting more ideas and suggestions from customers to benefit an entire car dealer organization. In each dealership, customer service groups were formed, consisting of representatives from sales, service, spare parts and administration. In this way customers could deal with the same familiar group for all their needs. This model simulates small entrepreneurial companies which are able to maintain close contacts with their clients.

This reorientation ran into considerable opposition at the start. Union representatives objected to team work, and the usual lack of coordination between sales, service and parts operations within the dealership was not helped by a lack of real enthusiasm at the top administrative level.

A turnaround occurred when customer representatives were invited to take part in team activities. They participated in discussions about the results of service surveys, brainstorming sessions, visits to plants and open house activities for customers. This was expanded to include attendance at rallies

A. Strategy
- strategic direction continuously rethought and expressed
- strategies based on visions
- top management as direction givers
- institutionalizing innovativeness

B. Orientation to
- markets, customers
- unmet, latent needs
- business opportunities
- solving complex problems
- long-term targets
- profitability, growth
- intrapreneurship, entrepreneurship
- quality, re-engineering
- excellence in performance

C. Information
- superb knowledge in strategic areas
- market need assessment systems
- information and documentation systems
- databanks, ideabanks
- links to external information services
- abundance of publications
- networking-based contacts

D. Resources
- competent innovative management and personnel
- outstanding R&D facilities
- hiring researchers, experts, inventors
- high level of core technologies
- availability of capital
- innovation champions
- effective use of local resources
- use of telematics

E. Structure
- flexible organizational structures
- clear, simple forms
- flat organization
- few status differences
- grouping into core groups, and competing units
- attractive forms

F. Development
- internal and external collaboration
- mainly decentralized but centrally supported
- continuous change processes
- purchased know-how (joint ventures, licences, patents)

G. Systems
- team work
- use of projects, taskforces, quality circles, etc.
- network-based communication
- intensive interaction between management and employees
- interactive learning
- continuous training
- cooperation
- individual and group rewards
- suggestion, patent, licence system

H. Organization of work
- flexible, possibility to enlarge
- enrichment of work by socio-technical means
- work rotation
- shared responsibility, delegation
- relatively ample roominess
- controlled freedom

I. Culture
- free-wheeling
- risk taking and tolerant of mistakes
- respect for people
- sense of pride
- ideas and innovations valued
- drive for improvements and continuous development

Figure 10.1 The Characteristics of An Innovative Organization

and trial runs of new car models. Customer participation reduced internal resistance at the dealerships and made personnel more willing to participate.

The planned interaction and informal contacts with customers generated many new ideas and solutions to practical problems. Some were at the practical level, concerning ways for quicker and better servicing of cars. Other suggestions dealt with strategic matters such as business locations and information management.

In retrospect, dealers agreed that the main learning experience had been how to build up productive internal participation to provide close relationships with customers. This, in turn, improved their ability to respond quickly to customer needs and expectations and give each dealer the distinctive differentiation they seek. All car manufacturers are trying to institute programmes of "Customer enthusiasm" and would be delighted if this kind of programme was instituted.

DEAL SUCCESSFULLY WITH UNCERTAINTIES

Change and innovation are rather like two faces of the same coin: change requires constant innovation from the organization. Innovation requires from the organization the ability to change. This all takes place in the presence of a great deal of uncertainty. Numerous studies[21] show how many factors determine the success of an innovation process. These begin with mapping out and understanding customer needs, the integration of technological resources, the extent and level of R&D, and the level of technology in the company. Consideration must also be given to the organization of innovative activity, the corporate climate, incentives to innovators, training and acquisition of new information, marketing skills and the ability of staff to exploit their own creativity. The processing of technological innovations in particular is so complex that directing these processes is a real test of company management skills. A small or medium-sized company depending on a single invention may well be able to take care of further development and utilization by team work. Large companies, on the other hand, are often faced with problems because of the great number of new ideas, discoveries and inventions.

Special problems are caused by innovations that are outside a company's main business line. "Individual discoveries tend to be highly individualistic and serendipitous, advances chaotic and interactive, and specific outcomes unpredictable and chancy until the very last moment", says Quinn[22]. No wonder that many large companies acquire successful innovations from smaller companies which are better able to manage the cumbersome process of innovation.

Peter Drucker[23], in his noteworthy article on innovation, poses an interesting question: "Can the management at all make plans or calculations of a process which itself greatly depends on creativity, inspiration or just sheer luck?" Drucker goes on to point out that only a few innovations are born in a flash of genius. Most innovations, especially successful ones, are the outcome of conscious research and development and are clearly bound to a certain time and certain conditions. According to Drucker these processes can be planned and monitored. Lovio's[24] study of the creation process for innovations in the electronic industry supports this view.

Uncertainty about innovations may often be caused by a lack of understanding about needs and preferences on local, national markets. Innovations made by ingenious headquarters laboratories may fail simply because they do not correspond to the needs of overseas customers. Bartlett and Ghoshal[25] have drawn conclusions about the factors behind Philips' innovativeness in mastering local conditions. Philips send their foreign subsidiaries a "cadre of entrepreneurial expatriates" who spend most of their career abroad and who are able to transmit ideas and suggestions to headquarters. Of equal importance is the fact that they are able to oppose inappropriate ideas emanating from headquarters.

The decentralization of authority and responsibility and the integration of technical and marketing functions within each subsidiary stimulate local innovation and creativity. Consequently, *by building up effective linkages between innovative local national subsidiaries and company headquarters, companies are more able to depend on a continuing global stream of innovations.* We should not, however, underestimate the importance of innovative headquarters groups, neither centrally located ones nor the ones which consist of sub-teams from various subsidiaries which communicate via modern telematics. These groups and teams with superior resources and facilities (typical, for example, in 3M and Texas Instruments) actually generate most of the leading edge ideas and innovations for global markets.

* * *

NOKIA — CONNECTING PEOPLE[26]

Headquarters: Helsinki, Finland.
Three main business groups: Mobile Phones, Telecommunication Systems, General Communication Products. No. of workers: 31,000, operating in 40 countries, with production in 16 countries. Sales of mobile phones in 110 countries. Net sales, 1994: Over FIM 30bn.
Shares traded: NY Stock Exchange, London, Paris, Frankfurt, Helsinki. An FIM 2.5bn stock issue in 1994 was "oversubscribed" in New York.

The above statistics are all the more impressive when we consider that in the last decade the company has grown from a traditional forest-based operation into a high-tech global giant. Nokia Mobile Phones is second only to Motorola in the world, and Europe's number one in the field.

CEO Jorma Ollila, economist and engineer, was only 41 when he was appointed to the presidency of the company in 1992. Finland was at the time in one of the country's deepest recessions after the decimation of its trade with the former Soviet Union. Nokia had gone through several extremely difficult years in the late 1980s. Ollila (selected by *Business Week* in their 1994 "Best Manager category"), together with a young top management group, carried out a notable turnaround. Impressively high growth resulted particularly in the mobile phone sector.

THE NOKIA SPIRIT

From the outset in the 1980s, innovativeness has been encouraged in every sector of the company's activities. A pair of huge rubber gumboots — the company's Seven League Boots — stood in the then CEO Kari Kairamo's office as a symbol of a company which intended to move fast. Acquisitions, internationalization, market-oriented business planning and restructuring of the company's personnel and financial management were supported by intensive R&D and new product development.

According to the directors of the corporation, innovativeness has been one of the key success factors during the decade of growth[27]. "Flexibility and innovation are the way to success. Our philosophy encompasses constant change and strength through cooperation. Our slogan is: 'Feed the mind and you fuel the future'", said Kairamo. Simo Vuorilehto, also a former CEO, expresses the company's spirit in another way: "We make an effort to avoid bureaucracy and hierarchical management. Instead we are able to make quick decisions by reducing the distance between the highest and the lowest levels of the organization. We favour a flexible, fast-paced and open-minded management style at Nokia. Our success is mainly based on adapting existing innovations to new products and systems because our resources are scarce." Antti Lagerroos, a former managing director of Nokia Mobile Phones, says: "Our success is partly based on our flexibility to react to technological innovation and changes in the markets. We have experience and we are a young team. We invest in the quality and training of our personnel. Young blood, fresh ideas. Creative engineering is what keeping ahead is all about."

Although Nokia's acquisition policy in the early years did not meet with financial success, top management did not lose their commitment to organizational innovativeness. After taking over in 1992, Jorma Ollila said: "Nokia must quickly and efficiently adjust to take advantage of technological and market changes to run its business operations successfully. We strengthen the positive, open atmosphere that encourages new ideas and solutions"[28].

The years 1994–1995 have been characterized by the theme "Excellence in Performance". Translated into practical day-by-day action this means bracing the company's spirit on the basis of common values, achievement, customer satisfaction, respect for the individual and continuous learning. Employee commitment at all levels is demonstrated by productivity, innovativeness and enjoyment of their work.

NEW FOCUS

One of Nokia's greatest challenges has been to balance the necessity for decentralizing, which brings flexibility and motivation to people, with the maintenance of organizational integrity in order to achieve greater cost effectiveness. The concurrent engineering process links R&D, production and marketing and brings them closer to the customer.

Flexibility in Nokia's global production capabilities, combined with the position of trendsetter in product development, has provided them with strong weapons in the competitive price battle. In 1992, to strengthen their market position, Nokia Mobile Phones extended its partnerships to include the Tandy Corporation, and a year later two Japanese operators, IDO and Kansai Digital Phone. In 1994 an agreement was concluded with AT&T to deliver cellular phones and accessories. Nokia has become strategically more focused, with a long-term strategy based on clearly articulated visions which institutionalize organizational innovativeness.

STIMULATING ORGANIZATIONAL INNOVATIVENESS

Nokia's patent activities clearly indicate their drive for innovativeness. Nokia Mobile Phones applied for 80 patents in 1992, a logical development of the efforts begun in the mid 1980s to speed up breakthrough innovations. It was at that time that they started the Innovative Management Concept to exploit information and people's creativity more effectively.

Ollila regards management leadership as the role of "a coach with the responsibility of encouraging each player to develop to the best of his or her abilities while building a team that aspires to excellence"[29]. This reflects an understanding of one of the most powerful energizing forces within an organization; that the greatest motivation that an individual can have is the feeling that he/she is achieving personal goals, while at the same time making a real contribution to the organization.

THE ABILITY TO REACT FAST

How can an organization maintain the ability to react fast to changing market conditions and continue to meet customer's needs and preferences? Nokia's answer is that they intend to keep business units flexible and the organization flat and network based. This will continue to provide synergy between their corporate units. "Size will not be important in the future, speed will be the key", says Ollila[30]. Mastering time-based competition is a sustainable advantage.

NETWORKED R&D

An efficiently networked R&D structure in which 40% of activities are carried out in international cooperation projects guarantees continued awareness of the latest international trends and customer expectations. Nokia's acquisition of the British Technophone in 1991 and Philips' development centre in Denmark in 1994 strengthened R&D activities. Of the 6000 new employees hired in 1994, a considerable proportion went into R&D. The need for additional employees in 1995 has been projected to be at the same rate.

POTENTIAL FOR FUTURE GROWTH

At this moment (1995) there are about 650 million wire line connections and nearly 70 million mobile phones in the world. Yrjö Neuvo, Director of Nokia Mobile Phones R&D, who presently chairs seven units located around the world, predicts that the number of mobile phones will exceed that of conventional phones early in the next century. There will exist a mass consumer market for mobile phones and Nokia works hard in order to establish its name worldwide. It is already the first company to bring mobile phones to all major digital systems.

MASTER SEGMENTED MARKETS

Teamwork is the secret of Nokia's flexibility. The company must be able to meet the demands of highly segmented markets, responding with a huge variety of models and packages in many languages. Market segments include analogue and digital cellulars, mobile units capable of transmitting short messages and phones connected to laptop or palmtop computers for Fax and data transmission. Some customers, such as the elderly and also young people, require inexpensive easy-to-use phones. Business users demand more sophisticated features. In all these segments, user needs are different, ranging from the complex needs of brokers and investors wanting message and data transmission about particular stocks and securities to transport companies with a need for drivers to maintain contact with dispatchers.

Women's particular needs must also be considered. Nokia Mobile Phones came up with a creative marketing idea for this potentially large market when they offered free calls on their phones to the ladies who finished the

"Ladies Ten", a race held in Helsinki which now attracts over 30,000 women each year. As we were told, "Ladies were queuing up. Sales also went up very nicely afterwards."[31]

THE CHALLENGE FOR THE FUTURE

Foreseeing user needs for the future is an imaginative exercise. General manager Matti Heikkilä envisions millions of Chinese cyclists who may need phone chargers powered by turning wheels. People in tropical lands will want solar energy chargers. We would like to see a built-in loudspeaker to make audioconferencing possible. Nokia's essential challenge is to retain the ability to imaginatively anticipate customers' future needs, while maintaining creative differentiation from competitors' products and services. This means that the right new products must be introduced at the right time to the right customers faster than the competition. No doubt European and Far Eastern competition is getting stronger. While Nokia's size and globalization is a competitive advantage, the crucial question now is: Can they master continuous growth and keep their entrepreneurial flair without getting trapped by inflexibility and excessive control? Top management is acutely aware of this potential problem. One of their chief concerns is to continue the improvement of management communication skills and further their efforts to help new people to accept and internalize the Nokia Spirit.

In Arthur D. Little's August 1995 publication, *The European Best of the Best Companies in Technology and Innovation Management*, an international panel of 100 chief technology officers from leading European corporations selected Nokia as being among the first five companies. The statistics produced by MERIT data on R&D show that Nokia leads in patenting per 1000 employees within the telecommunications sector.

* * *

Chapter 11

Innovation Conference

Psychology professor John Magnus von Wright responded to the eager young students in his seminar when they severely criticized creative work done in an unorthodox way: "Folks, it is relatively easy to criticize work which has been done, but a lot more difficult to create a novel work, especially if the approach is to be original." (Lecture notes by KL.)

Perhaps it has been easier to critically analyze companies using the criteria of innovativeness than to construct a workable model of an innovative organization. We need a number of models because the environment and conditions vary greatly. A company's environment, size, position on the growth curve, the degree of internationalization, internal resources and traditions must be considered. We originated an unorthodox way of looking at the Innovative Organization and especially the various management strategies which have been used to build one. We organized a conference to which we invited some of the innovative managers who have already been introduced to the reader.

We first called our good friend Daniel Fabun and asked if he would be willing to sponsor the gathering in one of his "fabulous resorts". He was willing, and immediately suggested Bali Paradise, a small, luxurious resort in a village in the centre of that island. We found Bali Paradise to be aptly named — a magnificent place with a superb view from the hotel down the hill to the river. Morning and evening we could see the village people coming and going along the path down to the river. On the other bank could be seen the glistening water of the rice paddies. The hotel grounds were full of leafy palm trees providing peaceful shelter from the heat of the sun.

Each of us had a suite with its own separate living room, bedroom and bath. The king-sized beds were decorated with splended native handwork. There were two pools, a bar, a Balinese restaurant and a reading room. The tennis courts were still under construction. Daniel proudly told us that all the construction work had been done by the people of the nearby village and that they had worked on the project when they could spare time from their work in the rice fields. Of course the hotel had taken quite a long time to complete but it had gained the full support and acceptance of the village people, which was important for providing assistance and service to visitors.

Daniel had envisioned a retreat for executives and professionals who wanted something different, a place in beautiful and peaceful surroundings far away from the package-tour beach resorts. This vision had been fully realized. We knew that the relaxed atmosphere would not be conducive to very hard work, but we had asked each of our participants to give a short presentation at the conference regarding the various aspects of innovative organizations which they considered to be most significant. Let's listen.

DANIEL

Dear friends, it is my pleasure and honour to welcome you to the Bali Paradise, the fulfilment of a project that I've dreamed about for years, and a source of great personal pride. I hope you all feel at home here and please consider me to be your host and servant. I'm also very grateful to June Hayward who with her close relationship to BA could negotiate such advantageous terms for our flight here. I want to express my particular pleasure at having you here to discuss together a subject of intense interest to all of us. I personally have a strong conviction about the impact of management creativity upon the successful implementation of innovativeness throughout the entire company.

I strongly believe that the human mind is our central fundamental resource, in which nature has concealed creative talent and ability. As John Naisbitt, the author of Megatrends, *has expressed: "In the new corporation, creativity and individuality are organizational treasures." No wonder* Business Week *reports that over half of the Fortune 500 companies send their chief executives, as well as other managers and supervisors, to courses in creativity training.*

I am proud to say that my company has a reputation as a "prime mover" in the hospitality field. We are known for designing innovative services and opening up new markets. We have to move fast because of the dramatic changes that are continually taking place in our field. Personally, as the chief executive officer and president of the corporation, I am accountable to employees, customers and shareholders for ensuring the company's successful future. And that all depends on my ability to envision new and imaginative projects for my company.

Let me offer an example. You've all followed the dramatic changes in Eastern Europe and in China. It is clear that these changes already provide enormous opportunities within the hospitality business. Think of several hundred million people willing, able or required by their business to travel abroad for the first time. In the next ten years they will be one of the major groups of our customers.

You may think I am exaggerating, but please believe me when I say that I've personally created nearly a hundred different options of how to meet the needs and expectations of this revolutionary mass tourism that we anticipate from the developing parts of our globe. It has started a flood which will exceed all records in the history of tourism and business travel when the time is ripe. Perestroika and the subsequent events have opened the doors, and I promise that we will be able to move fast and flexibly to meet the demands. The hospitality field is very competitive today, and to quote Philip Wellons: "Successful innovators remain ahead in this industry scarcely longer than the twenty-four hours a Mayfly lives." There will always be imitators, but I want my company to remain a trendsetter in our industry. Certainly the ideas and innovations of top management are essential, but perhaps just as importantly, we must inspire and nurture the creative spirit of the whole company. There will always be room for new ideas, and we as responsible executives should be able to see new business opportunities in these new ideas. Our own example is decisive. Our people will follow the lead.

JUNE HAYWARD

Even though I've just met some of you for the first time in these marvellous surroundings, and particularly with Daniel's warm welcome to us all, I feel that we are friends, united by a common interest. I basically agree with Daniel about the significance of the creativity of top management. However, I would like to add an aspect of innnovation in relation to the organization itself. In my opinion, the highly innovative organization is not a structure or a collection of systems, but basically an environment where ingenious, creative individuals and teams can share a free-wheeling spirit. If you visit in this kind of environment you may find the atmosphere somewhat chaotic, quick in tempo with continuous movement and a high drive. The climate is sometimes as relaxed as a sauna, and sometimes as exciting and tense as a Stanley Cup hockey game. One moment, it seems that nothing is being done. People are just sitting and thinking. And then, suddenly it seems that the office has been hit by a hurricane.

We can build up highly innovative organizations if we first strive to recruit imaginative and talented individuals. We must then offer them an environment where they feel free to work according to their needs as creative individuals or teams. We must encourage a spirit of playfulness in these teams. Let them try new ideas and experiments. Let them make mistakes and fail. Many times it has been my experience with my teams that it is not the instantly accepted bright idea, but the at-first-rejected, foolish or wild or crazy idea that actually serves as a good base for working out original and successful marketing concepts.

We have to allow for fantasy. Edward de Bono used to tell in his seminars about the man who bought a watchdog, which unfortunately didn't bark at all. Turning his problem into an opportunity, he put a sign on his gate which read: "Beware of the dog which does not bark". That leads me to think: it's natural that one invents products for a dog's owner, but how about the neighbours? Especially if the dog is a bit mean and may bite. What products might we suggest? A strange question designed to evoke wild, crazy ideas that may be the starting point of something really new. I asked this the question of one of our teams. A very creative product manager thought for a moment and replied: "I'd sell him sprinting shoes, leather pants, tree-climbing cleats, a lunch basket in case he got hungry up a tree, and a mobile telephone to phone the dog-catcher."

As managers we have to learn to stimulate people's original thinking. We must avoid presenting them with our own ready-made solutions, and let them come up with their novel ideas. I would recommend the use of catalytic questions and problem formulations everywhere in your organization — in meetings, in memos and during planning sessions. If you are patient enough, because acquiring this style will take some time and effort, you will be surprised at how many solutions and answers people will find for themselves. Try this also with your customers. Involving them in the solutions to their own problems is an optimal way to strengthen the relationship.

Attractive rewards and incentives for individuals and teams, together with the setting of high goals, will maintain the excitement and enthusiasm necessary to create novel and original concepts. Our success as managers depends on our ability to stimulate our people with exciting visions of the future.

In my judgement, the optimal structure of an organization is simple, flat, flexible and changeable according to the prevailing needs and conditions. Avoid strict rationalism and rigid planning. Eliminate hierarchies, fight against red-tape, formal systems, standard operating procedures and deadly routines. Simplify things and processes. And please, no unnecessary control. All these things will kill the spirit of innovativeness and creativity within your organizations. The Innovative Manager is, in my opinion, a great STIMULATOR who gets people to work enthusiastically year after year, motivated to meet endless, new, challenging tasks.

MAX HOPPER

May I also express my gratitude to be here with you in this exciting place. The comments already made about innovative organizations and the manager's role in nurturing a creative atmosphere are very close to my own area of deep interest. My own experience is based on the management of expert organizations, where I have to lead engineers, scientists, and product specialists.

Experts are sometimes very original personalities. A distinguished speaker travelled round the US driven by his personal chauffeur. The poor driver had to sit and listen. Everywhere always the same speech and of course finally the driver could repeat that speech word by word. Once, being really exhausted, the speaker asked his driver to exchange the roles and to give the same speech, which he did very successfully. Unfortunately, one member of the audience asked an unexpectedly difficult question. After a short pause the driver said: "This question is so simple that even my driver here sitting in the first row can answer it . . .".

My personal dedication is to promote and manage internal creative development. The essential characteristic of our corporate culture is a high expectation of success. Our mission is to develop attractive products which are tailor-made according to the real needs of our very demanding customers. This means that we must come up with breakthrough ideas in a highly competitive market. As an inventor, one can devote one's thoughts totally to the product. As a colleague once remarked: "It may be difficult to learn to love somebody else's cruiser, but it's easy to get wholeheartedly involved in the painted mouse-trap you personally designed." As a manager, however, you must not only know your products very well, but also understand the production and marketing processes, and, of course, know your people and your customers.

Brilliant marketing ideas have always been with us. Thousands of years ago the Phoenicians carried on a lively trade with the Greeks and Romans, selling them, among other things, soap. *The Gauls, though not interested in soap's cleansing properties, readily accepted the product when it was marketed to them as a laxative!*

To successfully manage an expert organization, we must recruit top experts in our specific areas and give them the support they need to achieve the ambitious objectives we set together. My personal task is to make superior expertise available to them as well as new, original ideas. This can be accomplished by a combination of their own knowledge and experience and various external sources such as basic or contract research, licensing or in some cases acquisitions. I must ensure that my staff have the best possible advanced technology, such as computer aided design and other expert systems at their disposal. In our field of manufacturing, we seek to be always one jump ahead of our competitors.

Another important task is to keep our experts in continuous touch with our customers, because they are the final decision makers. By organizing technical conferences, customer meetings and maintaining contact through the network of local laboratories or global telematic networks we can get the necessary feedback and suggestions for improvement on our new products and processes.

What I want to emphasize is that a manager must recognize and value both new product development and also the efforts of staff to improve the cost effectiveness of the manufacturing and delivery operations. We must also reward those who are able to market our new products and earn a return on the investment. In an expert organization, you really need a collection of all kinds of expertise and your task is to encourage improvements in all areas. Naturally, everyone expects that I'll be able to find adequate capital resources for continuous development.

Finally, I'd like to express a personal opinion: in expert companies, the organizational structure should be lean and consist of relatively small units which are best able to profit from a creative spirit. Recently, I've worked very intensively to simplify our operations in order to get rid of those things which take time and energy away from the mainstream of our real business. For example, by encouraging decision making at lower levels, eliminating unproductive reporting and shortening approval cycles. These are some of the ways that we can encourage our people to use their talents and expertise most effectively.

WILLIAM MCPHERSON

What a pleasure to be here with you and Daniel in this lovely place! I can understand Daniel's pride as he told of how he worked with the local villagers to complete this paradise. This is the kind of approach that works if you have trust in people, the courage to take risks, and the patience to see it through. And by the way, I think I've just described the essential qualities of the Innovative Manager.

Personally, as the manager of a large plant, I consider our employees to be the key ingredients in the success of our organization. And I trust them. When I started to renew our operations some years ago, I understood that it was necessary to apply a process-innovation strategy. I had to find ways to rationalize and automate our internal working processes in order to increase productivity and flexibility and reduce costs.

The successful implementation of this kind of re-engineering strategy means that you have to get not only key engineers and supervisors, but also the entire organization committed to these objectives. This takes more than just putting suggestion boxes around the plant and waiting for ideas to flow into your office. People must be encouraged, supported and motivated to take initiative into their own hands. People cannot be creative if they have to ask permission every time they try to do something new. You have to give them freedom and independence to experiment with new things and to be willing to risk failure, obviously within certain limits. I mean, they shouldn't be permitted to make the same mistakes repeatedly, and there should be understanding as to the use of the plant's resources.

Some of my supervisors would still like to see our plant run like a military organization or merchant fleet where the management and staff should always be prepared for any sudden crisis in which absolute authority and a top-down chain of command resolves the problem. But even in these cases, a contrasting style may be productive.

I remember a good friend telling an amusing story about an Italian sailing ship that he had served on in his youth. On that ship, it seemed that the whole crew commanded whenever the ship had to manoeuvre in stormy seas. As he tells it: "In the darkness of a stormy night everyone shouted commands; the loudest of all was our massive cook's bellow. But the ship's manoeuvres functioned suprisingly well."

You should be careful not to try to formalize all innovative efforts. We soon found out that a lot of idea-rich work was done not in formal team meetings but outside the normal work day in informal meetings wherever and whenever people happened to meet each other. We encourage our people to bring these ideas, found informally, into the daylight.

But it must not stop there. Quite a few people will innovate over a period of years just out of natural curiosity or the desire to find something new, and they should be encouraged by a workable system of incentives and rewards.

Finally, I would like to emphasize the importance of good relationships between management and labour. If we can find ways to get the unions to support our efforts

at innovation, we are half-way to the goal. Whenever possible let's try to bring them
in at the early stages of change.

JARI SILTA

I'm reminded that John Muir once wrote: "It is astonishing how high and far we can
climb in mountains we love."
I think that Daniel has exemplified this in accomplishing this Bali Paradise
project. Here we are today in this magnificent natural setting, and I am convinced
that this represents the fulfilment of one of his early dreams. Yesterday evening we
learned of his decision to eventually retire here and concentrate on his favourite
hobby, painting. Certainly we can all understand how this place could stimulate an
artist and provide inspiration from this rich, abundant nature, and, permit me to
say, the beauty of the Balinese people, whom we all have admired.
Our visions are the basis for our actions. They create the intentions for our
activities. They are more than just objectives or targets. They interpret the future in
a promising, encouraging light. They cause us to strive for excellence and make us
feel that all the work and effort is worthwhile. It is through visions that we see light
even in circumstances that may seem hopeless.
A visionary leader is able to generate among his people a sense of adventure and
the firm will to step into an unknown future. Top management initiatives come from
visions. Without visions our companies cannot progress. I personally experienced
this when I became so involved in short-term daily matters that I lost the sight and
vision of long-term business needs. It was a hard lesson to learn. Now I try to
balance both of these important aspects of leadership. In my opinion the secret of
leadership lies in strategic thinking. This does not mean writing out a hundred
pages of plans, but concentrating on developing a clear strategy within the business
environment and the internal conditions that exist.
You have to get your managers and staff involved in the process, because in fact
the strategy will work only if people are committed to its implementation. It is this
particular area, the development and implementation of a company's strategy, that
makes the greatest demand on the creativity of top management. From my personal
viewpoint, I could never accept the idea that the top manager is a "lone wolf". By no
means!
Actually as managers we have many excellent opportunities to take part in
discussions about our visions and strategic plans. Not only do we have our executive
clubs and meetings where we can meet and talk with national and international
gurus, but we have continual opportunities for close contacts with our major
customers and suppliers, bank managers and important shareholders. And we
should never neglect the contacts and discussions with our own ingenious people.
These include scientists, engineers, marketing experts and ordinary people who work
closely with our customers or in plant operations.

Great ideas may germinate in silence and solitude, but to grow they need to be fertilized and stimulated in a living, busy world that is in touch with other thinkers and doers.

ROBERT HARTMAN

As the final speaker you may perhaps expect me to summarize what has been said about the Innovative Manager and management. I indeed planned to do so but found the task so demanding that I will gratefully leave the last words to our seminar leaders. Allow me instead to develop some personal thoughts regarding innovation.

You all know my interest in the leadership aspect of management. I found the presentation of Japanese innovation management by J & K awe inspiring and it stimulated my thinking on how we could integrate those ideas into our management systems. It also reminded me of my recent visit to Japan.

During that visit I had the rare opportunity of being invited by a Japanese businessman to visit his home, which in itself was an exceptional event since Japanese hospitality is nearly always offered outside of the home. He lived in a traditional house, where he proudly presented the ancient family possessions. My curiosity and enthusiasm were especially aroused by the presence of several miniature, though seemingly fully developed, trees placed on small tables in the living room. My host told me that they were Bonsai, which are ordinary trees but miniaturized by a system of careful gradual pruning of the roots and training into naturalistic shapes.

Planted in round or square-shaped pots, usually of earthenware, with or without a colourful exterior glaze, these Bonsai may live for a century or more and are often handed down from one generation to the next as valued family possessions. I became so interested in them that I now have several in my home and on my office table, as you who have visited me know. These trees inspire me. Every tree is an individual creation which has no counterpart. Like ourselves as innovative managers, we all grow up in different conditions and surroundings like Bonsai. We all have different kinds of experience, schooling and training and of course our successes and failures. Our management work is done in different contexts and cultures. We all have our strengths, weaknesses and opportunities: diamonds, stones and pearls as J & K call them. Each of us is successful in our own way at leading our organizations as an innovative manager. We all know that to consistently push for innovation within an organization despite the limitations and pressure of conformity and other restraints is not an easy task. But we are able to keep active and persistent in the most demanding and difficult circumstances, like the natural Bonsai which grow in rocky crevices of high mountains or overhang steep cliffs.

Many innovative managers who manage large, even gigantic organizations have learned one main lesson: "Keep it small even if you are big". We have to be able to administer the growth of our business. We must prune the organization when it grows too big. We can put size limits when the number of people in one unit grows too large. Every Bonsai tree planter has to have an anticipated image of his or her tree when starting to prune roots and branches. Innovative managers must have vision, a clear agenda, purpose and a focus upon results, as Warren Bennis has told us. And as he continues: "Their range might be very narrow, and outside of that they might be very boring. But within their range they are very intense. It is as if a bright filament is always burning."

The innovative manager is a designer. Like the Bonsai cultivator he or she follows a creative path according to his or her insight and through prolonged observation and learning produces ideas, connects one idea and experience to another, and aims to reach significant objectives and patterns.

I learned in Japan that Bonsai must be repotted every one to five years, depending on the root growth and species. We must admit that every so often it would be very useful for us as managers and directors to be taken from our organizational roots and planted into a totally new cultural and organizational environment. In old secure conditions we are too inclined to retain our customary habits and use only means and methods which have proven to be successful in the past. I assume that the new generation of innovative managers will be global movers who are able to act flexibly in different countries, diverse cultures and organizations. One of the secrets of their success will certainly be the ability and skill to master organizational culture changes, even to influence those with their bright ideas and insights, to fertilize the old roots with new seed ideas.

Innovative managers must be masters of art and handicraft. They build organizations with the most imaginative forms, structures, models and processes. Every organization which they touch deeply will have the landmarks of creativity and innovativeness.

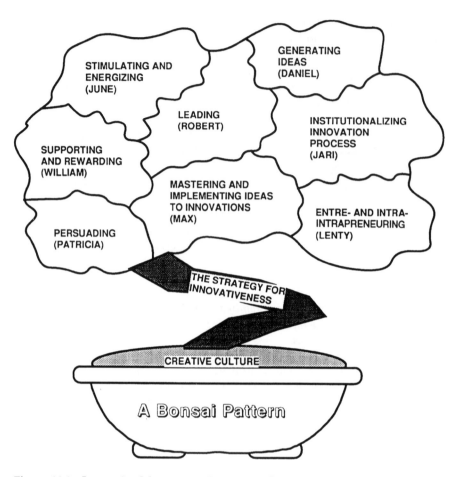

Figure 11.1 Innovative Managers in Innovative Organizations.

Chapter 12

Japanese Innovation Strategies: A Trend to Create and Innovate

A KEYNOTE SPEECH BY J & K

How would you explain the "Japanese miracle" of creating an economic superpower after the Second World War? Probably by giving a bundle of reasons. In the literature, some explanations are very simple like emphasizing the disciplined and industrious work force, while other experts present very complex constructions by combining cultural and historical factors with economic, organizational, societal and global factors.

In this context let's examine the often neglected aspect of strategies for innovativeness in Japanese corporations. It is easy to disregard this aspect by referring to mere imitation as the basic approach of Japanese companies. Certainly imitation of Western industrial processes, tools and products, in general of the whole model of the second industrial revolution in the West, has been an important phase in Japan as they reconstructed their whole industrial infrastructure after the war. However, Japanese corporations, mainly big ones, have long put emphasis on both creative and innovative forms and structures when searching for new businesses. "Creativity and innovativeness form the most important megatheme as Japanese corporations get ready for the Age of Creation", say Murakami and Nishiwaki at the Nomura Research Institute in Tokyo[1].

Western companies are now starting to reach the level of the Japanese both in quality of products and in lowered production costs, as well as in the speed of launching new products onto the market. Japan needs new strategic competitive assets and the newest one is internal and external innovativeness. Murakami and Nishiwaki call the new Japanese management style "creagement": schemes and set-

ups that stimulate full exercise of creativity at all corporate levels. They state unequivocally: "NRI are convinced that the practice of creagement will constitute both a necessary and sufficient pre-condition for corporate subsistence, growth, and advancement in the 21st century: the age of creation."

MASTER STRATEGY

The United States is generally accepted as the leading country for inventing and developing breakthrough products. Their creativity and innovativeness is based on high investment in basic and applicable research and development of new technologies. The culture of individualism is characteristic for the United States. Risk taking and admiration of entrepreneurial spirit and individual excellence are esteemed even in a research career. No wonder that the United States holds the record for Nobel Laureates in physics and chemistry — more than 80 compared with the Japanese figure of four. The predominant Japanese strength is that they have been able to adopt quickly the new technologies and have advanced in the further development of innovative production processes. They have been very effective in constructing a fast chain from idea-generation to successful launching of new products on the market. According to the MITI research[2] the average time from the basic research idea to commercialization is 5.5 years, and from applicative research to commercialization 3.7 years. The intense competition and very demanding customers in the Japanese home market have forced Japanese companies to develop sophisticated quality products which have beaten their competitors also on global markets.

Japanese companies have perceived that an absolute prerequisite for the success of really large-scale innovation projects is the integration of highly complex technologies through multidisciplinary teams from big companies and university research centres. Samuels[3] estimates that about one-quarter of these superprojects are executed with cooperation among competitive companies, often with public sector support as well. When the prototypes have been developed, the companies start to compete with each other by means of their own unique development and marketing processes.

Using the Delphi method, STA[4], the Science and Technology Agency, produces massive scenarios for the development of future technologies. MITI and other government offices also publish detailed reports of various industries which support the innovation strategy development in Japanese companies. Chisholm[5] emphasizes the value of these scenarios for the development of new businesses, describing them as a kind of future database and "lighthouse" which will guide innovative developments in the directions of the most promising potentials.

Japan has followed the Western model of creating science parks and centres around the country and also in foreign countries. Companies have headhunted talented foreign researchers for their laboratories. The international approach to innovation projects is at present intensive. Japanese corporations have even more power than their Western counterparts to create new businesses based on radical innovations because the control of capital and management decisions is more closely integrated than in Western countries.

Japan is increasing efforts to encourage individual excellence in higher and professional education as well as support a corporate culture in which creativity can thrive. All these developmental factors may help Japan to heighten its comparative status as a nation able to produce breakthrough innovations. In the future many Japanese companies and research units will be guided by MASTER-STRATEGIES requiring a MASTER kind of innovative management skill.

IDEA-GENERATION STRATEGY

According to the study undertaken by Fortune *magazine[6] Japanese companies invest more than US companies in the development of new products. They have learned the PIMS lessons which tell us that "early birds" have gained 29%, early followers 17% and late followers have gained only 12% of the total market share[7]. In addition, pioneers in a market will get about a 30% bigger return on their investment in new products than late followers. The Japanese home market competition not only encourages but actually forces companies to invest heavily in new product development. Egan and McKiernan[8] refer to a McKinsey consulting study according to which nearly 10,000 new products will be launched yearly on the Japanese market. As in the West, only a fraction of them will survive; however, this fraction will give enough profit to the companies to encourage them to continue new product development activities. Baumol[9] describes competition between innovative companies as a continuous process of development of innovations and strategic sabotage. When companies move ahead, they soon observe strong reactions among the second ranks and follower companies which will not accept that the innovators take over their market share by offering more sophisticated or less costly products. They react by intensifying marketing campaigns, lowering product prices or by developing even more sophisticated product versions and searching for new market segments. These countermeasures weaken new product profitability on the home market, but in the process Japanese product innovations have reached new levels of excellence which can target the needs and expectations of the most demanding customers on the world markets.*

Japanese idea-generators invest heavily in R&D for diversification into new product areas. This heavy investment in R&D has allowed Japanese companies into the top of the United States patent list. New product idea-generation may often happen in Japanese companies through informal exchange of ideas among researchers and engineers. Many of these companies prefer to start the intrapreneuring process with informal teams; however, they don't have to "skunk-work" like their Western counterparts. Instead they often have a high status and access to the essential corporate information database, say Hamel and Prahalad[10]. Top management will later formalize the most promising developing ideas and search for the best corporate talents to make up the project teams. According to the study of Kono[11] about 60% of Japanese companies use project teamwork, either on a full time or part time basis. For example, Canon uses various teams such as new business study teams, corporate scenario teams and teams to search the future of different product divisions. Sharp names teams who search for new strategic products as "urgent product teams" and Sony name their top teams as "gold badge teams"[12].

TIME-BASED COMPETITION

Japanese companies have been very fast in introducing new products. The Government Economic Planning Agency[13] presented a comparative study of the adjusted lead time for automobile products in the early 1980s. Adjusted lead time is the time from concept development to market introduction required by the average company in each region to complete the average project in the sample. Japanese automobile manufacturers were incorporating continuous improvement as a crucial factor into the development process. Consequently, the development period was four years, one year less than in Europe and the US. This shorter development period was made possible by simultaneously performing product engineering and process engineering while maintaining a close relationship between the two.

George Stalk Jr and Thomas Hout[14] made a startling finding of how Japanese companies were introducing new heating and air-conditioning appliances at four times the rate of their US competition. Stalk and Hout present many advantages of time-based competitors' strategy which many Japanese companies use. It reduces production costs, innovative products can be priced higher because they are more modern and include the latest technology. Manufacturers can react more quickly to customers criticism and changing preferences. Especially the shorter lead time which will reduce the risk of product aging.

There is a negative side to an all-out commitment to a strategy of time-based competition. Stalk and Webber[15] criticize Japanese corporations for their technology-push approach. They are able to innovate faster because they encourage energetic and determined idea champions to come up with and sell their improvement ideas. "The company is faster, leaner and sharper", say Stalk and Webber. They are able to reduce costs and improve quality and liberate human and material resources which are needed for new innovative products. "Innovation becomes an addiction." However, customers may not be able or willing to accept these innovations at the speed the company wants and needs. This can weaken profitability and discourage innovations in the long run.

The solution for this dilemma, which some Japanese companies such as Daichi have found, is "double linking" (the concept used by Professor Burgelman), i.e. connecting the technology-push approach with the technology-pull approach. Customer expectations and preferences for improvements need to be examined in the context of decision making, even when time is short. What are needed are

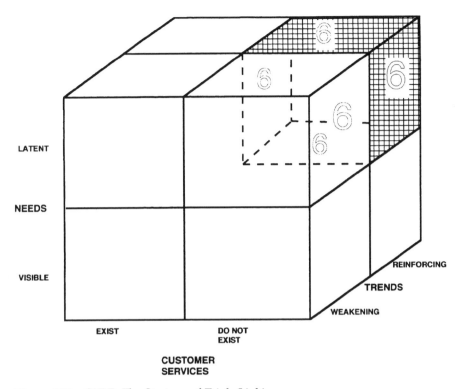

Figure 12.1   CUBE. The Strategy of Triple Linking

*innovations in faster information scanning systems of customer needs, expectations
and preferences. The most innovative Japanese companies have turned to the
strategy of "triple-linking", as we call it. They scan local, national and global
environments to find:*

- *growing trends, often a bundle of trends leading in the same direction*
- *latent needs which consumers or often customers have not yet expressed*
- *areas where there do not yet exist products or services*

*Accordingly, companies idea-generate and develop technologies to create solutions to
the "cube's" most promising sectors, innovations which will cause a "big bang" on
the market. (See Figure 12.1).*

*Many of these innovations are winners of the Nikkei Annual Awards for Creative
Excellence. A number of the successful developers have looked for applications to
daily life and have been able to end up with a viable consumer product or service.
Examples of these are: Mitsubishi Bank's "money capsule", a high yield financial
instrument; "Tabi Tabi", a travel saving plan; Shinjuku Washington Hotel's*

Automatic Front Desk; and "Secom", a medical emergency alarm[16]. Our favourite is "Kanban Musume", a self-heating sake in a can. To activate the heating process the can is turned upside down and the bottom pierced with the attached pin. The pin is removed, a lid is placed over the surface and the can is returned to its upright position. The heated sake is ready in a couple of minutes; especially fine in cold weather.

Japanese companies are able to direct efforts to the triple-linking strategy because of the intensive cooperation between marketing, R&D and the manufacturing sector. Job rotation is even typical for researchers and engineers. They have to spend a certain period of their work career in other departments, including marketing and sales. This arrangement gives them an excellent opportunity to learn to understand customer needs and behaviour and to perceive how they can get new product and product improvement ideas from customers. According to the Kono's research[17] Japanese companies get about one-third of new product ideas from their customers. Internally, the intensive information and idea exchange between different departments lead to the development of products which potential customers really need and want. Mansfield[18] has found that Japanese manufacturing and salespeople suggest much more R&D topics than their US counterparts.

Japanese production management favours incremental innovations, i.e. progressing in small steps in product improvement and manufacturing processes. The management expects, demands and encourages workers to produce ideas and to solve problems in their everyday working life and environment. They make suggestions concerning tools, working processes, working environment and product improvement. These suggestions will be passed up the line by foremen and engineers and the selected ones will be developed and implemented in practice. Because the role of workers and foremen is important in idea-generation and development, this kind of Japanese management practice has been called a principle of "bottom-up" management.

Japanese companies are very open to new ideas. About 80% of all Japanese workers in private companies have made suggestions. A great many of them have produced numerous ideas and have received quite substantial rewards for their efforts. At the top of the list in one year are Matshushita with 6.5 million suggestions, Hitachi with 4.6 and Mazda with 3.0 million suggestions[19]. Ideas have been generated both by individuals and by teams. One of the best-known, team-based working models for stimulating worker suggestions is the quality circle. Based on voluntary meetings, employee-initiated problem-solving tasks, structured methods of cause analysis (fishbone diagram) and systematic procedures for idea development and presentation as well as brainstorming, quality circles have been found to be particularly effective when dealing with practical problems in the working environment.

The Western work tradition favours ideas and opinions expressed by the individual as well as efforts which produce rewards for that person. The Japanese tradition, contrary to the idea of an individual seeking to display him/herself in an outstanding manner, in most cases expresses its creative spirit collectively. Japanese workers hesitate to say aloud their own ideas. They would rather express themselves by saying "it has been told–said–perceived–or worked out". The individual participant in the team listens to other participants, incubates others' ideas and tries to anticipate team members' probable and wishful solutions to problems. Consensus and compromise are valued. People in groups are conformistic and try to avoid expressing deviant, wild or far-out ideas. "People who generate deviant, wild or weird ideas will be punished by social sanctions", says Sheridan Tatsuno[20]. This kind of collective and conformistic attitude may be useful in producing incremental innovations but harmful when radical ideas and breakthrough innovations are needed.

Japanese companies have been able to turn the value of collectivism to advantage by pragmatic synthesis, however. According to Hofstede[21], it is more important to get things done than to argue about who has created what and who is right or wrong. Japanese workers are able to suppress ego and direct their efforts to collective objectives more than to individual interests. As a result they tend less to accumulate obstacles in the course of idea to implementation than their Western colleagues do.

It may sound odd that the present much discussed low productivity among Japanese white-collar people compared with manufacturing workers may hold some advantage when thinking about creativity in organizations. Rossander[22] writes that overmanning of companies with white-collar employees means that there are always people in offices who have time to prepare new initiatives, try even far-out ideas and support existing projects.

Still, the need for greater innovative productivity is acknowledged. Fortune[23] refers to the innovation paradox described by Hori, who says that Japan has a high productivity, but needs more individualism, differentiation of products and specialization and creativity as well as more effective use of white-collar manpower. The leading companies are putting forth great efforts to correct this situation. Good examples are Matsushita Electric's "Simple, Small, Strategic and Speedy" campaign and Toyota's "Task Force Program". Through extensive incremental innovation management these Japanese corporations have been able to boost productivity and efficiency, increase flexibility and streamline their operations not only in manufacturing but also in business administration and in management practice.

THE JAPANESE MANAGEMENT PARADOX: TO ACCEPT OR AVOID

Original thinking, idea-generation and radical innovations include a risk element. They often threaten existing patterns of operations or established systems and structures in the organization and they also may cause creative initiators to look ridiculous if they fail when implementing original thoughts and concepts in practice. Japanese management includes procedures designed to ease the creation process. Virtually all books on Japanese management today include a description of Ringi and Nemawashi. Ringi *means a procedure by which a suggestion or initiative will be circulated among people whom the suggestion concerns. Anyone of those can give one's approval to this suggestion by signing the paper.* Nemawashi *refers to a consultative planning. Before starting an innovative project all potential participants must accept the project initiative. In this way consensus will be reached and "the wings of opposition will be cut off".*

The president of the Japanese advertising giant Dentsu, Tamaru Hideharu, has expressed the importance of consensus in team work as follows[24]: ". . . the creative power that springs from solidarity is immeasurable. In teamwork, it is indispensable to listen carefully to what others say. By listening to others, you can eliminate discontinuity, remove prejudices and avoid dogmatism. The first step in producing excellent work is to give careful consideration to the feelings and opinions of others. Broadening your sphere is the seed of creativity." Still, in the context of the needed breakthrough innovativeness, Ringi *and* Nemawashi *may be harmful because they are likely to kill original and radical initiatives or lengthen the time chain from idea to innovation. Critical analysis of an emerging idea can easily destroy it before it has a life of its own. However, once a consensus has been reached it is easier to progress with a new idea because all parties are committed to the development project.*

Gert Hofstede[25] has provided much evidence to support the idea that Japan is a country with a strong uncertainty avoidance culture. He defines uncertainty avoidance as "the extent to which members of a culture feel threatened by uncertain or unknown situations". Hofstede indicates a number of areas of uncertainty avoidance in Japanese society. Those which have relevance in the context of organizational innovativeness are: "fear of ambiguous situations and of unfamiliar risks"; "emotional needs for rules"; "what is different is dangerous"; "emotional need to be busy, inner urge to work hard"; "precision and punctuality come naturally"; and "suppression of deviant ideas and behaviour; resistance to innovation".

Again we see that the conditions at Japanese organizations are problematic when thinking of the front end of the innovation process. However, when a decision has been made the qualities of precision, punctuality and sense of detail support the process of full-scale implementation — the prerequisite for manufacturing products with high quality and functionality.

It is paradoxical that other experts on Japanese management have provided evidence which contradicts the Hofstede position. Pascale and Athos[26] contend that Japanese managers don't feel disturbed by uncertainty in work situations as much as their Western counterparts. Western managers perceive problems as an organizational "sickness" which has to be cured by analytical rationality and assertive decision making. Japanese managers look at the uncertainty and disorders as natural phenomena of worklife.

In Japanese management literature the concept of chaos is often presented as a prerequisite for the creative process. It forces one to approach a problem from many angles and to search for solutions along various paths. Chaos can justify many mistakes. *Creative people are able to accept chaotic situations but they will create order from this chaos, while uncreative people are prone to avoid and leave such situations.*

Japanese managers understand when dealing with complex problems that it is not wise to try to sell ones own solution as the only acceptable one. According to Pascale and Athos[27], Japanese managers present the problem and ask for suggestions for solutions and possible experimenting. "Uncertainty legitimates experimenting", say Pascale and Athos.

When a Japanese manager wants a subordinate to improve an initiative or an idea he/she has submitted, he will start a dialogue through which he tries to get the subordinate to develop further the concept but he will not criticize the idea like his Western counterpart readily does, argue the authors.

Magoroh Maruyama[28] disagrees with Pascale and Athos, arguing that "for Japanese, problems mean shortcomings of those who are involved. It is shameful to mention them and they should be dealt with quietly and secretly, and under the table if necessary". He points to the typical Japanese tendency of "waitism". If someone just waits long enough, the problem will "disappear" or someone else will take an initiative. In Japan problems are often solved by non-verbal mutual accommodation.

How can we explain the Japanese management paradox — the tendency to accept or to avoid uncertainty as interpreted by different researchers? One possible explanation could be that Pascale and Athos describe a procedure whereby uncertainty avoidance is institutionalized in Japanese management. Managers when attempting to form structures and processes which could get events more clearly interpreted and predicted accept the coping with uncertainty as a part of everyday work praxis. A typical example is that of quality circles where "problems are put on the table". People discuss these openly and the goal is to change the rules and work practices, or even policies if necessary, in a way that the organization could be able to avoid similar problems in the future. Hofstede, on the other hand, emphasizes that the avoidance of uncertainty is conceptually not the same as the avoidance of risks. In societies where uncertainty is not acceptable, familiar risks are, however, tolerated, even sought after. These are the uncertainties inherent in working life.

CULTURAL EFFECTS

Paul Herbig and Cynthia McCarty[29] have explained differences of innovative activities between nations by cultural factors. They consider that a nation's culture influences their people's curiosity for new things as well as their tolerance for ideas and innovation willingness. They assume that the greater the individual liberty for researching new things and the liberty of opinion formation, the greater the probability of new idea-generation in the society. Given the individualism, acceptance of risks and entrepreneurial spirit, they conclude that the culture of the United States is particularly favourable for radical innovations.

The Japanese culture, as we have seen, prefers process and evolutionary innovations. Japanese people are hard working, they are responsible, skilful, ambitious and willing to work in groups and teams for problem-solving purposes; but collectivism, avoidance of new and unfamiliar risks, and homogeneous culture do not create a favourable ground for radical innovations. In the comparison between American and Japanese cultures, Miller and Sparks[30] add several factors to the list of negative aspects of Japanese life related to radical innovations. These include life-long employment with the same firm, slow career advancement and collective responsibility.

Tatsuno[31] emphasizes that the ideology of Buddhism has slowed down the development of breakthrough innovations in Japan. The heritage of Japanese creativity is predominantly in the design arts. Japanese designers are skilful in the use of "right-brain" thinking: the holistic approach, synthesis, use of imagination and visualization, all essential in planning and creating. But the emphasis upon tradition, the re-use of old ideas which respected predecessors have originated and the cross-fertilization of present day methods with the past, though conducive to evolutionary innovation, are in stark contrast to the Western values of original and unique ideas.

Desphandé et al.[32] examined the Japanese corporate culture by interviewing members and customers of the same companies. They found a predominant clan-culture in which the following characteristics are typical:

- *dominant features: cohesion, participation, teamwork, belongingness to the common family*
- *management style: mentoring, supporting, adult gestalt*
- *commitment: loyalty, tradition, cohesion among people*
- *strategic emphasis: development of human resources, commitment, moral values*

The researchers also perceived the emergence of other cultural types in the companies surveyed. An especially interesting finding is the market culture in which such features as competitiveness, achievement orientation, productivity, entrepreneurship, risk tolerance and innovativeness dominate. These features are typical of those big Japanese companies which have been able to develop into globally successful players. This, together with the changes taking place in Japanese society as a whole, must be put into perspective as we look to the future.

Hofstede[33] observes that individualism is gaining a greater foothold in Japanese society. As Japanese households have acquired more economic resources they have been able to get along more independently without involvement of parents or relatives. Life-long employment at the same firm is no longer as common as it used be. Lu[34] estimates that the real figure of lifelong employment at the big corporations is about 35–40%. Especially noticeable is that the attitudes among young employees are changing. A substantial part of young Japanese are no longer willing or able to enter into lifelong employment with the same firm. The high unemployment figure

(8% of the age-category 15–24) and part-time employment (10% of high-school graduates) are self-explanatory reasons for them to seek whatever work is available[35]. *Present surveys tell us that about half of high-school graduates will change their firm within three years after starting their work careers. Many of them want to get better jobs which are more suitable to their talents and preferences. In this respect, Japanese youngsters are coming closer to their Western counterparts.*

The tendency to leave their old firm is also growing among Japanese middle managers. In the leading 100 Japanese corporations, nearly 40% of middle managers interviewed said they would be willing to accept a new job in another company[36]. *However, it is not easy to change jobs in Japan. People cannot easily get another job at the same level they hold at present. Top management attitudes do not favour this kind of solution. The directors of the big corporations prefer to select executives from within their corporation or from among their major stakeholders.*

In the context of innovativeness, life-long employment has both advantages and disadvantages. When a Japanese engineer or marketing manager has worked for a long time in the many sectors and functions of a company, he has learned to know all the resources and work procedures necessary to process ideas to innovations. This is certainly helpful for incremental innovative progress, but the Western model of radical innovations shows that they quite often have been sparked by people who have been working in various corporations, even in many different industries or industrial branches.

Maybe the increasing Japanese mobility will give better ground for innovativeness. What the most innovative Japanese companies understand is that there is a special need for work experience and career development in the international context. A lot has already been done. The most famous example of the Japanese spirit of doing business abroad is that of Akio Morita, the former chairman of Sony, when he moved to the United States to start business there. He understood the necessity of gaining first-hand knowledge of North American markets, especially customer behaviour, in order to be able to offer innovative products.

Also other kinds of traditional attitudes in Japanese working life are changing. People are no longer willing to work as hard and long as earlier. The Federation of Japanese Economic Organizations performed an extensive study among Japanese workers[37]. *Almost 80% of those interviewed considered the opportunities for developing their personal talents and interests to be more important than advancement in their work career. About 85% of them preferred some kind of norm regulating working time and about half of them said that the company is involved too much in their private lives. The strength of the Yen on the international exchange and the accompanying material advancement has caused a situation where the Japanese people are anxious to get more here and now, and they tend to have less confidence in the future. The challenge to Japanese management is to solve creatively these new kinds of problems in working life. What are especially needed are social innovations which will respond to the changing needs, preferences and attitudes among the Japanese people.*

Japanese society values education. Parents not only encourage, but literally force their children to get good marks at the lower school levels so they can get into one of the best universities. Graduation from one of these elite schools means a good chance to be recruited by a major company. The employer will make a considerable investment and ensure that a newcomer gets a good start to his/her company career, which perhaps may last a lifetime. In this way the company will also see a return on their investment in continuous career development of their personnel.

While from one point of view this may seem to be an enviable education-career path, Japanese schools are not the best to educate for later creativity. It is well known that they emphasize memorization of facts, terminology, definitions and principles rather than the important creative skills of interactive speculation, debating, synthesis and idea-generation. Japanese schools reward obedience, carefulness and conformity rather than initiative or originality. They provide excellent mathematical training and in general emphasize the sciences and engineering more than Western schools. The system turns out large numbers of trained scientists and engineers. This will continue to insure a sound base for developing technology.

Many Japanese companies have understood the need for advanced business studies and they are sending their managers in increasing numbers to foreign universities to earn, for example, an MBA degree. Continual training of all ranks remains a high priority. Lorriman and Kenjo[38] in their extensive study of corporate training, concluded that the development of personnel is the most important responsibility area of management. They report that Japanese managers use from 20–30% of their time to develop and train their subordinates. This is somewhat in contrast to Western practice. Western managers seldom realise that their main job is to help their subordinates to do their jobs better.

Granted that these seemingly contradictory dynamic forces exist in Japanese society and in their industrial complex, it is important to understand that at the highest levels of government, business and industry the Japanese have set themselves very high targets for innovativeness. The image and status of imitator no longer applies. The report of the Japanese Economic Planning Office predicts that they will be leading in 29 technologies and sharing the first position in another 24[39]. Japan has initiated superprojects in high-tech areas such as HDTV, neuro-computers, intelligent robots, bio-sensors, PDA, super-conductor materials and telecommunications.

This is their challenge. We would do well to take it seriously.

Chapter 13

Managerial Innovativeness in a Situational Context

Innovative management behaviour is one of the strongest determining factors affecting a company's prevailing activities, attitudes and motivation. This is evident especially in those cases where some particular management style is strongly emphasized. For example, emphasizing the role of Stimulator usually leads to high idea-generation among people, and idea-penetration is fast because interaction between manager and subordinates is lively. The Stimulator's role model fits particularly well in certain situations such as the early phase of idea-collection, where you need initial reactions and first ideas and suggestions. The Stimulator is also an effective leader at brainstorming sessions where he or she needs to stimulate people's thinking and give continuous sparks to ideation. Strong emphasis on the role of Master may result in high idea-generation among experts and in development teams but demotivate "floor-level" staff's willingness to participate and take initiatives.

Companies and consequently managers also operate in different situations created by internal and external circumstances and pressures for change. It is obvious that the optimal emphasis on roles is also determined according to a company's situation. In an entrepreneurial company, especially one which is just getting started and mainly managed by the inventor/entrepreneur, the Creator's drive is decisive. Other people are inspired by his ideas. In an established company the usual tendency is to distance the CEO from the staff as the company grows. The hierarchic and horizontal levels have enlarged and direct interaction has decreased. The Course-keeper role is urgently needed in this situation. In the stages of growth, for example, through acquisitions and mergers, top managers should have Course-keeper's and Creator's skills in order to identify and predict the advantages of synergy with new businesses. During negotiations, top managers should also be able to act as Stimulators. They can assist in obtaining the information required to analyse the strengths and weaknesses of possible target companies, and make proposals on how to maintain existing profitability or return loss-making situations to profit. Furthermore, someone acting in the role of a Persuader is needed so that companies can be purchased at acceptable price levels.

In crisis situations, a balanced selection of roles is the key to successful survival. There is an urgent need for short-term idea-generation which will give immediate results. Strong Leader characteristics are needed to keep key persons committed to the organization. Competitive spirit and self-confidence need bolstering. However, people may experience high insecurity, meet complex problems and be driven into conflicts. The Consultor role will be greatly needed. *Top management's concern here may be the identification of those managerial profiles which best suit the company and consequently recruit and train managers to respond to these expectations.*

Role behaviour is influenced by a manager's *position* in the firm. The CEO acts mainly in the Course-keeper role. The R&D director favours the Master role. The sales director often operates in the Persuader's role. Successful assembly of a good mix of managers in a management group requires a clear understanding of managers' role behaviour. Different managers make different kinds of input into team activities and can be organized to complement each other when generating business ideas, stimulating creative discussion, consulting about complex matters, mastering the development of ideas into innovations and giving strategic direction. The most effective management style is probably provided by groups of innovative managers in which some members emphasize the Creator's, Stimulator's or Master's roles while others show their strength in the Consultor's or Course-keeper's roles.

Chapter 14

Re-creating Management

It is a normal academic practice to describe business as a continuous process of monitoring the business environment, specifying targets and objectives, developing, choosing and implementing strategies and tactics, controlling activities and executing corrective actions.

Traditionally, managing is a science of planning, organizing, maintaining and controlling. Development in this context means directing, honing and improving existing activities. Management work is done by CEOs, individual senior and middle managers and management groups or corporate management boards. Their work is based on generally accepted knowledge, traditions, norms, rules, policies and published strategies. Management operates within the implicitly or explicitly accepted understanding of "how our business functions" and "how it should function". Above all, rational thinking and acting are valued and promoted. While this approach is of course still valid for the maintenance of operations in a stable business environment, most CEOs and managers operate in an environment which is far from stable.

As a CEO, your working day may not actually leave much room for following systematic procedures. Your secretary organizes a morning meeting with a key customer who wants to negotiate a change in an existing deal with your company. After this, you are to attend a meeting of industry leaders where you will present a paper on EU transportation directives. Back in your office, one of the division heads calls to inform you about the delay in delivery of material promised by a supplier. One of your business partners asks advice about a very tricky problem, your electronic mailbox is full of non-answered messages, the phone rings . . . the secretary is waiting at the door. . . .

Someone may advise you to pay more attention to time management. The issue is, however, not so simple. It may be very difficult to avoid the daily "business maintenance" tasks. The CEO and senior management are responsible for resolving the major operational problems, and trying to restrict their number as much as possible. For companies, whatever consequences recessions have caused, one positive effect has been that managers have had to simplify operational policies. Downsizing has reduced the number of hierarchical levels and departments and bureaucratic procedures. People have had to learn to do their core tasks under time pressure. One negative side effect is that operational timespans have shortened.

Actually, *improved managerial innovativeness* is a much more profound solution than time management. You may need a fundamentally different approach in order to solve your problems. Your improved ability as a Creator in defining the essence of a problem and generating solutions is the primary time saver. Developing your skills in empowering people and in managing creative projects and teams may leave you much more room for strategic matters.

Total quality management will prevent quality problems by giving people a sense of pride in their work. Re-engineering may offer you the opportunity for effecting radical structural change, for example the establishment of new strategic business units to improve profitability or the redesign of jobs to improve productivity. Implementing new information technology solutions can radically diminish the need for face-to-face meetings. A surprising number of problems in companies can be avoided by skilful communication. Lastly, institutionalizing the innovation process in your company will simplify your attempts to lead your company and people into new unexplored territory.

In all of these areas, managerial innovativeness is a core issue. It is evident that most of the new entrepreneurial companies have a lot of managerial creativity. They might have problems in implementing ideas and inventions into business practice but the owner/manager should act as an enthusiastic idea-generator even there. It is an often experienced fact that as companies grow older they lose their creative and innovative flare, the very quality that made them outstanding in the first place. The key element in maintaining and promoting innovativeness is the continual process of *re-creating management*.

ESTABLISHED COMPANY

Our experience confirms that management and people at innovative companies will be very responsive to the strategy of innovativeness—if the problem of timing can be solved. Key people are busy people. When a business is running well and things seem to move forward smoothly managers may claim to be too busy for new ways of thinking and acting. Some of them might ask, "Why should we, we are doing well?" They may be right when pushing forward their mainstream business. Or are they? Why not seek to become an exception to the "Wilmot 80/20 rule of management" which says that 20% of time is spent on high value-added activity, and 80% on relatively low valued activity. *Innovativeness allows managers to increase the proportion of their high value-added activities.* A general responsiveness seems to prevail here. According to studies referred to by Bob Tricker[1] top directors would usually like to increase the time their board spends on strategy issues. Phil Hanford[2] uses the SLIM priority setting technique to guide managers towards a more strategic and realistic set of priorities for their organization. He differentiates four elements of management priority, urgency (critical; the item should be dealt with now), relevance (essential; to achieve higher-order goals), growth (meaning; to get a longer-term positive effect) and ease (easiness; the item can be accomplished in the short term).

More energy, enthusiasm and management time is needed in the arena of new businesses, especially when penetrating into new territories. Accumulated experience demonstrates that only a part of acquisitions and mergers is successful. Venture managers have found that they will not get far with innovations unless the corporate culture and systems around them support their activities. Innovation is often associated with significant risk, which division or department managers may be unwilling to take if they are fearful of failure and possible loss of status. Without real commitment and support by top management great business ideas are doomed to vanish into thin air. This is where management behaviour especially needs to be re-created. It is not enough to assume that new businesses are the responsibility of some experts or managers in the company. "Innovative companies understand that it is not a valid strategy to put all the eggs into one isolated new ventures division where they tend to be forgotten or squashed when their top management sponsor moves on", says Christopher Lorenz[3].

The strategic approaches discussed earlier in this book such as empowerment of people, re-engineering, TQM, learning organization and institutionalizing the innovation process are some possible means of unleashing managerial innovativeness. For example, in empowerment of people, significant delegation of problem solving and decision-making authority substantially reduces management's routine tasks and transforms managers from daily problem solvers into Course-keepers and direction givers. Phil Hanford[4] recommends that the managers' perspectives should include radical changes from "micro and macro" levels to mega aspects (business environment, marketplace, society). "Chances are the big issues you're wrestling with are at the mega level", says Hanford.

TROUBLED COMPANY

In times of recession many companies find themselves with sales figures dramatically down and inadequate cash flow to cover expenses. You may have campaigned more intensively than ever, your sales force has redoubled their efforts. You put visits to your key customers on your priority list. But the "slow-down-cost-reduction-brush-fire-buy-out" consultant still knocks at the door. Of course, *the whole process of retrenchement can itself be a masterpiece of innovativeness since it affords a multitude of areas for being innovative.* Many companies react to difficulties by radical restructuring of the entire organization while others try to overcome troubles by stepwise procedures[5]. As an innovative manager you can search for turnaround by employing the following action pattern:

- Act as a Creator. Focus on resolvable problems and issues. Instead of worrying and constantly speaking about the most difficult and at the time most unsolvable problems, try to creatively solve more immediate problems. These solutions serve as promising examples to your people. Look for immediate opportunities. Creative short-term thinking often pays off. Some demonstration of your company's ability to actually increase sales or to win new contracts may give both customers and creditors an encouraging indication of your wholehearted efforts to keep business going. Discover also whether you could reduce your cost structure by outsourcing and benefiting from supplier competition. In bigger businesses, buyouts may in some cases be a successful way of restructuring the company portfolio
- Act as a Course-keeper. Build a task force. Use a consultant. In a very difficult situation people are normally too troubled to be able to make long-term plans for the future, even though this could be the most important thing for the company's survival. They are usually eager to put all their energies into creating some concrete outcomes from the crisis. In essence, they tend to behave like innovative people in sudden life and death situations: how to get the hell out of here? A task force works fast and solves problems efficiently and innovatively. A consultant may offer experience and fresh solutions to your problems
- Act as a Consultor. Promise fair rewards. People are interested in searching for creative solutions to problems they can handle, especially if they are rewarded for their extra efforts. The reward can be a very small fraction of the incremental return to your company. Consult people about their difficulties. Organize every kind of support they need to get their tasks done
- Act as a Master. Maintain your company's core capabilities. Do you really know what they are? Assign your most competent innovative people to a

survival task force. Challenge their creative spirit. Put everyone in teams to create solutions to problems. Create an innovative management culture which supports the efforts made by these teams

- Act as a Persuader. Ask your people to provide you not only with information and plain figures but also with suggestions on how to improve things. Communicate with your people, owners, creditors, suppliers and customers. They want to know where the company is now and where it is going, they will find out later anyhow. They can give you invaluable ideas about improving your situation. Network with innovative people, ask their creative advice

- Act as a Leader. You are the role model. Nothing destroys the process of creative development more quickly than a top manager's deeply worried face and ultrapessimistic statements. Many companies have been able to achieve turnaround — the numerous case studies written about them are worth reading. It is typical that the guys at the top have been able to overcome apathy and mistrust through their own drive and personal optimism

- Imagine a promising future. The recession will not last forever. There will be better times. What then? Now may be the time to design improved strategies. John Kay[6] recommends recognition of a company's distinctive capabilities in the markets in which it operates. He has pithy observations, for example, about BMW, where one influential shareholder, Herbert Quandt, following BMW's bankruptcy, recognized the company's distinctive capabilities such as the quality and image of their high-performance saloon cars and the company's attractiveness to young affluent Europeans. This gave a powerful impetus to the real business success which is now BMW.

RE-CREATING YOURSELF

Young people raised to managerial positions are usually eager to try out new innovative approaches. Many senior managers have become more sceptical under the constraints of short-term profit requirements, strict planning and standard operating procedures. A sceptical attitude may not only kill the needed innovativeness of their subordinates but also cause them to act as non-innovative managers. "Routine mindness" is an insidious enemy. Allowing each work day to follow the same paths, although it includes routine problem-solving tasks, may lead to a vicious circle which is very difficult to break.

BREAKING OUT FROM THE SHELL

Managers are often prisoners of their own paradigms, the frameworks of understanding about their work and environment. They define their needs and future expectations from these paradigms. Learning offers alternatives of thought and action breaking the established patterns. It means rethinking the needs and assumptions of what is necessary and beneficial for themselves and their company. *Re-creating means generating alternative ideas different from the existing ones to build up alternative action frameworks.* They may represent totally different views or ideas of reality.

Managers who have lived for a long time within a constrained organizational environment seldom take the opportunity to perceive or even imagine alternative ways of functioning. They regard change as a threat to security and predictability, disrupting the hard earned equilibrium of the organization. Change brings with it the need to acquire new knowledge and skills, using resources of time, money and energy. Some managers strongly resist being first to do things differently, others exercise their talent for envisioning disastrous results. In some organizations the conservative culture views change as the enemy.

Experience has shown that although it may not be possible to force change or new paradigms upon managers, they can be challenged by organizing learning experiences. General Dwight Eisenhower is said to have illustrated this concept by placing a length of cord on the conference table. He demonstrated the futility of trying to "push" the cord ahead. It could only be "pulled" or "led" in the desired direction.

"Action learning" is a popular method of guided learning. Selected managers from different companies participate in a development project. This involves "set sessions" held in one of the participant's companies. The set tries to solve selected problems under the leadership of a set leader, who can be a trainer, a consultant or one of the company's senior managers acting as a sponsor. Alternative solutions are put on the table for questioning and discussion. Participants are encouraged to find unusual, alternative view-points and to ask very pointed "impertinent" questions, avoiding conventional solutions. This method has been found to stimulate a creative attitude toward problem solving in the managers' own companies.

Listening to experts and successful managers operating in totally different fields can be a stimulating experience. Since the Gulf war General Schwartzkopf has been a much-sought-after speaker at top management conferences. Curre Lindström, the Swedish manager of Finland's 1995 world champion hockey team, has become one of the most popular speakers on aspects of leadership. The famous Russian hockey manager Jursinov took his entire team to watch the training and rehearsal of ballet dancers to get them to train and play in more creative ways.

One of the authors was involved in the marketing of a new opera house during its construction phase. All present were convinced that performances would be sold out for the first few years when it was a novelty, but were also anxious to come up with ideas for long term viability. Idea-generation teams were selected in which very few members actually had any experience of the opera, but who did have a lot of experience in marketing consumer goods and services. These teams quickly generated hundreds of marketing ideas, most of which had never earlier been thought of in professional opera circles. Many of the ideas are now successfully in use.

SELF-ANALYSIS

What are the underlying assumptions of my action framework? Idea-generation techniques such as IMAGINE!, Scenario Writing or Storyboard[7] are useful imaginative approaches which can assist in your own personal development. Although their use may be too demanding on an individual basis, friends and colleagues might be enlisted to work with you in a small team. We suggest the following approach:

- Examine your past: Where have I been? What is my background? What effect does it have on my present assumptions and working habits? Which people have had the greatest effect on my present values, preferences and viewpoints?
- Make clear your present state: What assumptions, values and preferences characterize my present working life? At what level are my capabilities as an innovative manager?
- State your goals: Where do I want to go? What elements in my managerial *assessment matrix* should I strengthen and improve in order to be more innovative? What features should I try to diminish or eliminate which seem to be obstacles on my road to innovativeness. Take advantage of available test and survey instruments. State your learning objectives
- Make a commitment: Imagine positive outcomes and consequences of reaching your objectives. Imagine your new working system, how your company will function as a master innovator. Change requires a real investment of your time and energy in the new way of thinking and acting. Your commitment cannot be a temporary one. It may even last for your whole career, especially if you are able to link together your deep personal interests and the company's growth. If you can't do this, you should probably leave the company
- Generate ideas on how to get there: Imagine various paths leading to your goals. Examine various learning approaches to managerial innovative-ness. You might profit from internal company training programmes or external seminars and courses. Computerized creativity programmes could provide one solution. Contact a managerial innovativeness consultant. Read cases about top innovative managers and companies. Try to meet great innovators. Try networking. Start a survey or research project. *Try to have a personal effect on institutionalizing innovativeness in your*

company. This can in turn have a positive effect upon your own personal innovativeness.

- Overcome the obstacles. When visiting Singapore our guide told us about the Japanese invasion of Singapore. The British troops concentrated all their resistance along the main roads but the Japanese troops simply evaded these obstacles by travelling by bicycle through the marshes. They met hardly any resistance. Fact or fiction, one of our Japanese friends told us that the idea came from the historical event of the Trojan horse! Overcoming obstacles requires creativity

- Examine your results: What have you really accomplished? Have you used genuine measurements, real indicators which tell you what progress you have achieved. Re-creation is a surprising process. It can be initiated by a sudden event which leads to genuine insight and opportunity. Re-creation can also be stimulated by an unfortunate situation involving loss of position. Many top innovative managers tell that they have been able to radically increase their proportion of high value-added work when forced to re-examine their priorities in life. The stepping-stones are not easily perceived by outsiders. The motivation to act as an innovative manager is kept high by direction and willpower

RECREATING THE TOP MANAGEMENT GROUP

Many established companies try to recapture the entrepreneurial and innovative spirit which they had when they began. To accomplish this *it is often necessary to break down the entrenched habits and behaviour of top management*. The past few years offer many examples of major corporations which have had to make a clean sweep of top executives and bring in a new group who understood market conditions, new technologies and above all possessed a strong drive for achievement. The change was necessary in order to institute a renewal strategy which fundamentally altered the company's structure. In some cases, institutional investors use their power to restructure the management when they want to achieve totally new strategic directions.

Radical reshaping of an organization rocks the established patterns of behaviour. For example, a couple of years ago 3M transformed its European organization by forming "European Business Centres" bringing managers to work in cross-border teams. As a consequence, managers had to learn new forms of cooperation and teamwork.

It is of critical importance when changing the top management team that the decision makers who remain are open to consideration of proposals by newcomers who bring badly needed insight to the re-creation process. The CEO should also give a helping hand to newcomers to learn, in particular, the Course-keeper's role. Here, the CEO should be a Consultor who coaches them in the adoption of innovative management roles.

In some cases change has been accomplished by assigning individual managers to chair task forces, or by appointments to foreign subsidiaries or secondment to social projects which offer a prestigious alternative to corporate activity. Working abroad is an accepted part of a manager's career path in innovative companies. Seventy-five per cent of 3M's top 135 executives have worked in foreign countries for at least three years and usually more, according to Marshall Loeb[8]. Most of Philips' directors are quite used to working anywhere in the world, continuing a centuries-old Dutch tradition.

A large proportion of companies use management training as an integral part of their strategic planning. In addition to the classical internal or external seminars, some companies have incorporated internal MBA studies. A steadily growing number are making use of the new information and communication technologies, particularly those companies in the IT&T, financial services, airline and travel services sectors. In Europe some of the strongest users of telematics in management training are Siemens-Nixdorf, Bull, Philips, Olivetti, Deutsche Bundespost and France Telecom. In the UK telematics and particularly distance education has made enormous strides. As we look to the future, "virtual" universities and management schools will take advantage of satellites and electronic networks to connect managers in a worldwide communication web.

REVIEW YOUR WORKING METHODS

Time: Find enough time for creative approaches. Why not sometimes start the meeting or perhaps stop the debate by saying: "Well, let's suspend critical judgement for a while. Generate new business ideas, the more and far-out ideas you create the better. For an hour let's just hang out. . . . Don't hurry the discussion." Producing creative solutions take its own time.

Chairing: Chair meetings effectively but in a relaxed way. Unblock tensions, unleash creativity and accept conflicting opinions. If creative chaos results, restore order. Remember that as chairperson your main task is to stimulate open discussion. This involves encouraging healthy competition, while discouraging destructive rivalry. Encourage participants to express their thoughts in positive form, rather than as negative criticism, and to support their ideas by relating them to the company's objectives.

Procedures: Vary the nature of management meetings. Peter Drucker suggests dedicating one meeting per month to innovation. Include idea-generation phases in the meetings. Build up creative task forces to solve complex urgent problems. Ask some team members to come to meetings with preliminary ideas and suggestions, not just with problem descriptions. Bring in external idea-rich experts or other key persons to spark the creative flame of discussion. Even a short (and inexpensive) interactive audioconference with an external expert could provide material for rethinking conventional issues. Many present problems in management groups can simply be reduced or even totally eliminated by renewing the whole organizational structure and system to be more self-managed. The coventional involvement of the management group as such will then not be so intense.

Use *hypothetical* questions and problem statements. "What if . . . our pricing of products would be a quarter more/less . . . our production would be removed completely to another country . . . deregulation would bring us to . . . our competitors would launch radical new models onto the market . . . a new environmental law would be passed by parliament?" Questions such as these will shake up complacency and generate new initiatives in the group.

Take advantage of subcommittees by giving them challenging tasks. For example, in one company, after working out a renewed strategy, most managers were tired and not motivated to carry out the follow-up task of translating strategy into policies. The CEO asked each of these managers to select two key people from within the company to work with them to design a policy statement that would fit on a single A4 sheet of paper. The three best proposals—the most precise, the most communicative and the most innovative—were amply rewarded.

Some companies operating globally form cross-national management teams for strategic development projects. The members of the team, physically situated in a number of different countries, benefit from a networking system. They use bulletin board facilities to maintain intensive 24-hour communication and for solving difficult problems. Electronic brainstorming can be very useful. According to recent research performed by Gallupe and Cooper[9] it is an even better way of generating ideas than traditional brainstorming. Programs such as "GroupSystems" or "Software-Assisted Meeting Management" help management teams to produce more high-quality ideas, organize the flow of ideas more effectively and provide help with the sorting out and re-working of ideas. Furthermore, these programmes assist in overcoming idea-production blocking (censoring) and they facilitate interaction. Managers can participate in brainstorming from different locations and whenever they find available time.

Environment: Design your meeting room for creative activity by supplying it with wall papers, flip charts, Post-it Notes, microcomputers with scanners and high speed printers. Decorate the room with stimulating posters, models, prototypes and charts. Organize some meetings in different plants and subsidiaries so that team members are able to have closer contact with local issues. Take your managers out into nature to experience leadership and team management situations under difficult conditions. Consider common training experiences such as manoeuvring a sailboat, climbing in the Swiss Alps or survival camping in Finnish Lapland (at minus 40°C). (Our Russian colleagues tell us that for some foreign managers the best survival experience is simply travelling around Siberia — we can testify that it works!).

CREATING THE STRATEGY FOR INNOVATIVENESS

We have observed that many companies lack a conscious strategy for raising the level of innovativeness. If there is thinking about innovation, it is only a "by-product" of other strategies such as new product or production planning. In other cases, innovativeness is planned as an adjunct to "hot" management techniques such as re-engineering, intrapreneuring, learning organization and time-based competition. Fine, if the importance of innovativeness is strategically emphasized. However, innovativeness in these programmes is more often a spin-off than a centrally intended objective. At present, even though many chief executives may express the desire to strive for higher innovativeness there is seldom any explicitly documented strategic thinking about how to get there.

Planning the strategy of innovativeness is in itself a creative problem-solving process. It seeks to match management behaviour with the objectives, conditions, resources and qualifications of the company in order to optimize the innovation output. A strategy is an intentional, planned search for higher innovativeness articulated by the chief executive and the top management group. We defined earlier the *strategy for innovativeness* as a deliberate and targeted activity for accelerating ideas and innovations in all or a selected number of action spheres, functions and levels of the company. Superb creativity as such is not enough for a business organization. It will need innovativeness which will target and guide people's creativity into measurable business objectives.

Top management may start a specific *project* to create a strategy for innovativeness in the company. Depending on the present state of innovativeness, it may be targeted more selectively for attainment through a strategic development project, a training project or the formulation of a policy of innovation in the company.

The company's current state of innovativeness can be determined by special *assessment forms* which evaluate the company's position in relation to their competitors. Further numerical assessment will increase management's understanding of the nature and characteristics of innovative processes and factors in their company. One example follows.

A high level of innovativeness will be reached in our company by:

- Identifying core skills and knowledge gaps
- Recruiting top creative talents and supporting them in their creative and innovative efforts

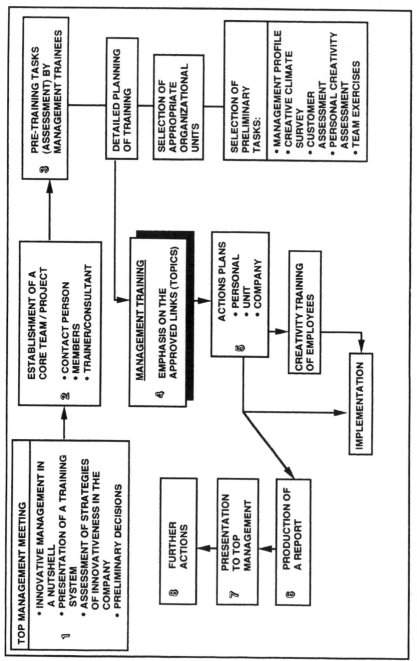

Figure 14.1 Strategy Development for Innovativeness. (Printed by Permission of IMA)

- Offering proper career paths to innovators
- Granting measurable privileges such as slack-time and extra rewards to intrapreneurial persons
- Attaching specific importance to the development of managers' creativity and innovative skills
- Attaching great importance to product innovation activities
- Devoting special attention to borrowing and buying ideas
- Developing and maintaining formal internal innovation programmes
- Stimulating operational and situational creativity and a readiness to grasp opportunities
- Maintaining effective idea management

(Part of the Assessment Form of Corporate Innovativeness. Reprinted by permission of IMA.)

The innovativeness assessment is a great help in formulating the objectives of a strategic project. Top management brings the necessary commitment to the project and helps to formulate the following stages. They also select a *project leader* who then puts together a *core team* of key persons who will have the responsibility of carrying on with the project. The team should include people from different units, levels and functions of the company. In addition to the necessary expertise they should also possess imagination and a strong drive to solve problems. Knowledge of the company's innovative activities is a strong plus.

Strategies for innovativeness include guidelines for methods, procedures and systems as well as behavioural suggestions about how to reach the objectives of innovativeness. The strategies actually decided upon may vary a great deal. Each approach will include its own specialized and different route to innovativeness. Some companies create and skilfully apply a highly complex composition of selected strategic approaches. Other companies apply a certain main strategic approach backed by a few support strategies. Some companies may emphasize internal development (development of their own experts', staff's and managers' creativity and investing in internal new business development and R&D). Other companies may rely on "purchased creativity" (acquisitions, buying licences and patent rights, hiring creative researchers and inventors). A few companies focus on developing an innovative elite, while others may try to maximize the creative input of all their people. There is a crucial difference between companies which aim for long-term innovative results in new markets, products and technologies and those who want to achieve immediate results through day-by-day super-creativity.

Some companies seek innovativeness by letting the wheels revolve freely while other companies prefer to formalize and structure innovative activities and innovation programmes. A mixed strategic approach can be effective especially in large and medium-size companies which have more complex structures.

MANAGEMENT TRAINING FOR INNOVATIVENESS

Once there has been a decision on a *training project*, the team works out a detailed training plan, selecting appropriate instruments for preliminary analysis:

- management profile tests
- surveys of the innovative climate (how people in the company evaluate the innovativeness of the organization)
- personal creativity assessment

The team recommends special training for selected target groups, usually for senior and middle managers as well as for experts and other key persons. The training is organized in stages. Each stage represents a link in the chain of innovativeness, which encompasses managerial behaviour, creativity techniques, innovative systems and operative and strategic development. After each step the participants assess their company's or business unit's position and develop a *plan*: "How to achieve greater innovativeness". The plan covers three issues: at personal level, unit level and company level. After one year the assessments are usually repeated in order to evaluate the effect of training. In some cases the main target group includes the company's entire personnel. The main topics are analysis and problem solving, development of personal and team creativity and creativity techniques.

Chapter 15
Conclusion

Managers, especially chief executive officers, have the decisive influence on a company's innovativeness. Although ideally the entire staff are involved in creating and renewing strategies it is the top brass which finally makes the important decisions which shape life and work. Even though top management's power is to a great extent controlled by the shareholders, CEOs are usually able, within certain limits, to guide the decisions in the direction they prefer. This is due to their special knowledge of the company's resources, competitive situation, development in the external environment and future plans. In addition, compared with the other key managers in the company, they usually have the closest relationships with the board members and can therefore influence events. This power carries with it the responsibility of exercising their creative talent.

Top management builds the company's organizational structure and determines operational policies which provide the framework for the staff's everyday operations. This includes the necessary prerequisites for innovation and creativity within the organization. These qualities are influenced by management, not only through the decisions they take concerning strategy and operational tactics, but also through their observed behaviour. It is in this respect that middle management and supervisors have additional influence on the creative climate within their organization.

Development of innovativeness within a company does not necessarily mean building up a new organizational structure, but rather re-creating management and revitalizing the organization. Consequently, the company's strategies will be re-thought and the organization remodelled to be more competitive in a fast-paced, increasingly changing business environment. Together with their people, innovative managers set ambitious visions, goals and objectives for idea-creation and establish continuous profit and quality improvement projects. They encourage and support their staff in solving problems and exploiting opportunities. Managers as "doers" must also make things happen in their companies and get results by championing ideas so that they get implemented.

Innovative managers are more leaders than administrators, because their actions clarify and strengthen company values, and inspire their people to follow their visions and examples of *successful business Creators*. As we approach the twenty-first century, the corporate game will be a struggle for survival. In business as in nature the most successful life forms, those which have prospered, are not those which have reached a comfortable equilibrium, but those in which imbalance has necessitated a continuous fight for survival. The need to adapt continuously to changing circumstances is the greatest stimulus to growth. It is promising for the future that even in the most difficult times, whether it be severe recession or the painful process of reorganization, the top innovative companies resemble the Phoenix, the legendary bird which is consumed by fire only to rise again from its own ashes.

References

Chapter 1

1. Evans Paul, Bartolome Fernando (1980) *Must Success Cost So Much?* Grant McIntyre Ltd., London.
2. Lampikoski Kari (1992) *The Innovative Manager*. Project report, IM, Helsinki.
3. Drucker Peter (1954) *The Practice of Management*. Harper and Row, New York.
4. Desphandé Rohit, Farley John U., Webster Jr Fredericke (1993) Corporate, culture, customer orientation and innovativeness in Japanese firms. *Journal of Marketing*, **57**, January, 23–27.
5. Peters T. (1991) Get innovative or get dead. *California Management Review*, **33** (1), 9–23.
6. Kay John (1993) *Foundations of Corporate Success*. Oxford University Press, Oxford.
7. Plender John (1995) Balanced vision for tomorrow. *Financial Times*, Wednesday, June 7.
8. Plender John, ibid.
9. Larson Cynthia M. (1993) Bridging the innovation gap—An interview with Robert Johnston. *Journal of Creative Behaviour*, **27** (2), 130–142.
10. Murakami T., Nishiwaki T. (1991) *Strategy for Creation*. Woodhead Publishing Limited, Cambridge.
11. IRDAC (Industrial Research and Development Advisory Committee of the Commission of European Communities) and ERT (European Round Table of Industrialists) 1994. A report presented by Tuula Kautto-Koivula, Nokia, Finland.
12. Quinn James Brian (1985) Managing innovation: controlled chaos. *Harvard Business Review*, May–June, 73–84.

Chapter 2

1. Schnaars Steven P. (1994) *Managing Imitation Strategies—How Later Entrants Seize Markets from Pioneers*. The Free Press, New York.
2. Rumball Donald (1989) *The Entrepreneurial Edge*. Key Porter Books Ltd, Toronto.
3. Hequet Marek (1992) Creativity training gets creative. *Training*, February, 41–46.
4. Davis Stanley M. (1989) *Future Perfect*. Addison Wesley Inc., Woburn.
5. Carson-Parker John (1986) A potential "coreholding" that's often overlooked. A special report on Nestlé. Supplement to *Euromoney*, July.
6. White Jerry (1988) *Intrapreneuring*. Penguin Books, Ontario.

7. Ornstein Robert E. (1977) *The Psychology of Consciousness*. Harcourt Brace Jovanovich Inc., New York.
8. Ornstein, ibid.
9. Arieti Silvano (1976) *Creativity — The Magic Synthesis*. Basic Books Inc., New York.
10. Arieti, ibid.
11. Lampikoski Kari, Korpelainen Kari. IMAGINE! A Creativity technique for solving business problems. Unpublished paper.
12. IFR, Review of the Year 1994.
13. Fry Arthur (1989) How to create an environment for innovation. Presented at the AMA's New Product Conference. American Marketing Association, February 16.

Chapter 3

1. Hampden-Turner Charles (1994) *Corporate Culture. From Vicious to Virtuous Circles*. Judy Piatkus , London.
2. Nolan Vincent (1984) The Creative manager. Abraxas Management Research. Unpublished paper.
3. Kanter Rosabeth Moss (1986) Creating the creative environment. *Management Review*, 75(2).
4. Murakami T., Nishiwaki T. (1991) *Strategy for Creation*. Woodhead Publishing Ltd, Cambridge.
5. Saporito Bill (1993) David Glass won't crack under fire. *Fortune*, February.

Chapter 4

1. Think — Innovation at IBM (1989). IMC Corporation, New York.
2. Fry Arthur (1989) How to create an environment for innovation. Presented at the AMA's New Product Conference. American Marketing Association, February 16.
3. Think, ibid.
4. Simon Herbert A. (1986) How managers express their creativity. *The McKinley Quarterly*, Autumn, 67–68.
5. Simon, ibid.
6. Benterude Per (1987) Future banking. SM, Oslo.
7. Dorman Lesley (1989) Original spin. *Psychology Today*, August, 46–52.
8. Corwing R. G. (1965) Professional persons in public organizations. *Educational and Administration Quarterly*, 1, 1–22.
9. Kay John (1993) *Foundations of Corporate Success*. Oxford University Press, Oxford.
10. Minkes A.L. (1987) *The Entrepreneurial Manager*. Penguin Books, Harmondsworth, Middlesex.
11. Kim Steven H. (1990) *Essence of Creativity*. Oxford University Press, New York.
12. Pryor Austin K., Shays Michael E. (1993) Growing the business with intrapreneurs. *Business Quarterly*, Spring, 43–50.
13. *Business Week*, 1994, November 7.
14. (a) Fry Arthur L. (1989) How to create an environment for innovation. Presented at the AMA's New Products Conference, February 16.
    (b) Kennedy Carol (1988) Planning global strategies for 3M. *Long Range Planning*, 21(1), 9–17.
    (c) Lehr Lewis W. (1988) Encouraging innovation and entrepreneurship in diversified corporations, in *Handbook for Creative and Innovative Managers*, edited by Robert Lawrence Kuhn. McGraw-Hill Book Company, New York, 211–219.

(d) Loeb Marshall (1995) Ten commandments for managing creative people. *Fortune*, January.
15. 3M Innovation Quiz. www. Internet Home Page, 3M.
16. Pryor and Shays, ibid., and Lynn Gary S., Lynn Norman M. (1992) *Innopreneurship*. Probus, Chicago.
17. Pinchot III Clifford (1985) *Intrapreneuring*. Harper and Row, New York.
18. Minkes, ibid.
19. Adams J.L. (1986) *The Care and Feeding of Ideas*. Addison Wesley, Reading, Massachusetts.

Chapter 5

1. Matherly T.A., Goldsmith R.E. (1985) The two faces of creativity. *Business Horizons*, **28**(950), 8–11.
2. Ahlbrandt Roger S., Leana Carrie R., Murrell Audrey J. (1992) Employee involvement programmes improve corporate performance. *Long Range Planning*, **25**(5), 91–98.
3. Osborne Richard L. (1992) Building an innovative organization. *Long Range Planning*, **25**(6), 56–92.
4. Bowen David E., Lawler III Edward E. (1995) Empowering service employees. *Sloan Management Review*, Summer, 73–84.
5. Dumaine Brian (1980) Creating a new corporate culture. *Fortune*, January 15.
6. Roy Mike (1988) Ideas in action. *Manager*, July, 8–9.
7. Roy Mike, ibid.
8. Dumaine Brian (1990) Who needs a boss? *Fortune*, May 7.
9. Senge Peter M. (1990) *The Fifth Discipline*. Doubleday Currency, New York.
10. Peters Tom, Austin Nancy (1985) *A Passion for Excellence*. Collins, Glasgow, Scotland.
11. Whitfield P.R. (1975) *Creativity in Industry*. Penguin Books, Harmondsworth.
12. Sjölander Sören (1983) *Innovation och Företagsnyelse*. Liber, Malmö.
13. Kamm Judith (1987) *An Integrative Approach to Managing Innovation*. Lexington Books, Toronto.
14. Miller William C., Rosenfeld R., Servo J. (1988) Innovation through investment in people. Unpublished manuscript.
15. Bowen, ibid.
16. French Jr John R. P., Raven Bertram (1968) The bases of social power, in *Group Dynamics*, edited by Dorwing Cartwright and Alvin Zander, Harper and Row, New York, 259–269.
17. Ketteringham J.M., Nayak P.R. (1986) *Breakthroughs*. Rawson Associates, New York.

Chapter 6

1. Brandt Steven (1987) *Entrepreneurial Drive in Established Companies*. New American Library, New York.
2. Goldsmith, Hickman Craig, Silva Michael A. (1984) *Creating Excellence*. New American Library, New York.
3. Richards Tudor (1985) *Stimulating Innovation*. Frances Pinter, London.
4. Wheatley Walter J., Anthony William P., Maddox Nick E. (1991) Selecting and training strategic planners with imagination and creativity. *Journal of Creative Behaviour*, **25**(1), 42–50.

5. (a) Cleick J.E. (1987) *Chaos: Making a New Science*. Heinemann, New York.
   (b) Lawrence P.R., Lorsch J.W. (1967) *Organization and Environment*. Harvard University Press, Boston.
6. Stacey Ralph (1993) Strategy as order emerging from chaos. *Long Range Planning*, **26**(1), 10–17.
7. McPherson Joseph (1985) The innovative organization. Unpublished paper.
8. Heap John (1989) *The Management of Innovation and Design*. Cassell, Guildford.
9. Hunsicker Quincy J. (1985) Vision leadership and the future of European management. *European Management Journal*, 3(3), 153–160.
10. Aaker David A. (1989) Managing assets and skills: The key to a sustainable competitive advantage. *California Management Review*, Winter, 91–106.
11. (a) von Reibnitz Ute (1988) *Scenario Techniques*. McGraw-Hill Book Company, Hamburg.
    (b) Sviden Ove (1985) Automotive usage in a future information society, in *Design and Innovation Policy and Management*, edited by Richard Langdon and Roy Rothwell. Francis Pinter, London, 27–43.
12. Argyris Chris, Schon Donald (1978) *Organizational Learning: A Theory of Action Perspective*. Addison-Wesley Publishing Company, Reading, Massachusetts.
13. Swieringa Joop, Wierdsma Andre (1992) *Becoming a Learning Organization. Beyond the Learning Curve*. Addison-Wesley Publishing Company, Wokingham.
14. Bandrowski James F. (1990) *Corporate Imagination Plus*. The Free Press, New York.
15. Fry Arthur (1989) How to create an environment for innovation. Presented at the AMA's New Product Conference. American Marketing Association, February 16.
16. Bennis Warren (1991) Concentrate on trust. Special report. *Fortune*, December 30, 40–47.
17. McGrath Rita Gunther, MacMillan Ian C. (1995) Discovery-driven planning *Harvard Business Review*, July–August, 44–54.
18. Clemons Eric K. (1995) Using scenario analysis to manage the strategic risks of reengineering. *Sloan Management Review*, Summer, 61–71.

Chapter 7

1. Bleicher J. (1979) *Contemporary Hermeneutics*. Routledge, Kegan Paul, Boston, Massachusetts.
2. Kamm Judith Brown (1987) *An Integrative Approach to Managing Innovation*. Lexington, Massachusetts.
3. Anna Kontek was awarded a special prize in the International Exhibition of Theater Scenographers and Stage Designers in Prague 1995.

Chapter 8

1. Levinson Robert E. (1983) *Making the Most of Entrepreneurial Management*. Amacon, New York.
2. Dixon Michael (1989) How innovators work and what stops them. *Financial Times*, March, 24.
3. Buchanan W.T. (1987) Managing to motivate. *Sam Advanced Management Journal*, 52(2), 16–18.
4. IFR, Review of the Year 1984.
5. Nicholls John (1988) Leadership in organizations: meta, macro and micro. *European Management Journal*, **6**(1), 16–25.

6. Clifford Donald K. Jr, Cavanagh Richard E. (1988) *The Winning Performance*. Bantam Books, New York.
7. (a) McClelland D., Burnham D.H. (1976) Power is the great motivator. *Harvard Business Review*, March–April, 100–110.
   (b) McClelland David (1961) *The Achieving Society*. Van Nostrand Reinhold, New York.
   (c) Miner John B. (1978) Twenty years of research on role motivation theory. *Personnel Psychology*, **31**, 739–760.
   (d) Stogdill Ralph (1974) *Handbook of Leadership: A Survey of Theory and Research*. Free Press, New York.
8. Buchanan W. T., ibid.
9. White Jerry S. (1988) *Intrapreneuring*. Penguin Books. Ontario.
10. Tuominen S. (1993) Satisfied customers are key to success. *Vaisala News*, 123, Helsinki.
11. Lorriman John, Kenjo Takashi (1994) *Japan's Winning Margins*. Oxford University Press, New York.

Chapter 9

1. Pryor Austin K., Shays Michael E. (1993) Growing the business with intrapreneurs. *Business Quarterly*, Spring, 43–50.
2. Houlder Vanessa (1995) R&D placed under the microscope. *Financial Times*, Monday, May 22.
3. Kennedy Carol (1993) Changing the company culture of CIBA-GEIGY. *Long Range Planning*, **26**(1), 18–27.

Chapter 10

1. (a) Baumol W.J., Blackman S.A., Wolf E.N. (1989) *Productivity and American Leadership: The Long View*. MIT Press, Cambridge.
   (b) Denison E. (1974) *Accounting for United States Economic Growth 1929–1969*. The Brooking Institution, Washington DC.
2. Botkin James, Diamancescu Dan, Stata Ray (1984) *The Innovators. Rediscovering America's Creative Energy*. Harper & Row, New York.
3. (a) Sjölander Sören (1983) *Innovation och Företagsnyelse*. Liber, Malmö.
   (b) de Brentani Ulrike (1991) Success factors in developing new business services. *European Journal of Marketing*, **25**, 33–59.
4. (a) Cooper R.G. (1980) Project NewProd: What makes a new product winner? Centre Québécois d'Innovation Industrielle, Montréal.
   (b) Cooper R.G. (1984) New product strategies. *Journal of Product Innovation Management*, June 1, 151–164.
   (c) Cooper R.G., Kleinschmidt E.J. (1987) Success factors in product innovation. *Industrial Marketing Management*, August 16, 15–23.
   (d) Maidique M.A., Zirgler B.J. (1984) A study of success and failure in product innovation. *IEEE Transactions in Engineering Management*, August 23, 116–123.
5. Gephart Martha A. (1995) The road to high performance. *Training & Development*, June 29–38.
6. Groenhaug Kjell, Kaufman Geir (1988) *Innovation: A Cross-disciplinary Perspective*. Norwegian University Press, Oslo.
7. *The European Best of the Best Companies in Technology and Innovation Management* (1995). Arthur D. Little International Inc., August, Brussels.

8. (a) Roberts E., Fusfeld Alan R. (1987) *Staffing the Innovative Technology Based Organization in Generating Technological Innovation*, edited by Roberts E. B., Oxford University Press, New York.
   (b) Richards Tudor (1974) *Problem Solving Through Creative Analysis*. Gower Press, Letchworth, Hertfordshire.
9. Gannes Stuart (1987) Merck has made biotech work. *Fortune*, January 19.
10. Udell Gerald G., Pettijohn Linda S. (1991) A retailer's view of industrial innovation: An interview with David Glass, President and CEO of Wal-Mart Stores Inc. *Journal of Product Innovation Management*, **8**, 231–239.
11. Citicorp, Annual Report 1986.
12. Citicorp, Annual Report 1992.
13. Citibank, www. The Citibank home page, Internet.
14. Citicorp, Annual Report 1994.
15. IFR, Review of the Year 1994.
16. Citicorp, Annual Report 1994.
17. Citicorp, ibid.
18. Buzzell Robert D. (1984) Citibank: Marketing to multinational customers, in *Global Marketing Strategies*. Harvard Business School, Boston, Massachusetts, 489–518.
19. Buzzell, ibid.
20. Ghoshal Sumantra, Bartlett Christopher A. (1995) Changing role of top management. *Harvard Business Review*, January–February, 85–96.
21. (a) Rothwell R. (1977) The characteristics of successful innovators and technically progressive firms. *R&D Management*, **7**(3), 191–206.
   (b) Maidique M.A. (1987) *Entrepreneurs, Champions and Technological Innovation in Generating Technological Innovation*, edited by Roberts E. B., Oxford University Press, New York.
   (c) Kamm Judith (1987) *An Integrative Approach to Managing Innovation*. Lexington Books, Toronto.
22. Quinn James Brian (1985) Managing innovation: controlled chaos. *Harvard Business Review*, May–June, 73–84.
23. Drucker Peter F. (1985) The discipline of innovation. *Harvard Business Review*, May–June, 67–72.
24. Lovio Raimo (1989) *Suomalainen Menestystarina*. Hanki ja Jää, Helsinki.
25. Bartlett Christopher A., Ghoshal Sumantra (1988) Organizing for worldwide effectiveness: The transnational solution. *California Management Review*, Fall, **31**(1), 54–74.
26. Nokia, Annual Reports, 1988–1994. Information Bulletin of Nokia Group, 1988–1995. www. Nokia homepage. Internet.
27. Nokia, Annual Reports, 1988–1994.
28. Information Bulletin of Nokia Group, Spring 1992.
29. Nokia, Annual Report 1994.
30. *Fortune*, March 21, 1994.
31. Information Bulletin of Nokia Group, No. 2, 1995.

Chapter 12

1. Murakami T., Nishiwaki T. (1991) *Strategy for Creation*. Woodhead Publishing Limited, Cambridge.
2. Chisholm John (1994) *Turning Research into Wealth: The Japanese Way. A Foresight Article*. HMSO, London.

3. Samuels Richard J. (1994) Pathways of technological diffusion in Japan. *Sloan Management Review*/Spring, 21–34.
4. Chisholm John, ibid.
5. Chisholm John, ibid.
6. *Fortune*, December, 2.
7. Egan Colin, McKiernan Peter (1993) *Inside Fortress Europe. Strategies for the Single Market*. Addison-Wesley Publishing Company, Wokingham.
8. Egan and McKiernan, ibid.
9. Baumol William J. (1994) Innovation and strategic sabotage as a feedback process. *Japan and the World Economy*, 4, 275–290. North Holland.
10. Hamel Gary, Prahalad C.K. (1994) *Competing for the Future*. Harvard Business School Press, Boston.
11. Kono Toyohiro (1988) Factors affecting the creativity of organizations — An approach from the analysis of new product development, in *Innovation and Management* edited by Kuniyoshi Urabe, John Child, Tadao Kagono, deGruyter, Berlin.
12. Hamel and Prahalad, ibid.
13. *Economic Survey of Japan, 1991–1992*. Economic Planning, Agency of the Japanese Government, 1992, Tokyo.
14. Stalk Jr George, Hout Thomas M. (1990) *Competing Against Time. How Time-Based Competition is Reshaping Global Markets*. The Free Press, New York.
15. Stalk Jr George, Webber Alan M. (1993) Japans dark side of time. *Harvard Business Review*, July–August, 93–102.
16. *The Best of Japan* (1987). Kodansha Ltd, Tokyo.
17. Kono, ibid.
18. Mansfield Edwin (1993) The diffusion of flexible manufacturing systems in Japan, Europe and the United States. *Management Science*, 39(2), February, 149–159.
19. Lorriman John, Kenjo Takashi (1994) *Japan's Winning Margins*. Oxford University Press, Oxford.
20. Tatsuno Sheridan M. (1990) *Created in Japan. From Imitators to World-Class Innovators*. Harper Business 1990.
21. Hofstede Geert (1991) *Cultures and Organizations Software of the Mind*. McGraw-Hill Book Company, Cambridge.
22. Rossander Olle (1992) *Japanskt Ledarskap, Harmoni och Hot*. Svenska Dagbladet, Stockholm.
23. Schlender Brenton R. (1994) Japan's white collar blues, *Fortune*, March 21, 33–37.
24. Lu David J. (1987) *Inside Corporate Japan*. Productivity Press, Cambridge.
25. Hofstede, ibid.
26. Pascale Richard T., Athos, Anthony G. (1981) *The Art of Japanese Management*. Simon and Schuster, New York.
27. Pascale and Athos, ibid.
28. Maruyama Magoroh (1992) Lessons from Japanese management failures in foreign countries. *Human Systems Management*, 11(1), 41–48.
29. Herbig Paul A., McCarty Cynthia (1993) The innovation matrix. *Journal of Global Marketing*, 6, 69–87.
30. Miller W.C., Sparks D. (1984) Theory Z: The promise for US schools. *The Educational Forum* 49, 1.
31. Tatsuno, ibid.
32. Desphandé Rohit, Farley John U., Webster Jr Frederick E. (1993) Corporate culture, customer orientation, and innovativeness in Japanese firms: A Quadrad analysis. *Journal of Marketing*, (57), January, 23–27.

33. Hofstede, ibid.
34. Lu, ibid.
35. *Training & Development*, September 1994.
36. Lorriman and Kenjo, ibid.
37. Future scope (1994) *The Futurist*, July–August.
38. Lorriman and Kenjo, ibid.
39. Lorriman and Kenjo, ibid.

Chapter 14

1. Tricker Bob (1995) From manager to director: Developing corporate governors' strategic thinking, in *Developing Strategic Thought, Rediscovering the Art of Direction-giving*, edited by Bob Garratt, McGraw-Hill Book Company, London, 11–28.
2. Hanford Phil (1995) Developing director and executive competencies in strategic thinking, in *Developing Strategic Thought, Rediscovering the Art of Direction-Giving*, edited by Bob Garratt, McGraw-Hill Book Company, London, 157–186.
3. Lorenz Christopher (1993) Corporate venturing back in vogue. *Financial Times*, Friday, July 2.
4. Hanford, ibid.
5. *Handbook for Creative and Innovative Managers* (1988) edited by Lawrence Kuhn, McGraw-Hill Book Company, London.
6. Kay John (1993) *Foundations of Corporate Success*. Oxford University Press, New York.
7. Higgins James M. (1995) Storyboard your way to success. *Training & Development*, June, 13–17.
8. Loeb Marshall (1995) Ten commandments for managing creative people. *Fortune*, January 16, 83–84.
9. Gallupe R. Brent, Cooper William H. (1993) Brainstorming electronically. *Sloan Management Review*, Fall, 27–36.

Index

Information regarding availability of IMA and SAI material, seminar leaders, and speakers is available from:

Europe
Jack B. Emden
Innovative Management Associates
Postfach 2303
D-65013 Wiesbaden, Germany

North America
Jack B. Emden
Innovative Management Associates
4965 Kestral Parkway, North
Sarasota, FL 34231